101 Favorite Play Therapy Techniques

Child Therapy Series

A Series of Books Edited by
Charles Schaefer

Cognitive-Behavioral Play Therapy
Susan M. Knell

Play Therapy in Action:
A Casebook for Practitioners
Terry Kottman and Charles Schaefer, Eds.

Family Play Therapy
Charles Schaefer and Lois Carey, Eds.

The Quotable Play Therapist
Charles Schaefer and Heidi Gerard Kaduson, Eds.

Childhood Encopresis and Enuresis
Charles Schaefer

The Therapeutic Powers of Play
Charles Schaefer, Ed.

Play Therapy Techniques
Donna Cangelosi and Charles Schaefer, Eds.

Children in Residential Care:
Critical Issues in Treatment
Charles Schaefer and Arthur Swanson, Eds.

The Therapeutic Use of Child's Play
Charles Schaefer, Ed.

Refusal to Speak:
Treatment of Selective Mutism in Children
Sheila Spasaro and Charles Schaefer, Eds.

Sandplay:
Therapy with Children and Families
Lois Carey

Helping Parents Solve Their Children's Behavior Problems
Charles Schaefer and Andrew R. Eisen, Eds.

Clinical Handbook of Sleep Disorders in Children
Charles Schaefer, Ed.

Clinical Handbook of Anxiety Disorders in Children and Adolescents
Andrew R. Eisen, Christopher A. Kearney, and Charles Schaefer, Eds.

Practitioner's Guide to Treating Fear and Anxiety in Children and Adolescents:
A Cognitive-Behavioral Approach
Andrew R. Eisen and Christopher A. Kearney

Words of Wisdom for Parents:
Time-Tested Thoughts on How to Raise Kids
Charles Schaefer, Ed.

The Playing Cure:
Individualized Play Therapy for Specific Childhood Problems
Heidi Gerard Kaduson, Donna Cangelosi, and Charles Schaefer, Eds.

101 Favorite Play Therapy Techniques
Heidi Gerard Kaduson and Charles Schaefer, Eds.

Saying Goodbye in Child Psychotherapy:
Planned, Unplanned, and Premature Endings
Donna Cangelosi

Short-Term Psychotherapy Groups for Children:
Adapting Group Processes for Specific Problems
Charles Schaefer, Ed.

101 Favorite Play Therapy Techniques

Edited by

Heidi G. Kaduson, Ph.D.

Charles E. Schaefer, Ph.D.

A JASON ARONSON BOOK

ROWMAN & LITTLEFIELD PUBLISHERS, INC.
Lanham • Boulder • New York • Toronto • Oxford

A JASON ARONSON BOOK

ROWMAN & LITTLEFIELD PUBLISHERS, INC.

Published in the United States of America
by Rowman & Littlefield Publishers, Inc.
A wholly owned subsidiary of The Rowman & Littlefield Publishing Group, Inc.
4501 Forbes Boulevard, Suite 200, Lanham, Maryland 20706
www.rowmanlittlefield.com

PO Box 317
Oxford
OX2 9RU, UK

First Rowman & Littlefield edition published in 2004

British Library Cataloguing in Publication Information Available

Library of Congress Cataloging-in-Publication Data

101 favorite play therapy techniques / edited by Heidi Gerard Kaduson, Charles E. Schaefer.
p. cm.
ISBN 0-7657-0040-9 (cloth : alk. paper)
ISBN 0-7657-0282-7 (pbk : alk. paper)
1. Play therapy. I. Kaduson, Heidi. II. Schaefer, Charles E.
RJ505.P6A14 1997
618.92'891653—dc21 96-31854

Printed in the United States of America

™ The paper used in this publication meets the minimum requirements of American National Standard for Information Sciences—Permanence of Paper for Printed Library Materials, ANSI/NISO Z39.48-1992.

CONTRIBUTORS

L. G. Agre, 6575 Hahndo Lane, Fayetteville, AZ 71901

John Allan, Ph.D., and Mary Anne Pare, University of British Columbia, Department of Counseling Psychology, 2125 Main Mall, Vancouver, B.C., V6T 1Z4, Canada

Judith Friedman Babcock, 4 Reeves Road, Bedford, MA 01730

Bria Bartlett-Simpson, M.A., 1251 East 30 Place, Tulsa, OK 74114

Helen E. Benedict, Ph.D., Baylor University Psy.D. Program, P.O. Box 97334, Waco, TX 76798

Sheldon N. Berger, Ph.D., and Jonna L. Tyler, Ph.D., 300 E. War Memorial Drive, Suite 106B, Peoria, IL 61614

Anne Blackwell, M.S., R.P.T., L.P.C., 711 Comet Drive, Beaufort, NC 28516

Marie Boultinghouse, Ed.D., A.B.P.P., Charlotte Counseling and Psychodiagnostic Services, 6213 Cedar Croft Drive, Charlotte, NC 28226

N. E. Brewer, 9080 Huero Road, Creston, CA 93432

Sueanne M. Brown, L.S.W., 1 Northgate Square, Greensburg, PA 15601

Neil Cabe, M.A., Rainbeau Northfield Counseling Center, 147 E. Aurora Road, Northfield, OH 44067

Donna Cangelosi, Ph.D., 786 Grange Road, Teaneck, NJ 07666

Sandy Carter, HCO1, Box 562, Goodrich, TX 77335

Michael Cascio, M.S.W., A.C.S.W., Carolina Center, 702 Johns Hopkins Drive, Greenville, NC 27834

Nancy H. Cochran, M.A., 605 North Main Street, Statesboro, GA 30458

Dolores M. Conyers, Ed.S., 221 S. Johnson Street, Bloomfield, NM 87413

Jo Ann L. Cook, Ed.D., 1316 Palmetto Avenue, Winter Park, FL 32789

Aileen Cunliffe, Ed.S., 113 Silver Lake Circle, Columbia SC 29212

Kathy Daves, M.Ed., N.C.C., 4940 Ridgewood Road, Apartment C-1, Jackson, MS 39211

Patricia H. Davidson, L.C.S.W., Family Service of Roanoke Valley, 3028 Hershberger Road, Roanoke, VA 24017

Kimberly Dye, M.S., A.D.T.R., BuddyBanz, 117 19th Avenue, Seattle, WA 98112

Sylvia J. Fischer, M.A., 3490 Buskirk Avenue, Suite A, Pleasant Hill, CA 94523

Richard Frankel, M.A., L.C.S.W., 32 Lewis Avenue, Arlington, MA 02174

Jackie K. Frederiksen, Elliot Elementary School, 1900 S. Story Road, Irving, TX 75060

Robert W. Freeman, Ph.D., University of Maryland at College Park, Shoemaker Hall, College Park, MD 20742

Teresa A. Glatthorn, R.P.T.-S., 211 E. Mill Road, Hatboro, PA 19040

Allan Gonsher, L.C.S.W., A.C.S.W., 12131 W. Center Road, Omaha NE 69144

Patricia Grigoryev, Ph.D., 3218 N.E. Turtle Creek Drive, Lowton, OK 73507

Lynn B. Hadley, Medical University of South Carolina, 307 Molasses Lane, Mt. Pleasant, SC 29464

Martha Harkin, Harkin and David Designs, 5601 Mapleleaf Drive, Austin, TX 78723

Mary-Lynn Harrison, M.S.W., L.C.S.W., 93 S. Victoria Street, St. Paul, MN 55105

Steve Harvey, Ph.D., 222 BFB, CMR 405. Box 1227, APOAE Germany 09034

Harold M. Heidt, Ed.D., 694 Jamestowne Drive, Garden City, SC 29576

Tammy Horn, Family Service and Guidance Center, 2055 Clay, Topeka, KS 66604

Mitch Jacobs, M.Ed., N.C.C., L.P.C., 8303 Skillman, Suite 274, Dallas, TX 75231

Debbie S. Jones, R.N., M.N., C.S., R.P.T., 921 Springdale Road, West Columbia, SC 29170

Heidi Gerard Kaduson, Ph.D., R.P.T.-S., 951 Route 33, Hightstown, NJ 08520

Stanley Kissel, Ph.D., 1655 Elmwood Avenue, Building 200, Suite C, Rochester, NY 14620

Norma Leben, L.M.S.W., A.C.P., A.C.S.W., Morning Glory Treatment Center for Children, 1207 Pigeon Forge, Pflugerville, TX 78660

Jennifer Leonetti, M.A., Jackson Memorial Hospital, 1611 N.W. 12 Avenue, Miami, FL 33136

Ann C. Levinger, Ed.D., University of Massachusetts, Room 159 Hills South, Box 34150, Amherst, MA 01003

L. Jean Ley, L.P.C., R.P.T.-S. and Jean Howze, Suite 205, 4415 N.E. Sandy Boulevard, Portland, OR 97213

Alan Lobaugh, Ph.D., Monica Park Christian Church, 2600 Broadway, Garland, TX 75041

Leslie Hartley Lowe, M.A., M.F.C.C., Counseling and Mediation Services, 112 N. 5 Street, Klamath Falls, OR 97601

Berrell Mallery, Ph.D., and Randall Martin, Ph.D., Staten Island Mental Health, 669 Castleton Avenue, Staten Island, NY 10301

Jamshid Marvasti, M.D., 139 E. Center Street, Manchester, CT 06040

Linda Mattingly, Red Rock Mental Health Center, 1204 Manvel, Chandler, OK 74834

Christina Mattise, M.Ed., Brookline Elementary School, 22 Fairway Drive, Amherst, NH 03031

Barbra McDowell, California School of Professional Psychology, 373 W. Nees Avenue, Suite 219, Fresno, CA 93711

Joyce Meagher, L.P.C., R.P.T.-S., 10400 Eaton Place, Suite 110, Fairfax, VA 22020

Diane L. Murray, M.A., L.S.W., The Murray Organization, 206 Allegheny Street, Hollidaysburg, PA 16648

Carolyn J. Narcavage, M.S., 2200 Brown Street, Suite 312, Waxahachie, TX 75165

Kevin O'Connor, Ph.D., California School of Professional Psychology, 1350 M Street, Fresno, CA 93721

Violet Oaklander, Ph.D., 2929 Glen Albwyn Drive, Santa Barbara, CA 93105

Karen Pitzen, L.C.S.W., 3851 N.E. 33 Avenue, Portland, OR 97212

Mary Repp, M.F.C.C., Lavie Christian Whole Person Health Care, 26400 La Alameda, Suite 202, Mission Viejo, CA 92691

Sheri Saxe, L.L.P., 3119 Sleaford, Waterford, MI 48329

Charles E. Schaefer, Ph.D., R.P.T.-S., Fairleigh Dickinson University, Center for Psychological Services, 139 Temple Avenue, Hackensack, NJ 07601

Mary May Schmidt, M.S., M.A., N.C.C., Tri-Valley Central School, 75 Jefferson Street, Monticello, NY 12701

Aimee H. Short, M.Ed., L.P.C., L.C.S.W., R.P.T.-S., 3410 Corona Drive, Garland, TX 75044

Glenda F. Short, L.C.S.W., R.P.T.-S., 400 Maitland Avenue, Altamonte Springs, FL 32701

Stazan K. Sina, M.A., 3308 N. Vernal Avenue, Fresno, CA 93722

Tara M. Sinclair, C.S.W., 1044 Abbott Boulevard, Fort Lee, NJ 07024

Richard Sloves, Psy.D., Director of Short-Term Therapy, Kings County Hospital Center, 451 Clarkson Avenue, Brooklyn, NY 12203

David Snyder, Ed.S., L.P.C., 72 Cannon Road, Greensboro, NC 27410

Jessica Stone-Phennicie, M.S., California School of Professional Psychology, 2448 Lind Avenue, Clovis, CA 93612

S. Eileen Theiss, M.Ed., L.P.C., N.C.C., Justin Elementary School, 425 Boss Range Road, Justin, TX 76247

Catherine G. Tierney, L.C.S.W., R.P.T.-S., 156 Sibbald Drive, Park Ridge, NJ 07656

Barbara A. Turner, M.A., 884 Third Street, Suite D, Santa Rosa, CA 95404

Ruby Walker, 285 W. Judicial, Suite C, Blackfoot, ID 83221

Cathy Wunderlich, Silvis School District Counselor, 9118 217th Street N., Port Byron, IL 61275

Martha D. Young, Ph.D., P.O. Box 240, 810 Lincoln Avenue, Steamboat Springs, CO 80477

CONTENTS

PREFACE

A largely untapped source of ideas for improving play therapy practice is the experience of therapists who use play with children. The goal of this book is to facilitate the sharing of play therapy techniques by therapists in the field. To this end, we asked play therapists across the world to send us their favorite play therapy techniques. We were impressed with the number and variety of the ideas submitted.

The criteria for selecting techniques for this book were that they be specific, practical, relatively inexpensive, and be original or involve an innovative modification of a well-known procedure. A few widely used techniques were included because we had not seen them written up in detail before.

We have separated the techniques into eight sections for easy reference. Each author has included a description and/or application of the technique to illustrate and demonstrate how it is done. These sections are: Fantasy Techniques, which include pretend games and the use of guided imagery and fantasy; Storytelling Techniques, which illustrate the use of different games and methods to enhance verbalizations in children; Expressive Art Techniques, which include the various mediums used in art to help children cope with traumas and disorders; Game Play Techniques, which use store-bought or self-created games to help children with psychological issues; Puppet Play Techniques, which help in the expression of conflicting emotions; Play Toys and Objects Techniques, which illustrate the use of various toys and objects and how they are useful in therapeutic play; Group Play Techniques, which include various methods and play techniques to use in group settings; and Other Techniques, which are a group of miscellaneous techniques that are useful in many settings with many types of children.

This volume should be of interest to play therapy professionals and students across a number of disciplines including social work, psychology, counseling, child life, therapeutic recreation, and psychiatry. Hopefully, this endeavor will stimulate further development and exchange of practical techniques by all who use play to help children resolve their psychological difficulties.

Heidi Gerard Kaduson
Charles E. Schaefer

Section One

Fantasy Techniques

1

The Playing Baby Game

Charles E. Schaefer

INTRODUCTION AND RATIONALE

Sibling rivalry is common among preschoolers following the birth of a new baby. Stress reactions tend to be particularly strong if the sibling is less than three years older than the baby. Field and Rite (1984) found that first-born preschoolers tended to express feelings of envy, aggression, and anxiety in their play following the arrival of a sibling. From the perspective of an older child, having to share parental attention and possessions with a younger, cuter sibling is not a desirable situation. After the birth of a new baby, mothers play less with the older sibling. This is understandable since mothers are not only exhausted from meeting the needs of a helpless infant, but are feeling sleep-deprived and probably some degree of post-partum depression.

Whether encouraged or not, the older child will want to pretend to be a baby again to gain back some of the special attention he or she enjoyed as an infant. Rather than opposing this inclination, it is best to encourage it but to limit its expression to a certain time and place. A particularly effective way to do this is for a parent to engage the child in the "Playing Baby" Game.

DESCRIPTION

The Playing Baby Game consists of the mother setting aside 15–30 minutes a day with the older sibling so that the child and mother can play as if he or she was a baby again. In this way the older child can experience all the special attention and nurturance that the new baby is receiving, which should serve to reduce feelings of rivalry and resentment. During the special time alone with the older child, the mother does not answer phone calls, so that she can devote her full attention to the child. The session usually begins with the mother showing the older child pictures, videos, or clothes from when he or she was a baby. The mother then suggests they play some of the fun games they used to play when the child was a baby, like "Peek-a-boo," "This Little Piggy," or "Itsy Bitsy Spider." After the games, its time to snuggle together or rock in a rocking chair while the child drinks from his or her baby bottle and looks at baby books like *Pat the Bunny*. This is a time for the child to receive lots of tender hugs and kisses from the mother, perhaps even receiving a relaxing massage. Baby talk by the child and soothing lullabies by the mother are welcome at this time. From time to time, the mother comments, "When you were a baby, this is how I sang to you, played with you, held you, etc." "You were so cute; we all loved you as much as we do now; I remember one time that you. . . ." A good way to end is simply to put the "baby" to sleep on the sofa wrapped in a baby blanket. By these activities, the child is helped to realize that he or she was once the sole center of attention and received all the special treatment that the new baby is getting now. In this way feelings of jealousy should be reduced.

Materials that should be available to encourage regressive infant type play include a baby blanket, baby bottle, pacifier, rattle, cloth for peek-a-boo play, soft baby blocks, busy box, baby lotion, or squeaky rubber dolls.

GUIDELINES

Set aside a special place and time each day to play the game.

The game should not be played in the presence of other family members.

Keep playing the baby game until the child becomes uninterested in it. Then suggest that the child play with the toys he or she enjoyed as a toddler. Soon the child will be back to a normal developmental level again.

Fathers and other caretakers should play this game as well as the mother.

Ignore "babyish" behavior by the older child at other times during the day and indicate that you generally expect maturity.

Remember to remain accepting of babyish and immature behaviors during the game. In this way you can satisfy these longings without the child having to openly "admit" to these wishes.

At times tell your child how much you enjoy these games because although you are proud of how big the child is, you sometimes miss your little baby.

Keep offering to play this game even if your child does not initially accept it. For some children it takes time to overcome their defenses.

Reference

Field, T., and Rite, M. (1984). Children's responses to separation from mother during the birth of another child. *Child Development* 55:130–1316.

2

Using Guided Imagery to Augment the Play Therapy Process

Kevin O'Connor

INTRODUCTION AND RATIONALE

Within Ecosystemic Play Therapy, the modality practiced by the author, the primary goal of treatment is to help a child learn new and effective strategies for getting his or her needs met in ways that do not interfere with others getting their needs met. Children who exhibit problem behavior or emotional distress are seen as unable to get their needs met either effectively or in ways that are both effective and socially acceptable. To resolve this problem the child and the play therapist must identify the child's needs, identify current factors that prevent those needs from being met, and then identify and master effective new strategies that the child can use to get those needs met. Guided imagery can be used to augment many aspects of this process.

Guided imagery is similar to both many relaxation strategies and to hypnosis. One can envision a continuum with standard relaxation techniques on one end and hypnosis on the other and guided imagery somewhere in the middle. As used by the author, guided imagery involves having the child engage in some focused relaxation exercise and then using visual imagery for the purpose of either direct or indirect problem solving with respect to getting the child's needs met. Guided imagery brings two advantages to the play therapy process. One advantage is that it can be used to help children gain a sense of mastery over both their bodies and their feelings. The other advantage is that it can be used to augment generalization of other gains made in the play therapy by allowing children to use their imaginations to create hypothetical life situations in the play room so as to practice their newly acquired skills with the support of the therapist. In other words, guided imagery can be used to create an elaborate form of role playing. While the latter use can be very effective, it is the use of guided imagery to augment mastery that is the focus of this discussion.

DESCRIPTION

Guided imagery can be introduced at any point in the play therapy process. The child must be able to follow simple sequential directions and must be willing to relax in session. Although the ultimate goal is to provide the child with an increased sense of mastery the initial process requires that the child relinquish some control to the therapist, as the therapist will need to teach the child the technique. There are a number of ways the therapist may introduce the process to the child. Younger children often respond to the idea of taking an imaginary trip, while older children often like the idea of personal mastery including the concept of self-hypnosis.

However guided imagery is introduced, the therapist begins by teaching the child a basic relaxation strategy. If the child is willing, it is useful to have him or her lie down or sit in a recliner for the early training. Alternatively, sitting in a bean bag chair works well. Progressive deep muscle relaxation (Jacobson 1938) is probably the most effective way of preparing the child for guided imagery. In this approach to relaxation the child is asked to focus on one muscle group at a time while working to achieve maximum relaxation of that group. Groups of muscles are added in sequence with the goal of achieving total body relaxation. Younger children may have difficulty with progressive deep muscle relaxation because it is such a passive process. For them a sequence of contract–relax instructions that take them through all of the major muscle groups is usually more effective (O'Connor 1991). For example, the child might be told to curl his toes then relax them, push his knees together then relax, tighten his stomach muscles and relax, and so on. Each muscle group is contracted and relaxed several times in a slow sequential progression. While deep relaxation facilitates the guided imagery process it is not necessary; simply getting the child to focus and follow directions is sufficient. Note that the child should be encouraged to achieve relaxation with her eyes open. This will make it easier for the child to access the effects of the imagery later, in situations where full relaxation is not possible.

Once even minimal relaxation has occurred guided imagery can be introduced. The imagery used needs to be tailored to the child's needs, experiences, and developmental level. This is best illustrated through a case example.

APPLICATIONS

Michael was 8 years old when he was brought to play therapy for many anxiety-related behaviors. There had been many changes in his life and neither of his parents had been particularly able to address his needs because of their own distress. While play therapy focused on helping to identify Michael's basic needs and those factors that were preventing him from getting his needs met, guided imagery was introduced to help him achieve symptom mastery, thereby reducing some portion of his anxiety. Specifically, Michael found his nightmares to be so distressing that they were interfering with his getting a full night's sleep.

Because of his age a contract–relax procedure was used to initiate relaxation. Although the therapist wanted Michael to practice his guided imagery while lying on the floor using a pillow and a blanket, Michael found this setup too anxiety provoking, since he was afraid he would fall asleep and actually have a nightmare. For this reason Michael was initially trained while he sat in a bean bag chair and later moved to a pretend bed.

In an interview with Michael it was determined that one of the images he found very relaxing was swimming in a lake (so long as the water was clear enough that he could see the bottom and make sure there were no creatures about to get him). Once he was relaxed the therapist guided him through imagining lying in very shallow water by the side of a lake. The image was strengthened by making it multisensory. Michael was asked to imagine that the sand he was lying on was warm and very soft and that it felt and sounded like the shifting of the beans in the bean bag chair. Then he was asked to imagine the water as being quite warm as it flowed over his body. He was told to picture a bright blue sky with puffy white clouds and to hear the sound of very gentle waves as they moved past his ears. The ebb and flow of the waves was then synchronized to his breathing so that the waves came up as he breathed in and flowed out as he exhaled. Michael enjoyed the image very much and was more than willing to practice it at home. The therapist instructed Michael to begin by practicing in the morning after he woke up so as to reduce the chance that Michael would be so anxious about the possibility of falling asleep that he would avoid the task.

In session the therapist helped Michael learn to use the image as a way of regaining control when anxious material was discussed. If Michael became anxious in session the therapist would cue him to begin "breathing with the waves" in a slow and measured pace. As Michael reported achieving a more relaxed state he and the therapist began to introduce images from his nightmares into the process. At first Michael was told to remain lying in the lake and to practice seeing some of the monsters from his dreams in the clouds overhead. Since these were clouds, not monsters, they were not particularly threatening. Later the monsters were brought to life and Michael engaged in many mastery fantasies. He would have his own monsters rise up out of the lake to protect him. He would become a knight with magic powers. Or he would tell a joke and the monsters would laugh until they literally broke into pieces. At this time the therapist began having Michael use the imagery when he woke up from a nightmare during the night as a way of soothing himself. As Michael reported more success he was encouraged to use the imagery prior to going to sleep at night to create dreams that would not be frightening. In essence Michael scripted his dreams and took control over the expression of his anxiety.

As can be seen in the above description it is important for the relaxation process and the imagery to come under the child's control. The therapist moves from the role of instructor to one where he or she is simply cuing the start of the process, to one where he or she is simply reinforcing and helping to focus the use of the process outside of the session. If the children do not gain control of the process it is unlikely that they will be able to use it outside of session as they will remain dependent on the therapist. It should also be apparent that the process, at least in this case, also contained elements of cognitive-behavioral therapy and systematic desensitization. As stated in the introduction, guided imagery effectively enhances the therapeutic process.

In this case, as intense as his nightmares were, it took Michael only a few weeks to reduce them by 80 percent and then a few days to virtually eliminate them. Once he experienced mastery, rapid gains and generalization followed. This same process was used to help him master some other anxiety-related symptoms and to enhance his school performance.

References

Jacobson, E. (1938). *Progressive Relaxation: A Physiological and Clinical Investigation of Muscular States and Their Significance in Psychology and Medical Practice*, 2nd ed. Chicago: University of Chicago Press.

O'Connor, K. (1991). *The Play Therapy Primer*. New York: Wiley.

3

The Rosebush

Violet Oaklander

INTRODUCTION

I first came across the Rosebush exercise in a book called *Awareness: Exploring, Experimenting, Experiencing* (Stevens 1971) in 1971. This book has a variety of imagery exercises specifically for adults. I felt that this exercise could easily be adapted for use with children, and I have used it effectively for many years.

RATIONALE

I find that the use of guided fantasy and imagery is a powerful tool for helping children express blocked feelings, wishes, needs, wants, and thoughts in a safe nonintrusive way. It is often easier for the young person to respond to a metaphor for his or her life than to the harsh reality. The use of fantasy provides a bridge to the child's inner life. The child then can look at it, examine it, and, when ready, own it. This "owning" of the aspects of the metaphor that fit provides the child with self-support and strengthens the child's self.

DESCRIPTION

I ask the child to close her eyes, take a few deep breaths, and imagine that she is a rosebush. "Or you can be any kind of flowering bush, but we'll call you a rosebush."

"What kind of rosebush are you? Are you very small? Are you large? Are you a full rosebush or skinny? Do you have flowers? If so, what kind? What color are they? Do you have many or just a few? Are you in full bloom, or do you have only buds? Do you have leaves? What do they look like? What are your stems and branches like? What are your roots like? Or maybe you don't have any. If you do, are they long and straight? Are they twisted? Are they deep? Do you have thorns? Where are you: in a yard? in a park? in the desert? on the moon? You can be anywhere. Are you growing in a pot or in the ground or through cement? What's around you? Are there other rosebushes around, or are you alone? Are there trees? Animals? Birds? People? How do you survive? Who takes care of you? What's the weather like for you right now? Is there a fence or maybe rocks around you?"

As you can see, I do a great deal of prompting while the child is imagining herself as a rosebush. I give many suggestions and possibilities. I find that children, especially those who are defensive and often constricted, need these suggestions to open themselves up to creative association.

I then ask the child to open her eyes and draw her rosebush, including the scene it's in. I generally add, "Don't worry about the drawing—it doesn't have to be your best work. You will be able to explain it to me." Later, as the child explains the drawing to me, I write the description down. I ask her to describe the rosebush in the present tense, as if she were the rosebush. I ask questions, speaking directly to the rosebush, such as, "Who takes care of you? Are you lonely? Who lives in your house?" and so forth. After the child has described herself as a rosebush, I go back to my notes and read each statement, asking the child if anything she said as a rosebush fits in any way for herself and her life or reminds her of anything.

APPLICATIONS

I have used this exercise successfully with individual children, groups, and even families. Adolescents particularly respond to this exercise, both male and female. It is an effective self-defining exercise for them, as well as useful for bringing up deeper feelings. When one young man, age 17, talked about a rose that had fallen to the ground and was dying, he admitted to me, for the first time, that he felt he needed to die.

Eight-year-old Gina said of herself as a rosebush, "I have red roses, no thorns or leaves, and no roots. The soil helps me. I'm in Disneyland because I like to be happy. I'm protected. [There was a large fence around the rosebush.] The keeper takes care of me and waters me once a day. It's a sunny day. I'm pretty. Sometimes I'm lonely. I'm going to see my Daddy tonight. I'm small and bushy. It never rains, but sometimes it snows. I can see people. I'm surrounded by grass. I can grow easier if I don't have roots—if they want to replant me, it will be easier."

When we referred back to the list I had written of her responses, Gina said the following of her own life: (I'm protected) "not in my life." (Sometimes I'm lonely) "I'm going to see my Daddy tonight." (I'm small and bushy) "I wish I were small—I'm too tall." (It never rains, but sometimes it snows) "I don't like rain. I miss snow here." (If they want to replant me, it will be easier) "I don't know what's going to happen to me." Gina is adopted, and her parents have separated. Since the separation, she has evidenced many symptoms, such as crying, nightmares, inattentiveness at school, and clinging behavior. Through this exercise, it appeared obvious to me that she had many uneasy feelings about her situation—much anxiety about what would happen to her. She had been unable to articulate these feelings. Her identification as a rosebush made it easier for us to begin to deal with her worries.

References

Oaklander, V. (1988). *Windows to Our Children: A Gestalt Therapy Approach to Children and Adolescents.* Highland, NY: Gestalt Journal Press.

Singer, J. L. (1973). *The Child's World of Make-Believe: Experimental Studies of Imaginative Play.* New York: Academic Press.

Stevens, J. O. (1971). *Awareness: Exploring, Experimenting, Experiencing.* Moab, UT: Real People Press.

4

Pretending to Know How

S. Eileen Theiss

INTRODUCTION

Sometimes things just come to you when you are working with children. I don't know when I started using this method of instilling confidence, but when you work in an elementary school setting you tend to use whatever works!

How many times a day a teacher is asked by a child, "Will you tie my shoe?" I've seen many a teacher kneel down and tie that shoe without even a request! I realize that there is a safety factor involved here, but so often we miss an opportunity to involve the child in a lesson in skill-building, self-responsibility, and self-esteem.

When my own daughter was in kindergarten, I volunteered as a teacher's aide once a week. The teacher put me in charge of teaching the children to tie a shoe. Imagine those dozen or so young faces lined up and waiting for their lessons!

RATIONALE

Children need opportunities to develop a sense of confidence in their own ability. In the book *Raising Self-Reliant Children in a Self-Indulgent*

World, Stephen Glenn writes of the importance of allowing the child to become self-reliant. "There is a prevailing belief that good parents and teachers explain things to children. However, truly effective parents and teachers work with children to help them discover useful explanations for themselves" (Glenn, p. 76).

When a child realizes how much she already knows about a particular skill, even if the skill is difficult, she will continue her efforts, and also try out other skills that have seemed "out of her reach."

DESCRIPTION

I have found that when a child is learning to tie her shoe, she often knows some of the steps involved simply because she has been observing others. If you ask that child to tie her shoe, she will generally say, "I don't know how." But if you ask that same child to *pretend* that she does know how, and to *show* you how, she will perform a least some of the steps involved. What a great opportunity then to remark, "Wow, you know a lot already! Here's how you finish. . . ." Other phrases that generate a positive response include: "Gosh, you know almost all of it!" or "Hey, you were just fooling me! You really *do* know a lot already." By using a fantasy play situation the child can free herself to show what she knows without fear of failure.

Often that same child can then be enlisted in helping another child. Remember that the process is always more instructive than the product, and that the skills learned in helping another child may be more beneficial to both children than the actual ability to tie a shoe.

As with any activity, the therapist, kindergarten teacher, or parent will have an opportunity to observe how the child responds to a challenge or deals with frustration.

APPLICATIONS

I would offer this to both parents and teachers as a means of encouraging self-reliance and self-esteem in young children. I believe that this technique could be applied to other skills as well, although I have not tried it yet. You see, I hesitate to take my 15-year-old out and ask her to "Pretend that you know how to back the car out of the driveway."

Reference

Glenn, S. (1988). *Raising Self-Reliant Children in a Self-Indulgent World.* Rocklin, CA: Prima Publishing and Communications.

Section Two

Storytelling Techniques

5

The Feeling Word Game

Heidi Gerard Kaduson

INTRODUCTION

A common problem in doing psychotherapy with young children is their inability to verbalize their feelings. With direct questioning, many children find it difficult to answer accurately. They seem to be guarded against or unable to connect with feelings that are threatening to them. The Feeling Word Game is used frequently with the population of children I treat—mostly learning disabled and attention deficit. It allows children the distance needed in a storytelling format to enhance verbalization of feelings.

RATIONALE

Communication is best accomplished by children through play. It is their most natural medium for self-expression. Play is a special form of communication. When children are involved in a game, their defenses are reduced, and they are more likely to talk about their feelings because they are just answers to a question in a game. Play allows children to enact those thoughts and feelings of which they are aware but can't express in words.

DESCRIPTION

The therapist sits at the same level as the child, either at a table or on the floor. The therapist has eight 4" x 6" pieces of paper, a marker, and a cookie tin filled with poker chips. The introduction to the client and the game proceeds as follows:

Therapist: We are going to play a game called the Feeling Word Game. First I would like you to tell me the names of some feelings that a boy or girl who is [age of child] has.

Child: How about happy?

Therapist: Happy—that's a good one. I will write that on one of these pieces of paper. [If the child cannot read, the therapist should also draw a face representing the feeling.] How about another feeling?

Child: How's sad?

Therapist: Yes, that's a good feeling—sad. I will write that one here.

The therapist continues to collect the child's feeling words, making sure that each feeling that would be required to explore the problematic behaviors is listed. If the child does not provide a word (e.g., nervous or scared), the therapist can suggest it.

When all the feelings are written on the individual papers, the therapist lines them up in front of the child.

Therapist: Here are all the feeling words. I have in my hand a tin of "feelings." They may look like poker chips, but in this game they are feelings. I am going to tell a story first, and then I will put down the feelings on these words.

The therapist tells a story about herself. After the story is told, the therapist proceeds to put some poker chips on each feeling that is appropriate—changing the amount put on each, if necessary, and showing that one can have more than one feeling at a time. The therapist then tells a story about the child that is non-threatening. This can be about their sport or fun things they do, with a twist to allow for both positive and negative responses. The child is then given the tin of "feelings" and told to put down what they might feel under those circumstances.

Therapist: Now put down your feelings for that story.

Child: I would be this much happy.

Therapist: Happy, okay. Why would you be happy?

Child: Because I scored a goal.

Therapist: Any more feelings?

Child: Yeah, sad. [he puts down a lot].

Therapist: Oh, that's a lot of sad. Why would you be so sad?

Child: Because we lost the game.

The next story is told by the child for the therapist to put down his or her own feelings. Remember that a child will project his feelings into any story that is told, and the therapist should respond accordingly. This continues until the major issues of the presenting problem are talked about.

APPLICATIONS

This technique is helpful with all children, but especially useful with children with conduct problems or anxiety problems. It allows the therapist to talk about and question issues that are generally too threatening to approach. Many children with attention deficit hyperactivity disorder are able to communicate quite well when using this technique.

6

The Card Story Game

Norma Y. Leben

INTRODUCTION

In creating structured games for my clients (children as well as adults and parents), I like to use things that are readily available in their environment. A stack of playing cards is one of those things. With that in mind, I have created several card games with multiple objectives (Leben 1994).

Of the seven structured card games I designed, the Card Story Game is my favorite because it is simple yet the most reflective of what the client is thinking. Even the most reserved and quiet child participates with some degree of confidence. The process of the game works for one child, a small group of children, or family members. The task of the therapist is to listen with sensitivity to the theme each player is trying to unfold in the story.

RATIONALE

I consider this game therapeutic because it allows the player to express what is on or buried in his or her mind in the safest setting. Telling the story in a nonthreatening fashion enables each player to convey his or her own theme, if listened to by a trained ear. When the theme makes sense to the player, sometimes there are clues expressed that can shed light for solving their ongoing problems.

Another therapeutic element to this game is that the therapist also participates, giving therapeutic input at strategic moments that unobtrusively sinks in with even the most resistant clients. With the help of the numbers and letters on the cards, even the less imaginative player manages to say something. Since each stack has a fixed number of cards, players can clearly see when the game will end (i. e., when all the cards are flipped over). This avoids the needless anxiety of guessing when the game is over. From my experience, the players in a small group usually exercise their sense of humor by creating wild story lines, thus enlivening the process.

This game is effective for the following objectives:

to aid in diagnosis and assessment of the client(s),

to increase attention span of the players,

to enhance communication skills, and

to provide cognitive/academic skills training.

DESCRIPTION

The therapist puts down a stack of standard playing cards and explains that each player may flip over two cards during his or her turn. Each player will make up a story line incorporating the number or letter of the two cards. The therapist will start first to set the stage. If she or he flips a *Q* and a *9*, the therapist may say, "There once was a lovely *queen* who lived in a castle surrounded by *9* dragons. . . . The next player then flips over two cards and continues the imaginative story, building on his or her predecessor's story line.

As the story progresses, the cards are arranged in a spiraling pattern, as seen in Figure 2-1. The therapist listens to the players' story lines and gives therapeutic intervention when it is her turn. For example, after two turns a player continues to tell about the poor little dog who wandered *6* streets and looked into *8* trash cans in search of food . . . and was chased by *A* big man with a stick and *4* ugly farmers' wives. The therapist might give a therapeutic remark of assurance with her cards (e.g., "then *J* walked by and saw this hungry little dog and decided to take it home, give it a warm bath and *4* dog biscuits. . . ." Another example is a player who draws a *Q* and a *2* and says, "There was a *queen* bee who buzzed around and stung these *2* boys real bad." The therapist might continue the story with an attitude of assurance and problem solving." The boys ran to their neighbor's in Apartment *6*, who helped stop the bee stings with *8* spoonfuls of ammonia and sent them to the hospital emergency room."

Still other examples of violent themes such as guns, gangs, knives, and fights could be counteracted by limit-setting and law-and-order remarks. For example, "Suddenly there appeared *A* wise judge, who talked to these gang members and gave them a choice of going back to school or doing community service for *3* years."

When working with abused children, each player has either seemingly nothing or too much to tell. Sometimes there appears to be no continuity to a story because every player has his or her own theme. Even with turns, each player seems to return to his or her own theme. At those times, the therapist needs to exercise good memory skills and, if need be, take an extra turn to give therapeutic input.

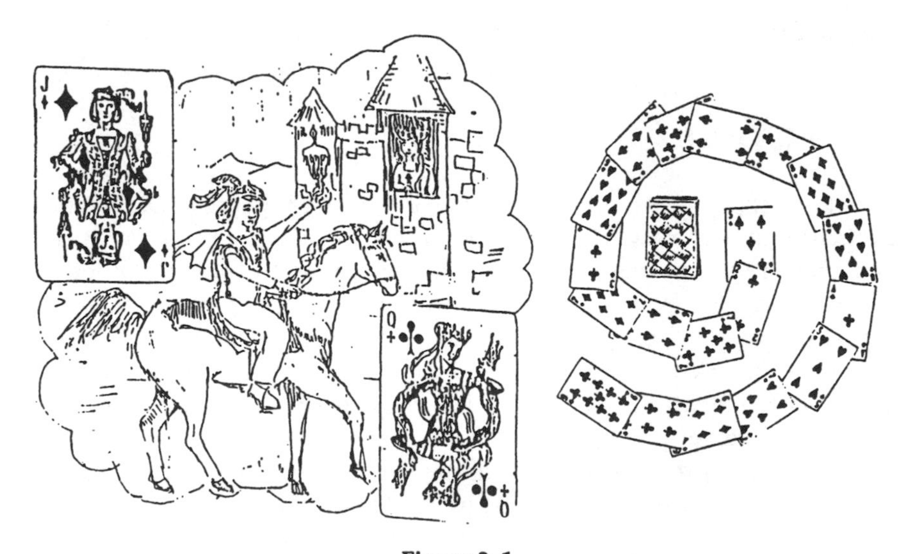

Figure 2–1.

APPLICATIONS

This technique applies to clients with ADHD, ODD, or low self-esteem, or who are aggressive, withdrawn, or depressed. It works with most individuals, families, and groups.

Reference

Leben, N.Y. (1994). *Directive Group Play Therapy—60 Structured Games for the Treatment of ADHD, Low Self-Esteem, and Traumatized Children*. Pflugerville, TX: Morning Glory Treatment Center for Children.

7

Storytelling with Felts

Linda Mattingly

INTRODUCTION

I was first introduced to storytelling with felts in Sunday School at an early age. Their use is so familiar to me that I may have a difficult time describing the story telling activity. The supplies are readily available for purchase at a book or hobby store. Felt boards are cardboard-like material covered with a piece of felt, usually black. The characters, scenery, and props can vary depending on the theme of the story. These objects adhere to the felt board like a magnet to a refrigerator. For example, in Sunday School the story of Noah and the Ark might be told with a large number of animals, rain clouds, a dove, characters representing Noah's family, and so on. This type of storytelling takes pictures and words from the printed page to give them mobility and individuality.

For the storyteller and his or her audience this allows for a wider range of interaction and participation. The Sunday School teacher might ask, "Who is this man with the hammer in his hand?" "N-O-A-H!" the children would reply. The teacher can have the children select and name the animals as they place them on the felt board in semblance of boarding the ark. The felt characters can be replaced and removed as the story proceeds.

RATIONALE

Storytelling with felts is effective in the classroom as well. I taught a kindergarten-through-fourth multigrade class at a private academy. Given the variety of skills and levels in the classroom, I allowed children to have their own felt boards and felts to tell stories verbally and visually so the younger students just learning to read and write were not at a disadvantage.

DESCRIPTION

Currently, I use felt storytelling in a diagnostic therapeutic nursery at a community mental health center. I work with 3- to 9-year-olds who are seriously and emotionally disturbed children. These children are victims of neglect and/or abuse. They often have additional difficulty communicating, which is a trust-based skill. I have found felts to be an effective tool to encourage verbalization and increase self-esteem. The use of this tool in therapy is very different from the church or school setting. The value is not necessarily in the story itself, but in the way a child presents it and the way the therapist perceives it. Children feel a great deal of pride in compiling a story of their own. Storytelling can encourage imagination and reveal their inner feelings and self-image concepts. The types of felts a child chooses and the manner in which they use them can indicate aggression, fear, anger, or phobias. The interpretive value of the stories can directly aid in the children's treatment process. They have freedom to express themselves without directly implicating anyone. However, to a trained eye and ear the stories become part of a much larger picture, similar to interpreting children's artwork. The media a child chooses—paints, pencils, markers, and so on—the way they use it— bold, hard, dark lines—where on the page they draw, and what is drawn are all part of interpretive value. As in art, stories have meaning beyond the surface that is revealing and useful to the therapist. If a child chooses to use characters typical of power in his story, he probably needs to have more control in his life. If she places an adult figure below a child-size character on the felt board she is indicating her own self-importance in relation to a parent or caregiver's position. These are contrasting examples, the first representing a child overpowered by adults, the second a child overpowering the adults in her life. Both circumstances in a home can cause a number of conflicts. When the child reveals his interpretation of his position in the family unit the therapist can work toward a balance in the relationship. A child doesn't have the understanding to say, "I feel superior or inferior to my parent, so I use bad behavior to communicate how angry I am."

The following list is a suggested guideline when interpreting storytelling with felts. I must emphasize that they are only suggestions. Each therapist must take into account a child's individual background and personality.

When used in storytelling,	indicate:
Trolls, witches, etc.	fear.
Wizards, fairies, unicorns	power.
Giants, dinosaurs, alligators	aggression.
A sun, flowers, birds	hopefulness.
Trains, cars, vehicles	escape.
Wind, rain, storms	turbulence.
Forest, jungles, darkness	emptiness.
Castles, palaces, mansions	an isolated world.

These are only a few examples of interpretive value. Some are more obvious than others: weapons are easily identified as aggressive feelings; dogs, cats, domestic animals mean security and affection. Some stories and art mean nothing at all. Therapists have a tendency to look for hidden meanings in everything, and they must be discriminating in their theories.

APPLICATION

The following story exemplifies a child who feels isolated from males and lacks an adequate father figure in his life. He views the world as revolving around the hierarchy of females. The story comes from a 7-year-old male who has been in multiple foster homes over a four year period. He and his 5-year-old sister were removed from their mother's care due to physical neglect and abuse. He is an angry, aggressive child. He has difficulty getting along with other children and is often in trouble at school. He was diagnosed with ADHD (Attention Deficit Hyperactivity Disorder) by a child psychiatrist, yet he was able to focus on his story for twenty minutes. While reading his story, incorporate the therapeutic interpretation for your own insight and evaluation.

The Palace of the Queen and King

There once lived a unicorn deep in the forest. A young girl was walking in the woods one day and met the unicorn. The unicorn told her she could have any wish she wanted. The girl wished to be a princess. And so she was. She met a prince and they got married. So now they were the queen and king. Then they had a baby, who was a girl, who grew up to be a princess. And the princess met a prince and they got married and the first queen and king died. And the princess and prince became the queen and king. The second queen and king had a baby, who was a girl. . . . [He repeats the process of birth, marriage, and death several more times.] Then one day a baby was born and it was a boy. So he grew up to be a knight and got a cat and a dog. Then the last queen and king died. And the knight returned to being the unicorn.

After conferring with a child specialist in interpreting creative activities, we arrived at the following theory: The child felt women had all the power, that is, the abuse by his mother he endured and witnessed for the majority of his life. He had also taken the role of primary caregiver to his younger sister during the chaos and uncertainty of their lives. It is unfortunate and confusing when children must take on adult roles. They view the world in a distorted way. It is impossible for them to enjoy their childhood once it has been stolen from them. He is being returned to his natural father, whom he has not seen in four years, but has recently visited with his sister. He is expected to accept two new adolescent stepsisters and a stepmother. His father drives a truck and is gone from home weeks at a time. The young boy is fearful and anxious knowing he will be the primary male in a four-female household. Considering the damage his mother left him to deal with, his fears are understandable.

The interpretation of his story was helpful to his treatment. We were able to address his fear issues in conjunction with the abuse history and released a fairly emotionally healthy young man to society.

In the story, the boy is the unicorn. He chose a figure representing power, but still feels unable to control his circumstances. Notice the female gender is always mentioned first. He was emphatic about the order. He does regain his position as the unicorn in the end when the last of the females in the cycle dies. Possibly he feels he will endure the cycle of females in his life and ultimately gain control. He believes there is hope for him after all. So do I.

8

The Box of Buttons Technique

Jo Ann L. Cook

INTRODUCTION

This play therapy technique evolved as a method to engage children and adolescents who were noncommunicative to initiate a communicative statement, particularly when they initially desired to remain nonverbal. While refusals may often extend to more traditional materials, many found the box of buttons, a large box full of pin-on buttons with varied statements and logos, unusual and intriguing. Most children and adolescents investigate and choose those which seem to portray a meaning or communication for them. Following some initial success with the material, it was later adapted as an icebreaker communication technique. It has been found to be particularly successful with children with reluctant speech and pre-adolescents and adolescents who initially are withdrawn and/or resistant.

RATIONALE

The Box of Buttons technique allows presentation of a material which, although familiar and acceptable to many children, does not appear childish and seems particularly identifiable with adolescents. The person can investigate and choose words, phrases, statements, or pictures which allow him to express emotions, attitudes, or opinions without taking the risk of verbal communication. By providing an initial opportunity to acknowledge or reject a variety of written communications, the interaction can move from silence to reading a written communication. It may frequently more comfortably enable the beginning of verbal communication which can move forward without the child viewing himself as having lost face for breaking his silence.

DESCRIPTION

Presentation of the technique has involved introducing the Box of Buttons as a collection of different sayings and ideas that may be of interest. The child is encouraged to review these, or they are read to him and scattered around the table. The therapist may invite the child to choose any buttons he feels express something he would like to communicate. This can be modeled as well by choosing a button, reading the inscription, explaining why it was chosen, and pinning it on one's clothing. The buttons have more appeal when there is a wide variety of different words or sayings ranging from serious to comical.

APPLICATIONS

The technique has been used successfully with individual children, in groups, and with families. Variations have included numerous spontaneous applications, such as people wearing multiple buttons, placing single to multiple buttons while their backs are turned and then turning to reveal their choices, ordering the buttons to create monologues or dialogues, as well as clarifications of the rationale for choices. Some phrases and sayings which have been collected and used successfully include: "No pain, no gain; I want to grow up, not blow up; Ask me why I am wearing this button; I know you know; One day at a time; I'm learning to like me; Cool your jets; Don't panic; Whatever; Kids need praise every day; I love you; I am loved," as well as blank and picture buttons. The option of choosing a pictorial button allows the person to describe what his button would read if it had a caption. Blank buttons allow for original inscriptions.

9

Computer Storytelling

N. E. Brewer

INTRODUCTION

This computer storytelling technique grew first from hearing Ruth Lampert (1989) describe her use of the computer with her clients on her audiotape when she asks her clients to generate a feelings list that she types into the computer. Secondly, I have successfully used mutual storytelling, which is a metaphoric counseling technique developed by Richard Gardner (1971, 1986), with some of my young clients. Children always seem interested in stories, both listening to and telling them on their own, and today the computer seems to be in many classrooms, schools and homes as well as offices. It is a fascinating piece of equipment to youngsters (and to me) and it seemed a natural evaluation to encourage my young clients to use the computer to tell their stories.

RATIONALE

This technique seems to aid clients in telling their stories with some distance, which is less threatening, while also seeing their lives in a more balanced perspective. Use of storytelling may also aid the child in generating alternative thoughts, feelings, and actions to some struggle she is having. I look for the character that represents the child, and what themes or patterns are revealed, especially relating to relationship interactions and problem solving, and I may ask a question or two about them. Children seem to feel important while working on the computer, either directly or dictating to me, and this seems to increase their self-confidence. Because they feel powerful and in control of their stories (their lives), sometimes for the first time, this technique seems to increase their sense of mastery in the universe.

DESCRIPTION

In the beginning, I suggest to the child that she may like to use the computer to tell a story with a beginning, a middle, and an end, not something that really happened or that she saw on TV or in the movies. Usually the idea of working on the computer excites the child and she may choose from a variety of ways in which to tell her story. She may work on the computer directly, typing in her own story; she may wish to type in a paragraph and have me type in the next paragraph, alternating turns at the computer until she feels the story is complete; or she may wish to dictate her story to me and let me type it into the computer like a secretary. One client would not write her story, but she wanted to be given words to spell, and every now and then she would use one to tell a story in one sentence. Sometimes I retell a story with a different but healthier ending, suggesting more constructive or appropriate ways of dealing with a life struggle or problem.

APPLICATIONS

I have used this technique with both withdrawn children and aggressive children. Withdrawn children seem to lose themselves in the computer and forget they are inhibited. When we work together creating their stories they feel connected to another person and encouraged to share themselves. The children like seeing words appear in front of them that they have created, as do I. Aggressive children appear to like having control and mastery over this machine, although they must work by computer rules or the computer won't work. They are free to change the story ending if it doesn't stand the test of time. Often the child asks to print her story and take it home to share with her family.

Sometimes children have asked to work on the same story with the computer week after week, and it is interesting to watch their stories change and grow. I never worry about spelling or grammar unless the child wants to have everything "correct," and I usually check this out with the client before we begin instead of interrupting her flow. Occasionally when a child talks about her story, she mentions that her mom is like that sometimes, and this can be an opening for some productive therapeutic work.

I believe the computer is a multifaceted tool that can be an enhancement to present-day play therapy techniques with children, and I welcome others to take this idea and improvise further techniques for the benefit of their young clients.

References

Gardner, R. (1971). *Therapeutic Communication with Children: The Mutual Storytelling Technique.* New York, NY: Jason Aronson.

——— (1986). *The Psychotherapeutic Technique of Richard A. Gardner.* Northvale, NJ: Jason Aronson.

Lampert, R. (1989). *Innovative Interventions in Child Adolescent Therapy.* Long Beach, CA: MaxSound.

10

Using Metaphors, Fairy Tales, and Storytelling in Psychotherapy with Children

Jamshid A. Marvasti

INTRODUCTION

The use of tales and storytelling for the purposes of learning and healing is an ancient phenomenon. In recent years, Milton Erickson (Zeig 1980), Peseschkian (1986a), and Bettelheim (1975) utilized metaphors, fairy tales, and fables as a means of therapeutic intervention. Peseschkian regards fables and parables as images and pictures in language (1986b) that have dealt with inner conflicts and alleviated emotional turmoil long before psychotherapy ever became an establishment.

Probably one of the first examples of the healing effects of stories is the well-known "1001 Nights" book. These tales were used by a captive Scheherazade to heal a tyrannical ruler's thirst for blood. Beside treating the ailing king, these stories are possible "treatments" for the readers and listeners, as they absorb lessons from them and integrate them into their consciousness (Peseschkian 1986a). Clinton (1986) attributed the success of Scheherazade's story to a "talking cure." Compared with the Freudian school, he stated that Scheherazade's storytelling "conforms to the expectations of Baghdad, not Vienna. That is, the doctor does the talking, not the patient and tells tales that address the patient's concerns" (p. 44). The first modern amateur psychotherapists were quite possibly hairdressers and bartenders, and their therapeutic tools, in addition to their listening skills, were anecdotes and life histories of other clients.

The *interspersed technique* was devised by Erickson in order to convey suggestions indirectly to his patients through the embedding of messages with different nonverbal aspects (O'Hanlon 1987, p. 167). *Interspersed suggestions* are underscored during the storytelling by shifting the tonal quality of the therapist's voice to a softer or lower timbre to the point that interspersed suggestions gain a "voice all their own" (Mills and Crowley 1986, p. 140).

The technique described in this chapter is very much influenced by Ericksonian psychotherapy and work of Peseschkian (1986a,b) and Mills and Crowley (1986).

RATIONALE

Stories can be used in play therapy to suggest new possibilities and to get a client's total attention (Wilk 1985), to evoke abilities (Lankton and Lankton 1983), to intersperse suggestions (Zeig 1980), and to establish hope and optimism by exposing the client to a happy ending.

Many clinicians believe that since tales and anecdotes are free from confrontation and direct approach to client symptoms, they may not trigger resistance. Children integrate the components of stories and develop a new attitude toward their conflicts. They may unconsciously borrow the skills and the solutions that the metaphor protagonist uses in order to overcome their problems.

The justification for the utilization of metaphors relies upon the premise that metaphors may pass the conscious level and enter into the unconscious of the child. Although no scientific research or data is available to prove or disprove this theory, many case histories and anecdotal statements demonstrate the influence of metaphors on the unconscious level (Marvasti 1996).

Metaphors aid us in the utilization of knowledge or experiences we have had already in order to make sense of new experiences (O'Hanlon 1987, p. 72). The direct application of a "therapeutic metaphor" via storytelling produces therapeutic results. In general, the story is a complex interweaving of observations, learnings, intuitions, and goals that transfer to the child an important message (Mills and Crowley 1986, p. xix).

Children need not attempt to deduce the story being presented; they easily enter into it with their imaginative powers. These imaginative powers are the elements of change and healing. The metaphors of the story activate the child's imagination for the purposes of healing through strength, self-knowledge, and transformation (Mills and Crowley 1986, p. xxi). The stories change the type of learning from abstract and theoretical concepts to vivid and imaginary modes of thought.

DESCRIPTION

With the help of psychodynamically oriented play diagnosis, the therapist will see the child's world from the child's point of view, and will identify the child's interpersonal needs, assets, conflicts, heroes, and fears (Marvasti 1994). Then, based on these diagnostic findings, the therapist will create a story with a hero (protagonist) who owns the same conflicts, behavior, and ego weakness, but will overcome them by learning new skills and coping mechanisms. The ends of the stories are always positive and successful. The emphasis is on assets rather than losses, potential rather than weakness, hope rather than despair, solution rather than problem, and healing power rather than pathology. In this technique, the therapist's doll takes the child's doll into the doll house, and, with the help of the child's doll, creates a story. The therapist's doll directs the story's outcome toward a successful, happy, and positive ending. Storytelling may occur in the doll house as a group of dolls encircle a fire and listen to a story, or in a playroom with stuffed animals sitting in a circle next to the child. The therapist's doll gradually closes the other dolls' eyes, relaxing them to the point that they appear to be in trance-like states. This may help the child to fall into a trance as well. The dolls and stuffed animals are then left to relax and listen to the puppet's story about "good days" and "happy endings." The puppet's story may contain metaphors and ***interspersed suggestions,*** emphasized in a slow, rhythmic voice, with vocal changes such as tone or volume shifts.

Clinicians have used various sources of material for story-making, such as fairy tales, movie, and cartoon themes, and at times the imagination of the therapist or the child. Several basic ingredients of story-making offered by Mills and Crowley (1986) required in creating a metaphorical storyline include: (1) presenting a ***metaphorical conflict*** similar to that of the child conflict; (2) ***personifying unconscious processes*** via various characters such as heroes and villains, which represent the potentials and fears of the protagonist; (3) integrating ***parallel learning situations*** that result in the protagonist's victory and success; (4) presenting a ***metaphorical crisis*** that eventually becomes a turning point in the resolution of the conflict; (5) developing a ***new sense of identity*** for the protagonist since his victory; and (6) culminating this resolution into a ***celebration*** and a ***sense of new identity*** (Mills and Crowley 1986, p. 138).

APPLICATIONS

This kind of technique may be useful with those children who have the power of imagination and the capacity to fantasize. This technique has been used for treatment of neurotic children: phobia, depression, anxiety, aggression, and victims of emotional or physical trauma.

The therapist's qualifications may be as important as the client's qualifications. The therapist should be creative, intuitive, and imaginative, and familiar with the culture of the client and its metaphors, fairy tales, and parables.

References

Bettelheim, B. (1975). *The Uses of Enchantment: The Meaning and Importance of Fairy Tales.* New York: Knopf.

Clinton, J. (1986). Madness and cure in the Thousand and One Nights. In *Fairy Tales and Society: Illusion, Allusion and Paradigm,* ed. R. Bottigheimer, pp. 1–65. Philadelphia: University of Pennsylvania Press.

Lankton, S., and Lankton, C. (1983). *The Answer Within.* New York: Brunner/Mazel.

Marvasti, J. A. (1994). Play diagnosis and play therapy with child victims of incest. In *Handbook of Play Therapy, Volume II,* ed. C. Schaefer and K. O'Connor, pp. 319–348. New York: Wiley.

——— (1986). Ericksonian play therapy. In K. O'Connor and L. D. Braverman *Play Therapy Theory and Practice: A Comparative Case-Book.* New York: Wiley.

Mills, J. C., and Crowley R., (1986). *Therapeutic Metaphors for Children and the Child Within.* New York: Brunner/Mazel.

O'Hanlon, W. H. (1987). *Taproots: Underlying Principles of Milton Erickson's Therapy and Hypnosis*. New York: Norton.

Peseschkian, N. (1986a). *Oriental Stories as Tools in Psychotherapy*, Berlin: Springer Verlag.

——— (1986b). *Psychotherapy of Everyday Life*. Berlin: Springer Verlag.

Wilk, J. (1985). That reminds me of a story. *Family Therapy Networker* 9(2):45–48.

Zeig, J. K. (1980). *A Teaching Seminar with Milton H. Erickson*. New York: Brunner/Mazel.

11

Art or Verbal Metaphors for Children Experiencing Loss

Glenda F. Short

INTRODUCTION

Working with children where parents are divorcing, or children who have experienced a loss, gives a therapist ample opportunity to do work with direct play therapy techniques. One technique that I use is that of creating art or verbal metaphors so that children can use their cognitive, emotional, and creative skills to express themselves after a loss has occurred. The children are led to discuss what their lives were like prior to the loss and to compare what their lives are like after the loss occurred. They begin to understand what that experience was and what their current experience is at the time of the work with the metaphors.

RATIONALE

This type of work is therapeutic for children as it causes them to begin to reason and identify their feelings. It gives children an opportunity to express their feelings and own their feelings through the drawing of pictures, and gives them further expression when able to explain to the therapist what has happened in their lives. Often, I ask children to draw a picture that would describe how they felt prior to the divorce, then to draw a picture of how they are feeling now that the divorce is occurring.

I work on the premise that if the therapist is successful in helping children identify, express, and own their feelings, they will be able to take this skill and use it for their life processes when loss and confusion occur, no matter the age.

One example is enclosed and is labeled A. A flower with blue sky, yellow sun, and green grass. The other, labeled "a dead flower," speaks for itself.

DESCRIPTION

A child is asked about the feelings and life lived prior to the loss. He is asked to identify and express feelings he remembers about his life and even to tell stories about how his life was at the time before the loss occurred.

He is then asked to discuss how the loss has changed his life and what feelings he now has about his life. Again, stories are helpful for the child to tell so that he can put it into feelings.

The therapist then mirrors the child's words and asks the child to think of something in nature or in his life that he could make a picture of to show how his life was prior to the loss, then make a picture of how his life is after the loss occurred.

APPLICATIONS

I primarily use this with children who are experiencing a loss: of divorce, an illness of the child or a family member, or the death of a significant attachment.

Example A shows a picture of life prior to the divorce that a 6-year-old experienced. She drew a flower, sun, and green grass, telling the story that all was well and happy with her family. In the second picture (Example B), depicting after the loss or after her parents' divorce, she drew a picture of a flower with no color and labeled it "dead flower."

The child was able to share this metaphor with both her parents, who were able to better comprehend what the loss of the family meant to this 6-year-old child. The primary feelings that the child was experiencing were sadness and hopelessness.

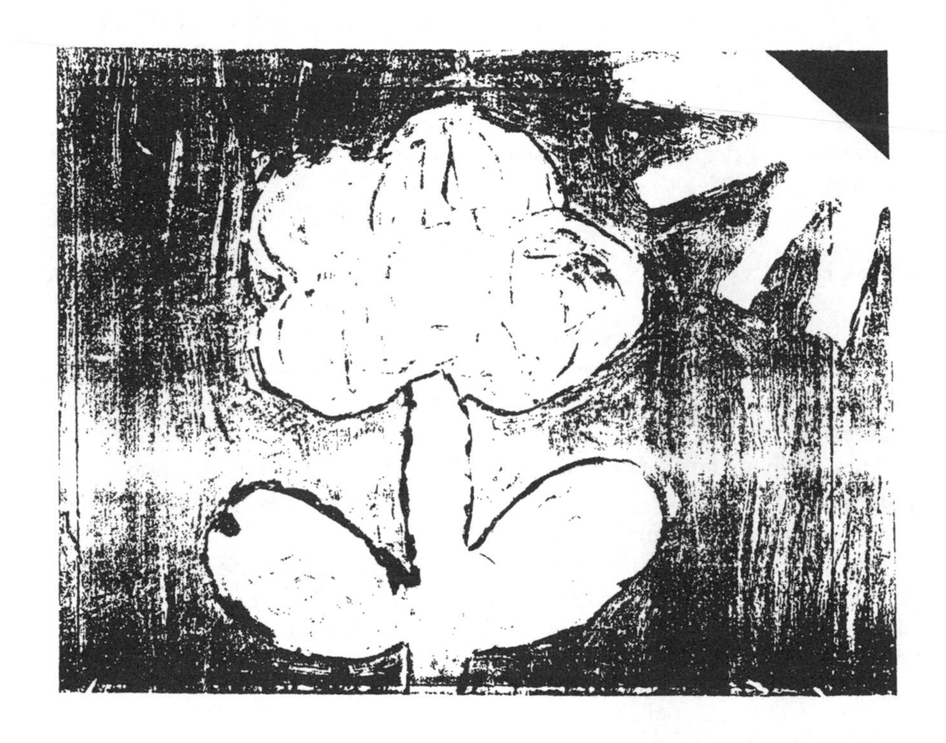

Example A: "the way it was."

Example B: "the way it feels now."

12

The Guess My Word Story Game

Mary Repp

INTRODUCTION

This game is close in form to Richard Gardner's Mutual Storytelling technique, with the added element of competition to encourage the child's interest and involvement. It provides a vehicle for story analysis. I developed this technique by improvising in the play room and putting together information from various workshops and seminars.

RATIONALE

Finding out what thoughts, feelings, underlying issues, themes, and coping patterns are occurring in children is often a daunting task. Generally parents bring in their children describing behaviors they are unhappy with (hitting, lying, fighting, etc.) with little awareness of what might be motivating that behavior. As clinicians we know that getting to more "process" issues will provide more comprehensive treatment as well as long-term results. Even if the child is able to verbalize these issues (e. g., "I am sad that my Mom left"), this game has the added richness the narrative form provides: symbols, complexities, metaphors.

Metaphors can indirectly communicate to the unconscious. The therapist can create a therapeutic metaphor to use as a focused treatment technique. The information gained from the narrative can sometimes be woven into other parts of the therapy and give direction for rituals and parent interventions.

DESCRIPTION

Each person draws a card that has a word written on it. Each person must then make up a story that has a beginning, middle, and end. Then the other person tries to guess what the word was in three tries or less. The therapist can assess for themes and content in stories, give therapeutic messages in his or her story, and get some idea of how well a child can put together and track a cohesive story. The words used can be individually tailored to the particular child, but generally include nouns such as mother, witch, baby, brother, monster, cave, and various feelings (afraid, sad, lonely, etc.).

APPLICATIONS

This technique is best used with a child who has beginning reading skills (6-7 years old through early adolescence). It can be used as a family play therapy experience if the clinician believes parents can participate on the abstract level in an appropriate manner. It is most useful with a child who is resistant to talking about painful issues. Children whom you want to reach through indirect methods can also respond well, since the child's focus is on guessing the word. As an assessment tool, it is helpful in revealing themes, coping skills, and feelings that might otherwise have gone undiscovered. This information might corroborate other information.

Reference

Gardner, R. A. (1979). *Therapeutic Communication with Children: The Mutual Storytelling Technique.* New York: Science House.

13

The Scarf Story

Steve Harvey

INTRODUCTION

Typically, a child therapist sees many children who have extreme difficulties controlling their bodily expression. This is particularly true with younger children, ages 3 to 7, though such difficulties can continue through the teenage years. Often such difficulties are described as Hyperactivity or Attention Deficit Disorder. While cognitive inattention clearly occurs with such children, often anxiety and other mood difficulties are part of the overall clinical picture. Further, such children have extreme resistance to verbal dialogue about their difficulties, making more traditional cognitive therapeutic approaches less effective. The Scarf Story is one of a series of approaches used in Dynamic Play Therapy to address this issue and to help young children develop expressive organization on a physical, nonverbal level, and to develop active metaphor-making from their more organized physical phrasing to help them develop emotional expression.

RATIONALE

Typically, children with impulsivity and distractibility appear to have little control over their bodily expression. This is particularly true when transitions from activity to activity occur, or in transitions in relationships between people. When observing such children's nonverbal expression, the general impression is that they simply don't stop. When looking more carefully at videotapes, it is clear that one gesture leads to another in such a way that this behavior can develop little nonverbal significance in interaction. Further, such children typically either cannot or will not verbally describe their emotional experiences. Interactive episodes tend to produce more tension and frustration than catharsis when these children are engaged with adults and their peers. Gaining these children's attention to form a therapeutic alliance is also quite difficult.

The Scarf Story was designed to address such difficulties and help such children become more organized in their nonverbal expression and in developing imaginative verbal imagery related to their actual body behavior. With these developments, the therapist can help such children use their play expression metaphorically to gain a better understanding and mastery necessary for resolution and integration of their affective experience.

DESCRIPTION

In the Scarf Story, the therapist, parent (when appropriate), and co-therapist use a large (eight to nine foot in diameter) canopy scarf that is made of a light material and is attractively colored. It is this therapist's opinion that scarves function better than parachutes in this activity because the material lends itself to more imaginative dramatic uses. When the Scarf Story begins, the adults present hold the scarf and make it go up and down while the child is underneath. The therapist then tells the story, initially stating exactly what the child does. The child is given the rule of moving when the scarf is up, and stopping when the scarf is down. Even with children who have extreme difficulty inhibiting their movement, most are generally able to slow or stop their movement when they are covered with the scarf. It appears that the scarf helps provide the appropriate condensing of energy to concretely signal more behavioral control.

Gradually, the child and/or parent is encouraged to add verbal imagery to the story itself. Over a series of sessions, the parent and child can usually develop a story of several scenes in length which can have a beginning, middle, and end.

Typically, the therapist's comments start off with, "Once there was a story of a boy/girl who [scarf is raised] jumped up [assuming the child is jumping toward the scarf]." The scarf is then lowered and the therapist states, "And then [scarf is raised] he/she jumped and grabbed the scarf [therapist following child's activity]."

Once the child is able to coordinate movement that begins and ends with the scarf's going up and down and is able to initiate movement that can be reflected verbally by the therapist and/or parent, the therapist can introduce different feeling states, asking the child to make a "happy/sad/angry story." During this time, the therapist reflects the child's body activity with the feeling state rather than asking the child to actually show a clear definition of the more socially acceptable expressions of affect. For example, a therapist might say that "this is a story about a happy boy who is happy *jumping*" as he reflects the child's actual activity. The therapist might say that "this is a *grabbing* happy girl" if the child were to grab the scarf during the activity.

Once the child is able to accomplish a "dance" around feelings that begins and ends in coordination with the scarf movement, the therapist then adds interactive words to the stories. This assumes the child's physical interactive activity with the scarf has some relationship to his or her interactions with significant people. Typically, such statements include things like, "In this happy story, this boy/girl is grabbing hold and not letting go of that scarf Mommy," and so on. Occasionally, a child may run out from under the scarf. At this point the therapist might add, "This boy/girl is running away from his/her. . . ." and then ask the child what is being run away from. The whole goal of these verbal statements and questions is to have the child begin to verbally equate physical interaction with the scarf to a story in a metaphorical way. At this point, the therapist is trying to help the child formulate a physical and verbal story that can express feelings about the relationship with family members.

In family therapy situations, this is a particularly good time to introduce the parent as the initial storyteller so that the parent can begin to use the child's interactive behavior with the scarf as a stimulus for a story of relationship. The parent typically needs to be coached to use the child's actually nonverbal behavior as a cue to influence the parent's actual verbal storytelling metaphor. In this way, the therapist's goal is to have the child's physical interactive behavior with the scarf directly influence his or her parent's verbal storytelling. This use of verbal and nonverbal expressive modes in a coordinated way to develop metaphors can be quite helpful in relationship enhancement.

APPLICATIONS

As in all techniques used in Dynamic Play Therapy, the Scarf Story can be adapted for use in families with children of any age. The Scarf Story has been used successfully with mothers and toddlers who are experiencing relational difficulties. The storytelling here, of course, is more for the parent's than child's benefit, and the therapist typically uses the scarf more as a metaphor for the attachment between parent and child in a direct sense to better focus the parent on his or her child's nonverbal expressions of need and distress. Clearly, when using the Scarf Story with preschool children, the therapist must have some knowledge of more concrete, direct, and simple stories that typically gain the attention of children this age. When using this technique with elementary school-aged children, the therapist must adapt the story to incorporate action and words to help these older children begin to have an interest in their actual body behavior for this technique to be successful.

14

Storytelling with Objects

Jackie K. Frederiksen

RATIONALE

Storytelling enables children to identify feelings and learn consequences to the situations they are involved in. It is a technique that can be useful to all counselors. It is easy to do and the results are extremely beneficial. Kids love to tell stories using this technique, and usually in one 30-minute session, they can tell up to four stories.

DESCRIPTION

First, gather five objects from a playroom, using a variety of objects such as a shark, toy drink cans, army soldiers, sunglasses, key chains, dolls, fake fingernails, a mirror and so on. Then lay out the five items and explain the rules of storytelling to the elementary-school-age child. According to the rules, the child must pick an object to use in his story. Second, he must tell a story that is interesting, because everyone wants to hear good stories. Third, the story must teach a lesson or have a moral. Tell the child that you are going to listen to what he says and then repeat the story back to him. The child then tells the story using an object of his choice. It is amazing what they will tell you. As the child tells the story, try to figure out who they are in the story, and what the conflict is about. Also try to understand which feeling the child is uncomfortable with: shame, vulnerability, fear, or other feeling. The child then tells the moral or lesson that the story teaches the listener. Then retell the story in a problem-solving way. Having to retell the story makes one listen intently and sometimes, if the ending does not teach a lesson, you can interject one in a nonthreatening way. The goal is to tell the story and retell the story to teach consequences and identify feelings. It is therapeutic because the child can describe to you what's going on in his life in a nonthreatening yet revealing way.

APPLICATIONS

This technique can be used with a wide variety of children. I have used it with children of abuse, aggression, withdrawal, and neglect. I worked with a girl who had recently reported to me in a regular counseling session that she had been molested by her mother's boyfriend. As a result of the Child Protective Services' report, the family had to go to the police and the boyfriend moved out. It turned out the girl was lying to me about the abuse to get rid of her mother's boyfriend. Her mother was very upset by the whole incident: having to go to the police station, the boyfriend moving out, and the fact that it had even been reported. She talked with me numerous times about the embarrassment her daughter had put them through. She also blamed me for reporting what the daughter had told me since it had caused the family so much shame. When I brought the girl in we did storytelling. All of the stories she told related to getting in trouble for stealing or lying. In each story, using four different objects, her mother was either mad at her for having to go down to the police station and all the hassle she had caused, or she and her mother were very embarrassed about feeling that everyone was staring at them. In one story she told using the mirror, she said that her mother and she had tried to go to a ball. Each time they arrived everyone was staring at them. First it was because they forgot their shoes, so they had to go back home and get them. When they went back to the ball they had forgotten their dresses, and then their makeup. But each time they went back to the ball everyone was staring at them. The mother was embarrassed, and it was the girl's fault. One of the lessons she learned was all about the embarrassment and shame she caused her mother. As she told the story I could see the things her mother had been telling her at home illustrated in the stories. The issues of embarrassment and of telling things she wasn't supposed to tell were very evident in the stories. The stories also portrayed the disappointment her mother felt toward her daughter, and I imagine toward herself.

Section Three

Expressive Arts Techniques

15

The Before and After Drawing Technique

Donna Cangelosi

INTRODUCTION

This technique was developed for use with children from divorced and separated families. It is an extension of the Kinetic Family Drawing (KFD) technique (Burns and Kaufman 1970) and can be used for diagnostic purposes and as an instrument for psychotherapy.

RATIONALE

Why this technique is helpful for children

Most children enjoy drawing and will find this exercise less threatening than talking about an upsetting experience or loss, which is likely experienced as overwhelming and extremely confusing. Furthermore, this exercise allows the child to share perceptions and feelings at a pace which is comfortable and safe.

Freud (1908) and Niederland (1979) note that everything lost must be replaced. They believe that creative expression, in and of itself, provides the individual who has undergone a significant loss with a self-healing, reparative experience. At both a cognitive and emotional level, this exercise helps the child to process changes that have occurred and to mourn the "before" while accepting the realities of the "after" or present.

Why this technique is helpful for therapists

Many children who have experienced parental divorce or other traumas develop a defense of pseudomaturity, or simply withdraw in order to cope with their experience. Accordingly, projective approaches often give a more accurate portrayal of their internal experiences and therefore, provide the therapist with a better understanding of defenses, conflicts, and ego resources. With this information, the therapist is better equipped to provide interventions that are attuned to the child's perceptions, concerns, and resources (both internal and environmental).

As a diagnostic tool this exercise can be used to assess the child's perceptions of his or her family dynamics and place within the family unit both before and after the breakup or change. In addition to its diagnostic utility, this technique can be used in therapy to promote a discussion of changes, losses, and adaptations that are brought about by parental divorce and other experiences of loss.

Before and After Drawings can be used to help the child (1) confront the painful situation that has occurred; (2) address the resulting realities; (3) acknowledge and work through losses, gains, and related feelings; and (4) develop coping skills. With regard to the last, therapists can use this technique as a vehicle for providing children with information about conflict resolution, problem solving, and skills that enhance adaptation.

DESCRIPTION

Materials:

This technique requires drawing paper, pencils, crayons, markers, and colored pencils. When working with children who have problems with impulse control, it is helpful to use smaller pieces of paper (8½ × 11) to help contain their anxiety and impulsiveness. When working with depressed or constricted children, it is helpful to use large sheets of paper to help promote spontaneity and expression (Kissel 1990).

Directions:

Ask the child to draw a picture of his/her family before the family breakup, loss, or change and another picture of the family afterward (i.e., in the present). Inclusions, exclusions, and the physical placement of family members provide valuable diagnostic information and a vehicle for exploration and problem solving.

APPLICATIONS

This technique was initially designed for use in my work with children from divorced or separated families. However, over time I have expanded its use to include any child who has undergone a major life change, separation, loss, or trauma.

In addition to addressing losses, this technique is helpful for assessing positive changes that have taken place following the traumatic event. It is useful to look for these in the "after" picture and to reinforce and build upon whatever healthy resources, relationships, and methods of coping are revealed. For instance, I have noted that children frequently bond with siblings after a divorce (e.g., they place themselves closer to one or more siblings in the "after" picture, or establish an apparent similarity which was not evident in the "before" picture). Such a bond can be reinforced to counter feelings of alienation, withdrawal, and isolation that may be experienced by the child. In addition, a close relationship with a sibling may help the child feel less alone in terms of his or her emotions. Knowing that at least one other person feels similarly about a situation can take away the burden of feeling uncomfortable with the mixed and confusing emotions that frequently result from parental divorce and other losses.

References

Burns, R. C. and Kaufman, S. H. (1970). *Kinetic Family Drawings (KFD).* New York: Brunner/Mazel.

Cangelosi, D. (in press). Play therapy with children from divorced and separated families. In *The Playing Cure,* ed. H. Kaduson, D. Cangelosi, and C. E. Schaefer, Northvale, NJ: Jason Aronson.

Freud, S. (1988). Creative writers and daydreaming. *Standard Edition* 9:143–153.

Kissel, S. (1990). *Play Therapy: A Strategic Approach.* Springfield IL: Charles C. Thomas.

Niederland, W. G. (1979). Trauma, loss, restoration, and creativity. In *The Problem of Loss and Mourning: Psychoanalytic Perspectives,* ed. D. R. Dietrich and P. C. Shabad, pp 61–82.

16

Feeling Balloons

Glenda F. Short

INTRODUCTION

This technique was first developed in order to give a child a visual prop to identify, express, and own his or her feelings.

RATIONALE

This technique is helpful for all children and provides some fun and creativity in seeing and understanding that there are many feelings that are available. There may be limited feelings that may apply to certain people and/or circumstances in children's lives.

DESCRIPTION

Three or more balloons are drawn by the child. In balloon number one, all feelings that this child knows about are verbalized and are placed in the balloon, which is called "all kinds of feelings." The additional balloons are also given names. For example, if a child is dealing with feelings regarding a divorce, the next balloon could be named "divorce." A third and fourth balloon might be labeled "Mom" and "Dad." The balloons can be named differently as needed to fit the issue needing to be addressed. From the "all kinds of feelings" balloon, feelings are placed in the "Mom" and "Dad" balloons. The child expresses and discusses the feelings. Sometimes the child has the same feelings or different feelings for the parents. Normalcy is established and anxiety often relaxes as the child begins to understand what he or she is feeling.

APPLICATIONS

This activity can be used with groups, families, individuals, and sibling groups. Schoolteachers can use this to discuss school situations and enable the children to discuss their feelings regarding the situation. All issues and life events can be topics of Feeling Balloons. In a classroom, a child can have an individual feeling balloon and stick his or her day-to-day feelings on the board. There are a variety of creative ways to use this technique at home, school, or therapy room.

17

Magic Art

Ruby Walker

INTRODUCTION

Projective techniques have been used to help understand people since late in the nineteenth century. Goodenough (1926) related intelligence to drawing, and Harris (1963) studied the development of human figure drawings by relating drawing maturation to intellectual development.

Rorschach's inkblots were among the first projective tests, where the person explores his inner feelings and conflicts by responding to a ambiguous stimulus. In the Magic Art technique, the child selects the color of paper and paint and, after making the picture, identifies the objects or feelings he receives from the picture. The significance lies in the colors chosen, figures, objects, or feelings described as they relate to the whole picture or individual objects picked out from the entire picture. After the child describes the picture, I ask him questions such as, "What makes it look like a ——— to you?" I relate what the child says to possible inner feelings and look at the color selection by the child with regard to the paper and the paints and the intensity with which the child prepares the picture. This tells the emotional reactivity of the child when he prepares and talks about his picture.

RATIONALE

The therapeutic value of this technique lies in the freedom to choose the colors, the manner of applying the paint, and the description of the figures. Children with control issues love the freedom and lack of control in their work. The success in making the picture is a significant boost for those youngsters who have low self-esteem. Therefore, I use this technique with children who are just entering play therapy, so they have positive feelings toward therapy and their work in the playroom. The delighted look on the child's face when he opens his creation is priceless.

DESCRIPTION

Have a wide range of colors of construction paper from which the child may freely choose a piece of paper. Have available red, blue, yellow, green, white, black, brown, and assorted colors of liquid tempera paint in bottles that have a very small opening in the top. My instructions to the child are: "You may select a piece of paper and use any of the colors of paint, at least three, to make a magic picture. You may use the paints to make any lines, dots, or draw any figure you'd like." A child who is not confident will want you to select the color of paper, the colors, tell him where to put it, and so on. Reinforce his selection of colors and where he is putting the paint. It is obvious that you need to have an area where you can clean up the paint if it is spilled or is squeezed out when you fold the paper. After the child puts on the paint, have him fold the paper (long ends together) and say, "Magic picture, what will [insert child's name] draw today?" Then have the child take hold of the edges of the paper and unfold the painting. I also keep several colors of glitter and allow the child to add sparkles to his picture if he so chooses. The child then tells me what he sees in the picture or describes the entire picture. I then ask him "What makes it look like a __________ to you?" (Cohen 1988).

The bottles selected for the paint are very important. Use bottles that have a very small opening, no larger than a round toothpick. If the hole is too large, too much paint is dispersed and children who tend to get overstimulated will use too much paint and make a mess. I try to keep the directions simple so the child is not corrected or told he is using too much paint. I like this to be a nondirective activity where the child is completely in charge.

APPLICATIONS

This is a fantastic icebreaker for a new client, but is also a favorite of all the children. It is almost impossible to make the same picture twice and it is a delightful activity for any child. Interestingly enough, I have had some pretty hard-core bullies sit down and make a Magic Art picture and leave with a better feeling about themselves. This is a projective technique that lets the child free associate and lets you experience his emotionality as he prepares and describes what he sees. I use it to bolster self-esteem in children, and it is also invaluable for a child who feels he has no control in his life. I use it to reinforce his selections and admire the finished product. It is not possible to make a "bad" picture. I use this technique with small groups as we discuss divorce or other issues. I begin with having them draw a caterpillar using any colors they want. Then, as I discuss the transformation of the caterpillar into a cocoon and finally into the butterfly, we fold our caterpillars and there is our butterfly. I characterize this as how a situation like divorce can end in a positive experience. I have also used this technique in abuse treatment as the child learns that he also makes a transformation.

References

Cohen, R. J., Montague, P., Nathanson, L., and Swerdik, M. E. (1988). *Psychological Testing—An Introduction to Tests and Measurement.* Mountain View, CA: Mayfield.

Goodenough, F. L. (1926). *Measurement of Intelligence by Drawings.* New York: Harcourt, Brace, and World.

Harris, D. B. (1963). *Children's Drawings as Measures of Intellectual Maturity.* New York: Harcourt, Brace, and World.

18

The Yarn Drawing Game

Norma Y. Leben

INTRODUCTION

Fourteen years ago, when I was an overworked psychotherapist and a treatment supervisor of a residential treatment facility, I had sixteen hyperactive multiproblem children to treat. The catch was there was no budget for therapeutic toys. Partly for survival reasons and partly for the challenge, I drew from my social group work, correctional, psychological, and recreation background. The result was the invention of low-budget, fast-paced games that sustain even the most hyperactive, low self-esteem, and traumatized child. The Yarn Drawing Game is one such game, along with 59 others described in my book (Leben 1994).

RATIONALE

This technique offers an alternative to paper-and-pencil drawing. For the low self-esteem children, their fear of criticism prohibits them from picking up a drawing utensil. With the use of yarn, if they don't like how the yarn is positioned, all they have to do is to reposition it. This is non-threatening yet engaging for even the most unsophisticated player. There

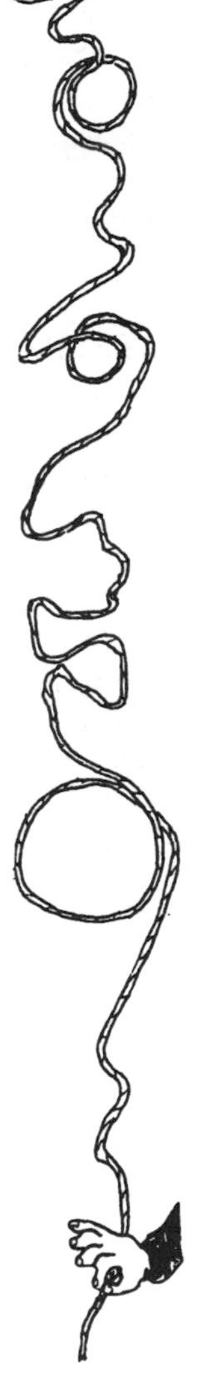

is no right or wrong design. This acceptance is empowering to most clients. The game also promotes creativity, self-esteem, and sense of observation. In the process of watching the child "draw" with the yarn, the therapist may have new information for diagnosis and assessment.

DESCRIPTION

The therapist makes available a ball of yarn or string; any color or thickness will do. The therapist demonstrates, unravelling a length of yarn and then coiling and shaping it to create part of the "drawing" on the table or floor. The ball of yarn is handed to the first child and the child is encouraged to continue with the "drawing." The first child holds his or her drawing in place while a second child further unravels the yarn and continues with the "drawing." After all the children have had a turn the therapist begins a discussion on the cooperative group "drawing."

At this point, the therapist may put several questions to the group for discussion about what is "seen" in the drawing. Each answer will be validated with reward (tokens) or verbal praise.

Examples of some of the questions:

Can you tell me what letters of the alphabet do you see?

What shapes do you see?

What numerals do you see?

What kinds of food do you see?

What does this whole picture remind you of: people, places, or events?

With the fast pace and rewarding the players, ideas come very quickly and the players' levels of confidence also improve. Some players gave me the feedback that during the game they picked up the impression that "anything was O.K.," and they felt encouraged with the visual validation of the tokens in their bowls.

For children who seem to be shy or slow with ideas, the therapist can encourage them to move around the table or step back to see if the extra distance jogs their imaginations. Therapeutic remarks made in those instances can be "Let's look at this problem from different angles and see if any ideas will come to you."

APPLICATIONS

This technique applies to ADHD, ODD, low self-esteem, easily distractible, impulsive, aggressive, and withdrawn clients in most cases (individuals, families and groups).

Reference

Leben, N. Y. (1994). *Directive Group Play Therapy—60 Structured Games for the Treatment of ADHD, Low Self-Esteem and Traumatized Children*, Pflugerville, TX: Morning Glory Treatment Center for Children.

19

Clayscapes

Lynn B. Hadley

INTRODUCTION

The clayscape is an expressive arts technique that incorporates the properties of clay work as described by Violet Oaklander (1988), and principles of world building in Sand Tray therapy (DeDomenico 1988). The use of this technique is based upon the theoretical and clinical recognition of art as an extension of the play process (Dundas 1978, Kramer 1977).

RATIONALE

This clinician has found the clayscape to be a powerful medium for facilitating expression and communication of significant issues and conflicts that had previously been inaccessible to the therapist and client. Oaklander describes modeling with clay as "promoting the working through the most primal of internal processes" (p. 67). The addition of figures and other materials allows clients the opportunity to select symbols that may stimulate creative expression of personal themes, experiences, and emotions. In addition, tangible symbols may encourage a child who may be resistant to or lack confidence in using clay.

DESCRIPTION

Materials needed: modeling clay, clay board or heavy poster board, clay tools, toothpicks and craft sticks, assorted figures and symbols. The client is first introduced to the clay and its properties, through active modeling and "warm-up" with the medium. The therapist proceeds to suggest to the client that he or she may be able to create a story or clay world with the materials. The basket of tools and materials is moved within reach of the client. The client is instructed that he or she may use clay and any other materials to create this world, and if something else is needed to ask the therapist or retrieve it from other materials in the play therapy room. (For example, a diabetic patient needed red paint to graphically illustrate blood.) Some clients may choose to form the clay directly on top of the existing figures. This process may promote confidence in utilizing the medium while allowing the client to select personal symbols and benefit from the manipulation of the clay. The emphasis is on creative expression, not artistic ability. All client-initiated methods are acceptable. The therapist uses appropriate techniques to facilitate the client's process, such as silence or supportive and reflective comments as the client works, in addition to observing the client's interaction with the materials and the clayscape as it progresses. Specific observations may include the quality and intensity of the client's use of the clay, sequence and selection of symbols selected or created, verbal and nonverbal behaviors before, during, and after the creation of the clayscape, including symbols that are removed, destroyed, or changed. When the client has finished, the therapist takes time with the client to look at the world or sculpture that has been created. The therapist then asks the client to tell about his or her clayscape. The therapist's philosophical orientation, stage of client's therapy, and client needs and goals will determine the next step. The therapist may focus on individual aspects or figures and central themes, or suggest an extension of the work, such as story writing. A therapeutic goal may be to assist the client in identifying and finding meaning in his or her representation. A photograph may be taken to preserve the work.

APPLICATIONS

This expressive arts technique may be appropriate in a wide range of cases in order to: facilitate increased self-esteem; increase client–therapist communication; remove the focus from verbalization when used to defend or to avoid contact with emotional content; bring concrete form to feelings, fantasies, fears, and experiences; maintain the client sense of control while reducing physical tension with anxious and aggressive clients. The clayscape is recommended for ages 10 and older, and seems to be particularly effective with boys.

References

DeDomenico, G. (1988). *Sand Tray World Play. A Comprehensive Guide to the Use of the Sand Tray in Psychotherapeutic and Transformational Settings.* Oakland, CA.

Dundas, E. (1978). *Symbols Come Alive in the Sand.* Boston: Coventure.

Kramer, E. (1977). *Art as Therapy with Children.* New York: Schocken.

Nickerson, E. (1983). Art as a play therapeutic medium. In *Handbook of Play Therapy,* ed. C. Schaefer and K. O'Connor, pp. 234–250. New York: Wiley.

Oaklander, V. (1988). *Windows to Our Children.* New York: Center for Gestalt Development.

20

Bad Dreams

L. G. Agre

INTRODUCTION

Bad dreams sometimes come up in the play situation. This technique was derived from reading about dream work in *The Centering Book* by Gay Hendricks and Russell Wills (1975) and about neuro-linguistic programming (NLP) in books by Grinder and Bandler (1982, 1985).

RATIONALE

Using this technique allows a child to understand that each of us creates our dreams and that we can choose to change our dreams if we so desire. A child is empowered by this technique, and this technique is open-ended: depending on the child's intellectual capacity, a child can go on to use NLP principles to develop goals and visualize himself performing tasks the way he would like to perform tasks.

When a child brings up nightmares, I talk about how we make up our dreams in our own heads and about how we can change our dreams. We can pretend to have our own remote control to squeeze to change our dreams.

DESCRIPTION

First the child is asked to describe his dream. Then we talk about how he would like his dream to end, how he could change his dream. Then I have the child draw a picture of how he wants his dream to end.

Next, I have the child close his eyes and tell me about the dream. When the child gets to the scary part of the dream, I have him squeeze his hand as if it held a remote control, and then the child finishes the dream the way he wants it to end.

When the child tells me he can see the new ending, I touch him lightly on the wrist or arm to anchor the new ending. The child is then told to open his eyes. We repeat this process at least three times.

I have the child take home his picture of the new ending to put under his pillow. I check with the child the next two or three days to see if we were successful. If not, we repeat the process.

APPLICATIONS

I use this technique with a child whose nightmare appears to be the result of scary movies or tall tales told by older siblings. The dreamer and dream cue me into whether or not the dream is of benign origin.

This technique seems to work with almost all children. However, it did not work with a severely emotionally disturbed child (as defined by special education guidelines) or with one other child. I rarely use this technique with children I know or suspect of having been sexually abused.

References

Bandler, (1985). *Using Your Brain—for a Change.* Moab, UT: Real People Press.

Bandler, R. and Grinder, J. (1982). *Reframing: Neuro-Linguistic Programming and the Transformation of Meaning.* Moab, UT: Real People Press.

Hendricks, G., and Wills, R. (1975). *The Centering Book.* Englewood Cliffs, NJ: Prentice-Hall.

21

The Personality Pie

Tara M. Sinclair

INTRODUCTION

The Personality Pie is a technique developed within the conceptual framework of Psychosynthesis. Psychosynthesis is both a philosophy of psychology as well as a therapeutic modality that was developed by an Italian psychiatrist, Roberto Assagioli. Assagioli, a contemporary of Freud, felt that the psychoanalytic framework excluded vital aspects of psychic life and needed to be expanded to include the full spectrum of consciousness. Thus, in addition to the lower unconscious and conscious mind, Assagioli posited the existence of the higher unconscious mind; the source of altruistic impulses, creative strivings, and the yearning for purpose and meaning in our lives.

Assagioli noted that, just as we repress lower unconscious, sexual, and aggressive impulses, we also repress higher unconscious wisdom and the drive toward life goals that transcend adaptation and survival.

The theory and practice of Psychosynthesis strives to facilitate the integration of the personality and to promote the expansion of consciousness in ways that infuse life with a sense of joy and meaningful direction.

RATIONALE

The Personality Pie is a useful technique to explore different facets of a youngster's personality. It promotes self-disclosure and self-awareness for the client and is a good assessment tool for the therapist. This technique can help the client become aware of the observing ego and enables the therapist to assess the client's capacity for such awareness.

The Personality Pie can be constructed for children as young as 7. Since at this age the capacity for abstract reasoning is limited, the technique is presented using more concrete, action-oriented language. For children aged 10 and older, more abstract terminology can be used.

DESCRIPTION

The Personality Pie is initiated by drawing the child into a discussion about the fact that we all act differently in different settings, depending on who we're with or how we feel. For instance, most kids act one way in school and another way with friends and family. Also, each of us has different abilities (i. e., athletic, artistic, academic) that we want to express. All of this suggests that we have different parts to our personality.

As this general discussion is underway, the therapist begins to draw what looks like a donut (illustration below).

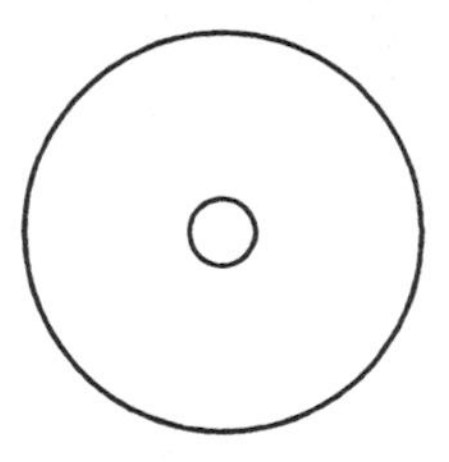

By the end of the discussion, the donut has been divided into four sections, as illustrated below:

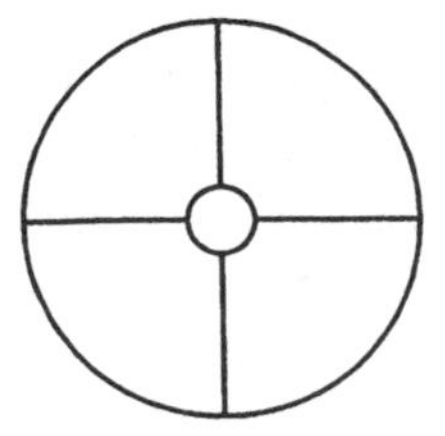

The center of the donut has not been intersected and, as the child is invited to draw a picture in each quadrant that represents a different part of his or her personality, the therapist casually mentions that the child should remind the therapist to explain what's in the center when the activity is complete. This creates a sense of mystery and also helps motivate the child to complete the activity.

Once the drawing is complete, the therapist can ask if anything has been forgotten or what needs to happen to complete the picture. The child will invariably mention the mysterious empty center of the pie. The therapist then reveals that this is the "eye of the pie" and draws an eye in the center as illustrated below:

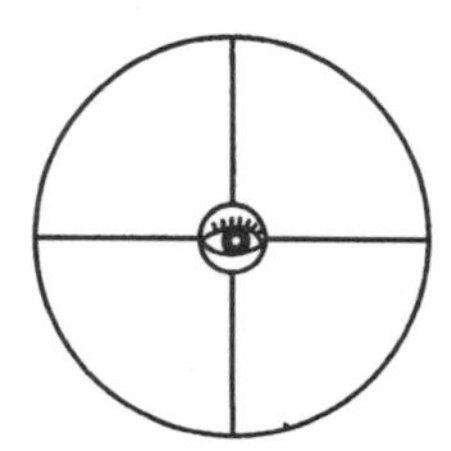

The therapist explains that we all have this inner eye, which gives us the power to be aware of each part of our personality so that we can see how we're feeling and what we're doing, and can therefore make choices about how to deal with our feelings and actions.

As a follow-up activity, the therapist can suggest that the next time the child is upset he or she remember the eye of the pie and that therapist and child can discuss this at their next session.

APPLICATIONS

If the therapist knows something of the child's core issues or areas of need, verbal prompts can be given to help the child express those issues as parts of the Personality Pie. For example, if the child is hyperactive, he or she can be asked to draw the part of the self that has so much energy and needs to be moving. Likewise, a child who suffers from school phobia might be asked to draw a picture in one quadrant that represents what it feels like to be in school and, in another quadrant, what it feels like to be at home. If the therapist knows that the child is artistic and tends to be a loner, separate drawings for each of these parts can be elicited to explore the relationship between solitude and creativity.

Since identity issues are key in adolescence, youngsters entering this phase of development can be directed to draw the image they think others have of them: how parents, friends, teachers, the opposite sex, see them. Another useful variation is to have the person draw an image that represents how they'd like to be seen, as well as a depiction of their present self-image. Questions can be asked that allow the therapist to gain insight into how fixed or fluid these images are for the person; does the adolescent imagine that, over time, these images might change?

Finally, there are certain aspects of the personality (the inner child and the inner parent or judge) that have gained recognition in popular psychology. These too can be incorporated into the Personality Pie.

EXAMPLE

The Personality Pie was used as an activity with a group of six adolescent girls who were having a great deal of difficulty getting along with each other. In the group, they were instructed to depict or describe the following in each of the four quadrants of the Personality Pie:

1. The Public Self: the part of yourself that you show to others.
2. The Private Self: The part of yourself that you don't want others to see.
3. The Inner Child: the part of yourself that carries your deepest feelings, both positive and negative, and that still feels like a child, even though you're growing up.
4. The Inner Critic: the part of yourself that may put you down, call you names or judge what you're doing.

All of the participants in this group were able to complete a Personality Pie and to share the results (optional) with the group. It helped the girls to realize that they had more in common than they thought and that they all shared vulnerable feelings and the need to act stronger or "cooler" then they felt. What was striking in their responses was the harsh words they were absorbing from the Inner Critic and the effect of this aspect on their self esteem and behavior.

References

Assagioli, R. (1965). *Psychosyntheses.* New York: Viking, 1980.

——— (1974). *The Act of Will.* New York: Viking.

Ferrucci, P. (1983). *What We May Be.* Los Angeles: Tarcher.

Fudgitt, E. (1983). *He Hit Me Back First!* Rolling Hills Estates, CA: Jalmar Press.

Hardy, J. (1987). *A Psychology With a Soul.* New York: Routledge & Kegan Paul.

Weiser, J. and Yeomans, T., eds. (1985). *Readings in Psychosynthesis.* Toronto: Ontario Institute for Studies in Education.

Whitmore, D. (1986). *Psychosynthesis In Education: The Joy of Learning.* Rochester, VT: Destiny Books.

22

Life Maps

Glenda F. Short

INTRODUCTION

The Life Map is a simple art technique where children draw four (or more) specific important life events they have experienced.

RATIONALE

This technique is used to allow children to comprehend a past, present, and future and to be able to identify, express, and own their feelings regarding their life events.

DESCRIPTION

The therapist can provide the child with a piece of paper with four circles on it, or the child can draw the four circles. Children are to draw in the circles four events they deem important in their life. This can be discussed before hand with the child, allowing the child to tell stories of his life events prior to drawing them. The drawings are then talked about in detail, giving feelings to each picture. Often parents are given a chance to listen to the children. Sometimes the child changes his story for the parents. It then becomes important for the therapist to explore with the child what his fears are if he tells his "true feelings." Pictures often give important information to the therapist about the family and the child's relationship with others.

APPLICATIONS

This activity is used with children beginning at age 4 years. It is used with all types of cases, as it helps children tell stories, identify feelings, and express those feelings. It helps children begin to see the process of life events and how there is a past, present and future.

Example A: Loss of father in the home and adjusting to a new baby sister and to school.

Circle number one: Shows his mother cuddling him and loving him. He tells that "I was the best baby. I was better than my baby sister."

Circle number two: Shows him scratching his father's back and with his swimming tube. He tells that if he scratches his dad's back, they will go swimming. He talks with the therapist about how much he misses his dad and that he doesn't see him enough. (When telling his mother about the second circle, he glosses over his missing his dad and does not elaborate about him and his dad swimming.)

Circle number three: Shows the child in school his kindergarten year. He tells, "I was scared. I didn't know much what to do and the teacher yelled." When telling his mother about the picture, the child states, "There I am in kindergarten doing everything I was supposed to do." His original words to the therapist are congruent with the look on his face.

Circle number four: Shows the child in school once again. He states, "This is me in first grade and I feel better about knowing what to do in school. Sometimes I like school." A general rule is that children who are older will often have more elaborate life maps and give more description of the events. It is important to write a story with each circle so the child can understand that he has a story. One step further to the Life Maps is to have the child talk about his control in the situations and what could the story have been if he or she made a different choice about the event. If the child has no control, talking about that is important, as the child will begin to understand that he sometimes does not have a choice about the event, but does have a choice about what he will do about how the event impinges on his life.

Explained to therapist:

1) "This is my mom. She loves me and helps me."

2) "This is me and my dad. When he was home, we scratched each others back in the morning." (Explained to mom. "You know how I had to scratch dad's back—glad that's over.")

3) "This is me in kindergarten. I was scared and didn't understand what to do. My dad left when I was in kindergarten." (Explained to mom: "This is me in kindergarten doing everything I was supposed to do.")

4) "This is me in 1st grade. I wasn't so scared." (Explained to mom: "This is me in 1st grade doing everything I was supposed to do.")

23

Play Art

Lynn B. Hadley

INTRODUCTION

This interactive art technique is loosely based upon Gardner's (1983) storytelling technique, and reflects the art therapy principles of Violet Oaklander (1988) and Judith Rubin (1978). The technique requires very active therapist participation in the child's expressive process.

RATIONALE

Interactive or "Play Art" combines the therapeutic aspects of play and art therapy. The client produces a symbolic representation of inner experience, and is encouraged through therapist responses to play with and elaborate on the themes expressed. The experience may be cathartic, lead the child to view the self in new ways, offer potential resolutions to conflicts, activate inner resources for healing, and actively engage the child in relationship and communication with the therapist.

DESCRIPTION

Materials needed: paint and brushes, markers, crayons, pencil, paper (may include various sizes). The child is presented with the art materials and is free to choose one or a combination to create a picture. Initially the child is allowed to work with the therapist observing but providing minimal verbalization. After the child has finished he or she is asked to tell about the picture. The therapist begins the interactive process by playfully giving a voice to a symbol on the page, or asking the child to do so and then responding, or by making a leading comment about some aspect of the story created (e. g., "How scary! What happens next?"). The therapist structures a storytelling format while encouraging the child to continually add to the picture with the available media. The client and the therapist are active partners in this play art. Symbols may be painted, drawn over, lines or shapes may be added to depict movement of characters around the page, and so on as the story progresses. The therapist must make verbalizations and interventions based upon several factors, including the child's affect, behavior, verbalizations, content of artwork, and story. The art process may span many pieces of paper, and requires that the therapist be available to immediately add a new sheet as needed. After the story is completed, the therapist may choose to review the story with the child, emphasizing important emotional or content themes.

APPLICATIONS

This clinician has found the technique to be effective in helping children work through acute trauma (such as painful or frightening medical procedures), significantly reducing anxiety in a single session. Play Art may also be successful with children who have difficulty expressing themselves with toys or unstructured creative arts materials. Recommended for ages 4–10.

References

Gardner, R. (1983). Treating oedipal problems with the mutual storytelling technique. *Handbook of Play Therapy,* C. Schaefer and K. O'Connor, eds, New York: Wiley, pp. 355–368.

Oaklander, V. (1988). *Windows to Our Children.* New York: Center for Gestalt Development.

Rubin, J. (1978). *Child Art Therapy.* New York: Van Nostrand Reinhold Company.

24

Gloop: Treating Sensory Deprivation

Neil Cabe

INTRODUCTION

One of the many unfortunate sequelae of abuse and neglect in children is the pervasive sensory deprivation so regularly seen in these children. The child lacks any sort of grounding based simply on his or her own five senses. Part of the focus of therapy with deprived youngsters lies in providing appropriate sensory stimulation in a safe environment where boundaries are clear and a caring play therapist can provide guidance and reassurance to the child.

Lusebrink (1990) describes a set of healing dimensions and emergent functions in children, and suggests that they move from most resistant to least resistant media. A child might progress from pencils, to crayons, to markers, to water colors, to poster paints, and then to finger paints. Urging the child toward less resistive media early in the therapeutic process is counterproductive. The earliest stages of the therapeutic process lie in animation, a kinesthetic stage developing consciousness and perception, and trust, a sensory and perceptual phase emphasizing assurance and security (Cabe 1995). Later, as the child becomes vested in the therapeutic process and learns self-efficacy and effective interaction with his environment, less resistive media may be introduced safely and with success.

RATIONALE

Two very successful exercises in my work with abused and neglected children have been the making of personal play clay and the making of personal silly putty we call GLOOP. In each exercise, the child and therapist are both fully involved. The exercise is a tactile one, and the play period is both pleasurable and healing for the child. The play clay is the more resistive of the two substances, and may reasonably be entertained earlier in the therapeutic process. The GLOOP is a very fluid exercise, and is appropriate only later. In practice, many of my young clients have been unable to even touch materials as fluid as finger paint and GLOOP early in treatment. Some are so sensationally deprived that the activities are simply too threatening, insisting on hand washings when even small amounts of paint or glue get on their hands. This changes later in treatment.

DESCRIPTION

The play clay is a simple, nontoxic mixture of flour, salt, water, and vegetable oil. Food coloring may be added, and flavors are appropriate if the child wishes. When the exercise includes coloring and flavoring, the child will excite his senses of touch, smell, taste, and sight. Further, since the therapist is actively involved with the child, the relationship continues to be built, and the child's imagination comes into play as characters and objects are constructed using the material after it is created. Finally, the child may take the play clay home with him, allowing for the possibility of the conservation of ground gained in this enjoyable and constructive session.

GLOOP is a mixture of Elmer's Glue™, water, and one tablespoon of Twenty Mule Team Borax™ laundry powder. The exercise allows for the same sorts of gains as the play clay, but is much more fluid. This is a messy activity but great fun, and has been one requested second and third times with some of the children I have seen. Food coloring may be used sparingly, but flavoring will not overcome the odor of the glue itself and is therefore not used. While Elmer's is non-toxic, and the amount of Twenty

Mule Team Borax used is minimal, it is also necessary to stress to the child that he or she should not eat the mixture. Flavoring may make the GLOOP more closely resemble some food source and is to be avoided.

On another cautionary note, both GLOOP and the play clay as it is being made may resemble certain bodily fluids. This can be extremely troublesome for some sexual abuse survivors, as it may trigger memories for him or her. The therapist should be aware of this possibility, and while it may be painful, the activity may also help the child to empower himself over a negative memory.

While the child is making each material, emphasize the contact functions including color, texture, roughness, smoothness, wateriness, smell, and taste if the child puts either material to his or her tongue—but discourage eating it. Note to the child how wonderful he is to have made something for himself, emphasizing his own self-efficacy. I often hide things in the GLOOP such as a plastic figure or a penny, and let the child keep the object when he finds it. Many sensory deprivation cases have problems with evocative memory and object constancy. This exercise is a beginning toward healing in those areas.

These are hands-on exercises, and the child should be encouraged to engage fully with the materials. My own approach involves making each material actively with the child. Most playrooms will already have the minimal equipment necessary. I also cover the play area with a plastic tablecloth as we make each substance together.

PLAY CLAY

Ingredients:

1 cup flour
1/2 cup salt
1/4 cup water (more or less)
1 tablespoon vegetable oil
several drops of food coloring
several drops of flavoring (avoid mint or cinnamon as these may burn)

In a small bowl, mix the water, oil, coloring, and flavoring. In a large bowl, mix the flour and salt with your hands. Gradually add the liquid to the flour and salt mixture until you reach a consistency you like. Your play clay will keep for some time in a zip-lock bag. It can be molded and allowed to dry, and then painted. NEVER EAT YOUR PLAY CLAY. IT MIGHT MAKE YOU SICK BECAUSE OF ALL THE SALT!

GLOOP

In one container, mix:
- 1/2 cup cold water
- 1 tablespoon of Twenty Mule Team Borax Powder

In another container, mix:
- 1/2 cup Elmer's Glue
- 1/2 cup cold water

Then mix the stuff in each of the two bowls. Pour them together. It will make a neat glob of stuff almost right away. When it turns into a large ball, pour off the water, let it set for a few minutes, pour off the water again, and keep this up until no more water puddles up on top. Then, just play with it. The consistency of the GLOOP will change, and become more firm, as your play with it. Store it in a zip-lock bag and your GLOOP will keep for several weeks. DO NOT EVER EAT YOUR GLOOP! THE GLUE WILL MAKE YOU SICK!

References

Cabe, N. (1955). *Grounded Play Therapy Processing.* Privately printed.

Lusebrink, V. B. (1990). *Imagery and Visual Expression in Therapy.* New York: Plenum.

Elmer's Glue is a trademark of Borden, Incorporated, Columbus, Ohio.

Twenty Mule Team Borax is a trademark of the United States Borax and Chemical Corporation and The Dial Corp., Phoenix, Arizona.

25

The Clay Squiggle Technique

Richard Frankel

INTRODUCTION

This play therapy technique, with a variant for both individual and group use, is based upon D. W. Winnicott's squiggle game as described in his book *Therapeutic Consultations in Child Psychiatry* (1971). Recognizing the profundity of Winnicott's squiggle game, this technique was developed to provide another way to facilitate the deep unconscious communication between therapist and client that Winnicott was able to bring about in his work. Having used clay in my therapeutic work with children and adolescents for many years, it seemed quite natural to devise a way of playing the squiggle game with clay.

RATIONALE

As a part of individual play therapy practice, this technique has maximum benefits for those children and adolescents who are too self-conscious to draw and for those who have internalized our cultural misconstruing of what makes good and bad art and thereby judge themselves to be "bad" artists, thus resisting the self-expressive use of drawing or painting. I have found clay to be a much less threatening medium, especially in this technique, where in the beginning state there are no requirements for having to "make" anything. This is analogous to Winnicott describing the squiggle game to a child as a game without any rules.

DESCRIPTION

The therapist and child begin by each taking a hunk of soft, air-dry clay. (I prefer air-dry clay because if hardens in a relatively short period of time and can then be painted with tempera paints). The child is given the following instructions: "Take your clay and make four or five different shapes out of it. There are no rules about what you should make. The shapes can be anything at all. I will do the same with my clay." (At this point, it can be helpful to have a few rudimentary clay modeling tools on hand which can facilitate shaping the clay).

Both the therapist and the child each separately make whatever shapes occur to them with their clay. This is the first step of the technique. When both are finished, the therapist gives the following instructions: "Now we will exchange what we each have made. You take my shapes and I take yours. The next step is for you to put together my shapes into any form that occurs to you. I will do the same with yours. You can use any additional clay if needed."

At this point, both child and therapist work at making an image out of the preexisting shapes. Having definite shapes to work with (especially those done by the therapist) gives the child more confidence to use the clay in a self-expressive way in creating an image, rather than if he or she were starting from scratch. This second stage can take only a few minutes or occupy the rest of the session, depending on the temperament of the child.

When both therapist and child are finished, they look together at the completed pieces and discuss what has been created. This discussion often focuses on the way each piece reflects both the work of the child and the therapist and how that is experienced in the context of the existing therapeutic relationship. It can be suggested to the child that the following week, after they dry, the pieces can be painted, thereby allowing a further elaboration of what the child intended to express.

APPLICATIONS

A variant of the above technique can be transposed to work in play therapy groups. It is especially effective when it is employed early on, for it promotes group cohesion and trust.

Each group member is given a hunk of clay. As in the above technique, there should be a few rudimentary clay modeling tools in the middle of the table to be shared by the group as well as additional clay. The group leader, who has a choice of participating or not, gives the following instructions:

"First, take the piece of clay in front of you and shape it into anything you want. There are no rules about this. It can be an abstract shape, a face, an animal, whatever comes to mind. Anything goes. When you are finished, take the scoring tool and mark your initials at the bottom of your piece. Then we will pass our pieces to the person sitting on our left. When your receive another group member's piece, you can change it by adding to it or marking it in any way that occurs to you. The only rule is that you cannot destroy the basic structure of what you receive. We will continue to pass our pieces to the left until we end up with our original clay piece. We will have a few minutes to work each time we are handed a new piece."

Thus everyone in the group gets the chance to shape and transform everyone else's work. At the end, the experience is processed by concentrating on the feelings that arose both in getting back one's original piece, now completely changed, and having to let go and share one's work with others. This discussion easily opens itself into a general group process around issues of trust and intimacy among group members. This exercise can be continued the next week once the pieces harden by having people paint the finished forms. A new group process is enacted in deciding who gets to paint whose pieces and who claims which piece to take home with them.

26

Expressive Arts Playdough

Lynn B. Hadley

INTRODUCTION

Play-doh™ is an invaluable tool in play therapy work with young school-age children. The addition of creative arts materials to be used with the dough opens new avenues for expression. The familiar and playful nature of the colorful dough, cookie cutters, and art materials helps to engage children while at the same time relaxing defenses. Basic play therapy techniques encourage maximum benefits from the process.

RATIONALE

The easy malleability of the dough and its transformational properties facilitates a child's ability to actually play with and give a form to significant issues while maintaining "control" over the material. The process of working with the dough as it changes form may serve as a helpful metaphor for change.

DESCRIPTION

Materials needed: playdough (assorted colors), cookie cutters (a preselected assortment including human figures, animals, angel, heart, skull, house, castle, etc., to represent a range of emotional themes), rolling pin, art materials (rhinestones, feathers, jiggle eyes, feathers, toothpicks, paper scissors, pencil, markers, craft sticks), hammer or pounding tool, plastic knife. As with clay work, the child is encouraged to explore properties of the playdough. The therapist's role may vary from quietly molding some of the dough to actively demonstrating a range of possible behaviors for the client (including fun, expression of feelings, and verbalizing while playing). There is typically an initial period of playing with the dough and cookie cutters, testing the materials and therapist responses, before the child enters the working phase of the session, in which symbols are selected and developed. The therapist may suggest in general terms how the art materials may enhance the images the child creates. Each child will approach the use of dough differently, and the therapist must be sensitive to cues from the child in determining the pacing and nature of therapist participation and interventions. This clinician has observed two major categories of behavior with the playdough: (1) creation of a primary symbolic figure or sculpture, and (2) creation of multiple figures and shapes that can be played with in much the same ways as toys. However, unlike toys, these figures can be transformed, elaborated, destroyed, and recreated. The therapist may use expressive arts playdough technique as a nondirected or directed therapeutic experience, depending upon philosophical orientation and client needs.

APPLICATIONS

The technique may facilitate therapist goals in the areas of relationship building, mastery over trauma and fear, understanding and coping with life changes, as well as enhancing self-esteem and increasing verbalizations. The therapist introduces the client to the materials, and suggests that he or she begin with the dough. Because of the regressive quality of the medium, this technique is especially helpful in allowing children to approach anxiety-provoking feelings, thoughts, and experiences. For example, an 8-year-old cancer patient was spontaneously talking about fears of death, when she became highly anxious and stopped talking. She immediately proceeded to carry out the theme with the playdough by decorating elaborate cut-out angels of different sizes. Recommended for ages 4–10.

27

Inner-Reference

Aimee H. Short

INTRODUCTION

The aim of the Inner-Reference method is to teach client-initiated problem identification, exploration, and resolution. The child uses his or her own intellectual resources to form new associations and ideas. The therapist becomes an important part of the child's process and helps to increase the learning potential.

RATIONALE

Inner-Reference is similar to the concept taught by the adage, "If you give a man a fish, he is fed for the day; but teach a man to fish and he is fed for a lifetime." With this method the child learns a systematic way to identify problems. Teaching a child to think for him or herself is crucial for healthy development. Encouraging a child to explore his or her own ideas helps the child to become more capable of making sense of the world according to the child's own unique understandings and experiences. With the guidance of the therapist, the child is helped to develop a positive inward focus. With Inner-Reference the solution belongs to the child and is therefore more meaningful. This method can increase self-esteem by teaching the child to believe in him or herself. It also gives the child a chance to show how much he or she knows and understands about his or her family situation. A good rapport and high degree of client comfort is essential for this task. The therapist should see the child for multiple sessions before attempting this technique. The therapist strives for minimal interference, but can share ideas which are relevant to a particular question. Because the therapist does not intrude with probing questions, this technique is nonthreatening.

DESCRIPTION

Materials needed include: large or small unlined white paper, a variety of markers, colored pencils, clay, and paints are optional.

The therapist starts the session by writing the topic "Questions about My Family" at the top of the paper. Next the child is invited to write down questions he or she has about family or parents. The therapist might say something like, "I know you have lots of questions about what's happening in your family. I wanted us to take time to write some of those down." Some children are eager to write and others may be inhibited, so the therapist may write the child's ideas down if necessary. Some children may hesitate and say they are unsure of what to write or that they can't think of any questions. If necessary it may be important to emphasize there is no right or wrong answer, and the therapist may need to remind the child about information brought up in previous sessions. The child is encouraged to think of as many questions as possible. If there are too many to cover in one session, the child is asked to number them in order of importance. The therapist's goal is to assess the underlying concern of fear to help the child organize a psychological and/or behavioral response. The therapist may share hypotheses about underlying meanings, restate questions regarding what the child really wants to know but doesn't have the words to ask, or encourage further exploration. For example, "No one may know this answer, but if you were to guess what would you say?" If a child has no ideas or seems particularly troubled by a question a redirection of medium may be helpful. Having clay and paper for drawing is useful when encouraging the child to explore deeper issues and increase awareness of wishes and desires.

Using the clay or drawing the therapist can suggest that the child show what his or her family would be like if the problem had never happened.

An activity that provides a segue into Inner-Reference is when the child is asked to draw pictures of someone who is sad, mad, happy, and scared. After the child has identified feelings associated with people in his or her life, it may be easier to form questions. The therapist may then ask the child to match one of the feelings with a question: "Tell me about how you feel when this happens," or "Tell me how you're feeling as we talk about this question now." When a child is able to associate an understandable feeling with the behavior of others in his or her family, then the child is better prepared (with help from the therapist) to separate him or herself from the cause of the behavior of others.

APPLICATIONS

This technique was developed to be used with children from homes where domestic violence has occurred and some type of separation from one parent has resulted. Inner-Reference is recommended for children ages 8 and up with a good capacity for verbal communication and logic. This technique works in one session but can be spread into several sessions or used as a reference in future sessions. Inner-Reference can be as flexible as the therapist is creative. Children coming from extremely authoritarian parenting styles, which is common in may families experiencing domestic violence, may need support and encouragement in order to initiate autonomous problem solving. The technique can be adapted for use with younger children and certainly is not limited to issues related to domestic violence.

EXAMPLE

LM is an 8-year-old female child client whose parents had been separated for approximately eight months, and her mother was filing for divorce. She was very close to her father, who visited only sporadically. LM would burst into a rage when her father would try to leave. The first three questions LM wrote were, "Why do my mom and dad fight so much?" "Why can't they share money?" and "Why did they make drugs?" In exploring each of these questions the therapist helped LM to understand her underlying wishes. LM wished her mom and dad could live together peacefully, she wished they didn't fight over money, and she wished her father didn't abuse alcohol (which was the cause of many of the parents' problems). By putting these important questions down on paper the therapist helped to make them less mysterious and more answerable. The therapist took this opportunity to educate LM about drugs and domestic violence in age-appropriate words, which helped LM understand that the separation was not her fault and was something her parents must solve. The questions helped the therapist talk about the child's role to help her gain a better understanding of her current living situation and identify feelings associated with the absence of a parent. LM was able to talk about her anger and how she goes into rages, hitting and kicking her mother and sisters. In the past LM consistently denied many feelings of anger. By using Inner-Reference LM was able to identify and own her feelings of anger. She successfully brainstormed with the therapist about what she would do to stay in control and express her anger appropriately.

28

Reworking

Sheri Saxe

INTRODUCTION

Reworking is an art therapy technique in which the child uses a large spiral sketch pad over a period of time, going back to previous drawings and adding or erasing elements.

This technique evolved naturally when children in art therapy were given their own sketch pads to use throughout the process of therapy. After the first few sessions, they would flip back, study previous drawings, and make changes. Sometimes these changes were corrections for greater accuracy, but more often they reflected therapeutic growth, reframing of past events, and different outlooks.

RATIONALE

Children are often faced with situations in which they feel helpless. Drawing about these situations can help restore a sense of power and control (Malchiodi 1990, Steele 1994).

Since therapy is a process, however, it can be even more beneficial to give children the opportunity to use their artwork gradually, over time, to regain a sense of control over their lives.

This can be accomplished by allowing children to "rework" their earlier drawings. Like free-form activities such as sandplay (Gill 1991, Oaklander 1988), reworking can imbue the child with a sense of power to reshape or repair his or her life.

The alterations to the artwork become a metaphor for imaginary or real changes in the child's life structure—including new ways of behaving or responding. One of the great symbolic advantages of reworking is that the child is altering his or her own original creation, often after a period of time has passed.

DESCRIPTION

Reworking is an art therapy technique that should take place over several sessions. The child is given a large artist's pad, at least 11" × 14", on spiral rings. Pencils, with good artist erasers, should be provided. The child is told to draw whatever he or she wants. It is best if the drawings are the child's own ideas, but if necessary the therapist can suggest something open-ended, such as "draw a wish" or "draw a dream you have had" or "draw something that scares you."

The drawings are all kept on the artist's pad. After a few sessions and several drawings, the child should be encouraged to look back over the drawings. The therapist tells the child that he or she can change the drawings in any way. This should become a regular part of the therapy.

In my experience, the child continually reworks his or her artwork, often reflecting therapeutic growth. For example, a picture of a scary monster may be reworked so that the child adds a huge drawing of himself on the same page eating the monster.

Another example might be for a child who has had a very restricted range of feelings to go back and add items to a picture reflecting more depth of feeling, such as tears running down a face or a fist raised in anger.

The reworking often included verbalizations that label, explain, or define the alterations to the artwork.

APPLICATIONS

This technique is appropriate for any art therapy client, but would be particularly useful for children who have experienced severe traumas during which they felt powerless. These children may require the slow gradual process of reworking to gain a sense of control, rather than just one session with a particular piece of artwork.

I used this method with a 7-year-old boy whose 2-year-old brother had died of cancer. I will use his first drawing as an example. He drew five super hero pictures on the same large page, all in different colors. Two sessions later, he went back and colored the in more thoroughly, telling me they were "bad germs." Two months later, he again flipped back to this picture and added three more super heroes, which he said were "good germs." After several more sessions, he added two more "good germs" so they would be "tied" (same number of each), circled the "good germs" in black and numbered them, and told the "good germs" that he forgave them for losing the battle, because he knew they had tried.

Thus, Reworking is a simple, inexpensive means of helping a child gain a sense of mastery over the past and power to change the future.

References

Gill, E. (1991). *The Healing Power of Play.* New York: Guilford.

Malchiodi, C. A. (1990). *Breaking the Silence: Art Therapy with Children from Violent Homes.* New York: Brunner/Mazel.

Oaklander, V. (1988). *Windows to our Children.* Highland, NY: Gestalt Journal Press.

Steele, W. (1994). *Kids on the Inside Looking Out after Loss.* Detroit, MI: Institute for Trauma and Loss in Children.

29

A Line Down the Middle of the Page

Dolores M. Conyers

INTRODUCTION

The Line Down the Middle of the Page is a technique that offers children a nonthreatening way to confront difficult concerns. For instance, when children see a sheet of paper divided down the middle by a line with *Good* and *Bad* headings at the top of each column, many are eager to participate and most work very hard at it. In addition to the nonthreatening presentation, the technique offers the child an opportunity to see more of the whole picture, and many children become quite involved in balancing both sides of the line. This is a healthier look at life issues than just dwelling on the bad.

DESCRIPTION

Basically, all that is needed for this technique is paper and pencil. Different size and colored paper, a ruler for drawing straight lines, colored markers and crayons, and scissors, pictures, and paste can be useful.

EXAMPLES

Good	Bad
Daisies, flowers	Storms and tornadoes
Birthday presents	Nighttime, dark
Mother and father	Ghosts
	(Fears often named here)

Me	
Happy	Sad
Well	Sick
Play ball	Broken leg
Get B in Science	Get D in History

Dad	
☺	☹
Fixes my bike	Yells at me
Takes me to ballgame	Drinks too much beer
Tells jokes	Throws things

APPLICATIONS

In addition to being a tool to create rapport, assess and identify, and work through concerns a child might have, this technique, given at intervals, can show the progress a child is making in therapy. One such case involves an 8-year-old who was identified as withdrawn. This child was clearly isolated in a rough-and-tumble classroom of third-graders. Initially, on the *Good* side of the line were drawn symbols of isolation and anger, including reading (alone), drawing (alone), army tanks, and monster figures. On the *Bad* side of the line were such things as spelling (and other school lessons), children, playground equipment, and the school lunchroom. After seven months of therapy, therapy for the parent, and work with the teacher on socializing the child, the subject matter on each side of the line was clearly reversed. The child who remained planted at the schoolroom desk inside an invisible shell all day became one who responded to the activities of the classroom as both an individual with contributions to make and as a member of the group, in which friendships were beginning to develop. Not only does the Line Down the Middle of the Page technique identify problems, but it clearly shows goals that the child very naturally originates and fills in when drawn to balance problems listed on the page.

Another use for the Line Down the Middle of the Page technique is the power it has to achieve a focus from children. Its simplicity seems to work well with ADD and ADHD children. One such child, who was also autistic, posed a great challenge when it came to any kind of assessment. The pressing concern was preoccupation with violent cartoon characters, and the child was beginning to strike out physically at family members. One task was to try to find out if the child understood the difference between cartoon violence and real violence. The columns formed by the line down the middle of page were topped by a picture of a superhero cartoon animal and a picture of a real animal of the same type. When asked to sit and work on this task, the child went from pacing and prattle to a highly focused, thoughtful taskmaster—goal-directed, verbally intelligent, and attentive. This is a child that even as a preadolescent no one could yet successfully evaluate fully. The child's work, including the categories of responses (i. e., creator, father figures), was completely generated by the child.

Picture of Superhero Cartoon Animal	Picture of Real Animal
Nonliving	Living
Latex Costume	Real Skin
"Name of a cartoonist"	God
[Creators]	
"Name of a cartoon character"	Boy (his pet)
[Father Figure]	
"Name of a food eaten in cartoon shows"	Pet Food/Grass Twigs, Leaves
[Food]	
"Name of a cartoon character"	Boy's Mom & Dad
[Friends]	
"Name of a cartoon character"	Crocodiles
[Enemies]	

Here was a child who to all appearances was uncommunicative, unreachable, and mentally handicapped. Indeed from the child's performance on the Line Down the Middle of the Page, the child *did* understand the difference, and therapy to begin the task of controlling physical outbursts could proceed.

When fears, confusion, inability to focus, poor communication skills, or sensitive issues are present and need to be dealt with the Line Down the Middle of the Page technique is recommended in play therapy with children.

30

Create-a-Community

Nancy H. Cochran

INTRODUCTION

Anger, distrust, and ambivalence over attachment to adult caretakers are common feelings of children who cope with abusive and neglectful parents. Although the need for individual therapy for abused and neglected children is becoming more clearly recognized, a change in the home environment is often considered sufficient intervention with the child who was abused or neglected as a result of domestic violence. The Create-a-Community technique was originally designed for children who were moving into new communities from a domestic violence shelter. The technique may be used by any therapist wanting to help a child better adjust to environment changes and feelings of insecurity during transition to a new community. It has been especially helpful in situations in which children are resistant or unable to talk about past and current family situations and tend to express their feelings more readily through action than verbalization. It is additionally helpful for those children who must frequently transition from one home to another due to being in foster care or other parental visitation arrangements.

RATIONALE

This technique is therapeutic in situations in which the child is clearly overwhelmed by and therefore resistant to discussing feelings and thoughts related to past experiences and/or the current stressful situation. By creating his or her own community, and manipulating fantasy situations from above with "a bird's eye view," the child is provided the necessary distance to feel safe and in control as he or she plays out situations and begins to express fears, wishes, and concerns. The technique allows the therapist to make several observations (colors used to draw and items chosen to include in each home or place, arrangement of the community, additions and deletions as sessions progress, and verbal expressions in role play) and reflect feeling and content as the child plays. Once established and accepted by the child, this technique may be used as a nonthreatening, familiar tool to help the child identify, express, and work through particular stressful events related to having moved to a new community and/or having separated from one or both parents.

DESCRIPTION

The therapist may choose to introduce this technique once the child has established trust and rapport and is actively seeking the therapist's assistance in an interactive role. Materials needed are: medium-sized poster paper, colored markers, small doll house people, and toy vehicles (cars, school bus). Structural limitations (i. e., "We have no doll house, so let's create one") may be used, as well as the suggestion, "Here's a fun way to draw a house." The first step is to introduce by modeling the drawing of a house by sectioning off a piece of poster paper into "rooms." This is drawn somewhat like a blueprint or layout of a house, with different shapes and sizes of squares for rooms and openings for doorways between them. The child is then asked to help decide on and draw in furniture and other items appropriate to each room. At this time the child may be encouraged to draw his or her own house, as well as other places (school, Dad's house, Grandma's house, courthouse, stores) that he or she needs for "a community." The child is then encouraged to decide where all the homes and places go and to place these around the playroom. Once the child has completed his or her community, various vehicles and dolls may be introduced, as well as the suggestion that the child, or the child and the therapist, put people in the houses and places and drive around and play in the community.

APPLICATIONS

This technique has been applicable in a variety of situations in which children were in transition due to leaving a domestic violence shelter, divorce, or placement in foster care. It is especially useful with abused and neglected children who choose drawing and play as a means for self-expression, and who behaviorally act out or withdraw when direct verbal communication about past experiences and/or the current situation are attempted. Additionally it is a helpful technique for those children who have been repeatedly questioned by Child Protective Services workers and/or police officers about their family situation and as a result are reluctant to verbally express any thoughts or feelings about their family or life situations. This is especially common if the child has recently been removed from the custodial care of his or her parent(s), or has reluctantly been involved in the court process during a divorce.

This technique was originally implemented with an 8-year-old female who was working through a number of issues related to neglect by her parents due to substance abuse and exposure to domestic violence. She had been removed from both parents while her mother was in a substance abuse treatment program. She and her mother had reunited and had recently moved to a new community after leaving a domestic violence shelter. Clinical symptoms included severe explosive outbursts during which she would physically attack her mother, as well as strong resistance to discussing feelings and thoughts related to past experiences or her current situation.

Initial client-centered play therapy sessions revealed a need for solitary play with the therapist's reflection of content and feelings in order for this girl to express intense hostility and anger, followed by a prolonged phase of developmental regression (becoming an infant and sucking a bottle; seeking nurturance). When the girl began a phase of more age-appropriate mastery play with doll figurines, the technique was introduced. It was at this time that the girl began to actively assign the role of "friend" to the therapist by handing her a doll figurine named "Sara." After being asked to play in this interactive mode, the therapist suggested the technique of "drawing houses for the two doll friends."

The girl became immediately interested and involved in this activity, and continued in the next five sessions to ask for assistance in drawing a school, "Dad's house," "Grannie's house," a skating rink, and different stores. Transportation vehicles (cars, a school bus) were used to transport the girl's doll, Jenny, and her friend, Sara, to school, to the store with Mom, and to visit "Dad's house" on weekends.

During these sessions the girl became increasingly able to express fears and concerns about going to a new school, riding the school bus, and visiting her dad's house. She expressed a need to feel safe and be able to "call Mom" while visiting her dad's house, and verbalized anger, and distrust of parental figures due to previous unmet needs. Both doll friends lived in their new homes alone, and "didn't need mothers" for the first few sessions. The doll friends were able to decide when they would or would not visit their dads' houses, and were able to care for themselves as well as their "baby sisters." When mothers were added to each home, the girl was able to try out a new relationship with her doll characters, explore the relationship between mother and daughter, and express feelings regarding her own needs as daughter. Eventually, though she had previously been reluctant to have her mother join sessions, she invited her mother into a session to play and talk. At this point the mother was able to begin to establish a nurturing, more communicative relationship with her daughter.

31

Outline Drawings of Boys and Girls

Barbara A. Turner

INTRODUCTION

The Outline Drawing of Boys and Girls is a simple technique that arose quite spontaneously in the course of working with a child in my office. As a tool to help children identify, express, and work through the feelings attached to particular events in their lives, it appears to have a broad range of applications and can be used flexibly to suit the particular clinical need.

DESCRIPTION

To use the technique I either quickly draw the outline of a boy or girl, about the same age and gender as my client, or use a stack of photocopied Outline Drawings I've prepared in advance (see Figure 1). The children appear to enjoy the hastily drawn imperfect drawings, which seem to put them more at ease, however, if the therapist does not feel comfortable drawing, the photocopied outlines work just as well. Referring to the Outline Drawing, I then make a rather general inquiry about how "this boy" or "this girl" might feel about something similar to what the child is presenting that day, and say, "Let's color it in and see."

APPLICATIONS

The Outline Drawing is used as a vehicle for the child's entry into his or her emotional experience and has application both with children who have the grasp and ownership of their emotions, as well as for those children for whom feelings are still unknown territory.

When an 8-year-old boy's father advised me that the child had just received the shocking news that his mother, now living in another state, intended to remarry, the Outline Drawing of an older boy was used, with the inquiry, "I wonder how this boy would feel if he got a telephone call like that? Let's color him in and see." In this case, this child was lacking in understanding of his feelings associated with this significant event in his life, so the Outline served as a learning and normalizing tool. When the boy covered the Outline Boy with question marks and jagged marks he identified as "lightning," I gave voice to the emerging expression of feeling, saying, "I'm so confused and I'm so mad I could explode like lightning!" Having his feelings identified and witnessed appeared to suit the child's therapeutic need at the time, so no further discussion or interpretation was initiated. In subsequent sessions we were able to refer back to the "Lightning Boy" and all those powerful feelings he felt.

When a 7-year-old girl appeared in session rather agitated, saying that her family had to sell their house and move because of her parents' recent divorce, the Outline Drawing was used to give vent to her pent-up emotions. In a highly energized manner she grabbed a handful of multicolored markers "Ten!" she pointed out, and hastily obscured the Outlines of several little girls with her "very angry feelings." After completely covering four Outline Drawings so that the figures were no longer even visible, she was noticeably calmer and commented, "Getting all of these angries out made rainbows!" The wisdom of her innocent comment was very touching.

For children who have less understanding of their emotional lives, I have found the Outline Drawing helpful as a teaching tool. While always watching for the child's lead, I might use the Outline Drawing and inquire, "I wonder what she might feel like if something like that happened in her family . . . maybe mad, or sad," while coloring or decorating the Outline to illustrate the feeling(s) we are discussing. This can then be a jumping-off place to talk about the particular feelings, what they are, when they happen, how they feel, and how we deal with them. The

Outline Drawing also provides the therapist an opportunity to model or play-act the feelings for the child.

The Outline Drawing flexibly allows the child the appropriate amount of distance from the trauma of the presenting experience. The emotional content of the experience can be first grounded in the Outline and need be made only as conscious as is therapeutically appropriate. The child need not assume ownership for the feelings until he or she is ready, yet the expression of the feelings on the Outline Drawing affords a certain normalization of what the child is feeling and facilitates movement into this fuller awareness of his or her experience.

EXAMPLE

As the child's understanding of his or her emotional life matures, the Outline Drawing affords the possibility of moving into deeper aspects of experience. A dramatic example of this occurred when a 9-year-old girl, with whom I had worked for about one year on the trauma associated with repeated sexual violations, came into her session one evening complaining that she hated a girl in her class because ". . . she is so perfect and snotty." Markers and typing paper were available on the table as we talked, so I drew the outline of a girl about the same age as my client and inquired, "I wonder what this girl feels like?" (Figure 1). The client colored in big blue tears and fiery red radiating from the chest area (Figure 2). She described this as "a perfect and snotty girl," then quickly asked me to draw another Outline. On this Outline she shaded in the dress and sketched in a face, saying, "a perfect, snotty girl changed into a regular girl" (Figure 3). She then took a marker, saying she wanted to draw her own Outline of a "fat girl." Drawing tears and a criss-crossed heart, she said this girl feels sad and bad (Figure 4). She then expanded the shape of this "fat girl" to huge proportions, verbalizing and writing on the drawing, "I feel this fat. Grandma said I was this fat. I feel sad." This cathartic experience continued with active mirroring on my part until it was worked through and the child began to verbalize, "I'm pretty because I'm just me," whereupon she had the therapist draw a final Outline, which she adorned with a huge red heart and radiant light around the face, strongly asserting, "I love myself!" (Figure 5).

In this case, it appears that the antagonism that the child had projected onto the girl she perceived as "perfect" was but a thin veneer over her own painful issues of body image stemming from her family experiences and her history of sexual molestation. The Outline Drawing provided an entry point to move beyond the projections, to reveal her own underlying pain, uncertainty, and anger about her perceived "imperfection." This child's use of the Outlines allowed a catharsis of these feelings, leading to a transformed image of her body and her self.

Whether it be used as a simple teaching tool, a device for emotive expression, or as a vehicle for catharsis and transformation, the Outline Drawings of Boys and Girls affords a broad range of clinical applications and is an enjoyable instrument for therapeutic exploration and engagement with the child's affective experience in the play room.

Figure 1. Outline Drawings of Boys and Girls

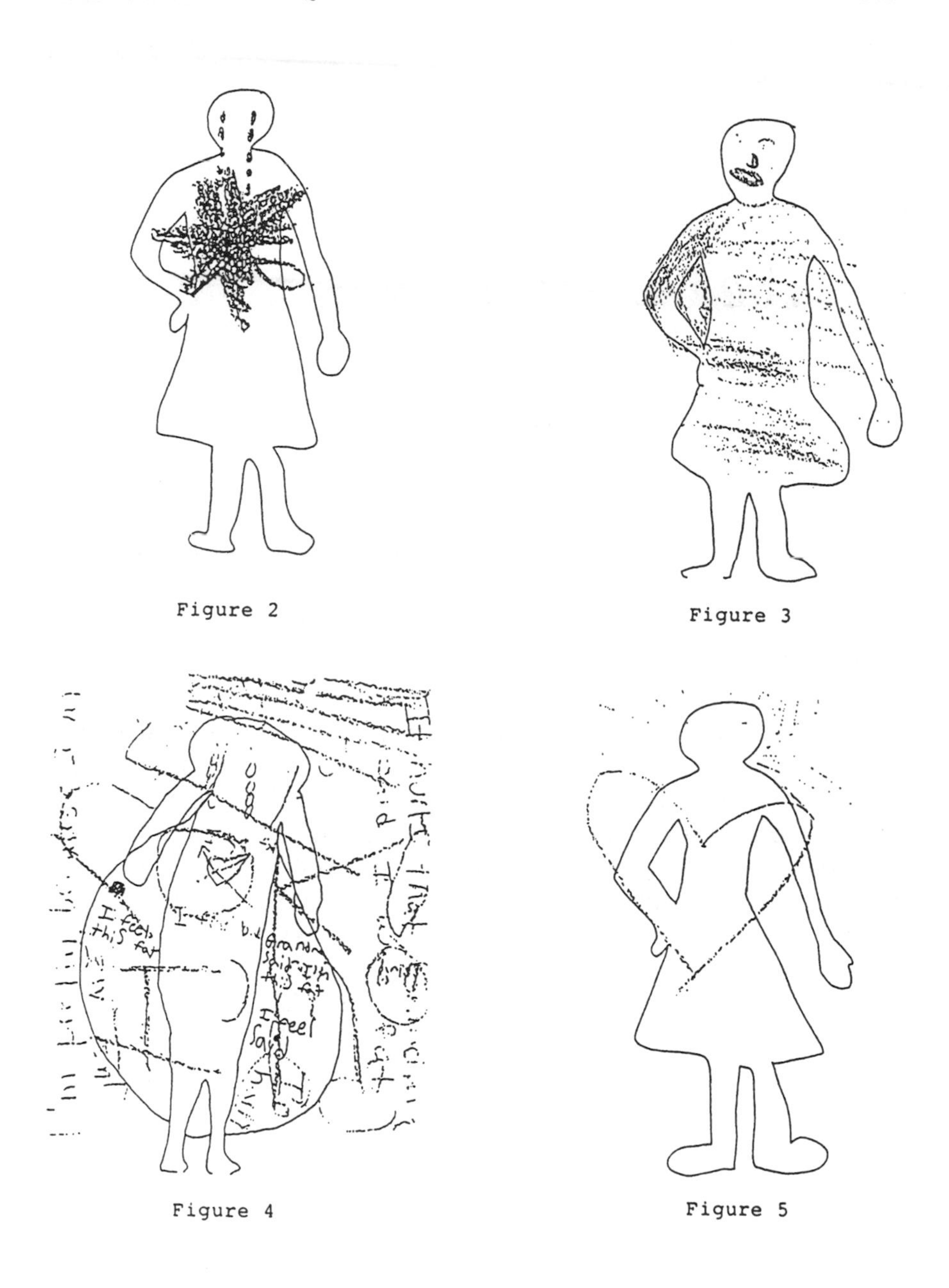

Figure 2

Figure 3

Figure 4

Figure 5

Figures 2–5. Clinical Example Outline Drawings of Boys and Girls

32

The Picture Drawing Game

Stanley Kissel

INTRODUCTION

The first time a child and therapist meet is usually anxiety-provoking. Some therapists suggest watching the child initially to see how he attempts to deal with the new situation (Greenspan 1981). Others advocate the therapist taking a more assertive stance by talking directly about the child's problems (Bernard and Joyce 1984). Feller (1992) advises the child therapist not to play directly with children but to reflect their request for direct involvement with them. Kissel (1991) believes that a major task of the therapist during the initial encounter is to reduce anxiety, and also to establish the therapist as an authority in the playroom. The Picture Drawing Game was designed to meet both these ends. It provides a way of quickly reducing anxiety while enlisting the child's involvement in an activity that is pleasant and nonthreatening (Figure 3-1).

DESCRIPTION

After introducing yourself to the child, ask, "Have you ever played a picture drawing game?" and immediately go to the easel, or on a piece of paper draw a square. Then say, "Once upon a time there was a house," and proceed to draw in the square two smaller squares for windows and one rectangle for a door as in Drawing A. Continue by stating, "It was just like any other house with two windows, a door, a roof, and two chimneys." Add a triangle to the top and then two chimneys coming off either side as in Drawing B. "In the house there lived a little [boy/girl]." To this point you have asked nothing of the child but have given some perceptual stimulation by drawing a picture and having presented some words in a child-oriented tone. Now ask the child for a name. After a sufficient period of time if the child does not provide one, you provide the child's name and ask for his or her acknowledgment. For purposes of our example, let the name be John.

"Okay now, John lived in this house with his parents. One day John's parents brought him a pet doggie. What did John call his pet doggie?" As before, wait for the child to provide a name and if he or she does not, you do so. For our example, let's call the dog Spot. "Every day as John would go to bed he would take his pet dog Spot with him. One day when John got up, he didn't find Spot in his room. He walked out in front of the house and did not see Spot there." Draw a straight line form the door of the house as in Drawing C. If the child responds "no," agree with him; if he responds "yes," say "John went to the door, and when he got close he saw the dog looked like Spot but it wasn't Spot." If the child makes no response after a reasonable time, state, "He didn't find Spot." The next part of the game consists of drawing a number of lines so that they look like feet as in Drawing D. While making these lines say the following: "John began to look for his dog Spot. He went on one street and up another and then to another." You can pause and ask the child if he sees his dog; the response in all cases you are looking to elicit is "no." Should the child say "yes," repeat as previously that he walked to the dog but it wasn't Spot. Get to the point where four legs are drawn and then tell the child, "John remembered that Spot liked to run in the park so he ran there," and draw a line which will become the tail. Ask the child if he found Spot; there the answer again should be "no." While asking him that question, draw a bushy tail and tell the child, "John kept looking and looking in the park for his dog, but could not find him," as in Drawing E.

Next, ask the child how John felt; the appropriate response is "sad." Then ask the child whether John walked home fast or slowly; regardless of what the child says, state that he felt sad and walked home slowly as in Drawing F.

Figure 3–1. The Picture Drawing Game

Upon drawing the final line from the tail back to the house, the child should be asked, "What happened to the picture of the house?" Some children will immediately say "Spot came home," others will say "It looks like a dog," and others will seem puzzled. In any case, let the child know that the house became a picture of a dog, and ask if he or she would like to take it home. Following this you can begin to talk with the child, suggest that he or she might want to play with some toys, or, as I often do, ask the child to make a picture for me, either of a person, his or her family, an animal, or whatever.

Basically the child has been given something to take home and has been engaged in a hierarchical fashion, as you first give and then demand a little, and then demand somewhat more during the interview. Finally, the child has been asked to produce something in return that can provide diagnostic information, and also has been related to in a less threatening, anxiety-reducing fashion.

APPLICATIONS

This drawing game can be used with children up to age 9 who are either too loose or too tight (Kissel 1991). Tight children—those who are anxious, phobic, depressed, shy, inhibited, or obsessive—are made especially uncomfortable by new situations. These children are provided with a fun activity, reducing their apprehension. Loose children—those who are impulsive, inattentive, oppositional, or actively aggressive—need direction and structure. The Picture Story Drawing Game provides this to these children in a way that is nonthreatening and yet establishes the authority of the therapist.

References

Bernard, M. E., and Joyce, M. R. (1984). *Rational-Emotive Therapy*. New York: Wiley.

Feller, D. (1992). Assessing children through play. *American Journal Of Orthopsychiatry* 62: 26–35.

Greenspan, S. L. (1981). *The Clinical Interview of the Child*. New York: McGraw-Hill.

Kissel, S. (1991). *Play Therapy: A Strategic Approach*. Springfield, IL: Chas. Thomas.

33

The Color-Emotive Brain

Sheldon Berger and Jonna L. Tyler

INTRODUCTION

We have found that in the course of doing play therapy there is frequently a need for a shorthand method of determining how far the child has come and what progress has been made, emotionally and cognitively. As a result, we have formulated a visual model that we have found to facilitate such a determination.

DESCRIPTION

In our model, the child is presented with a picture of his or her own brain, with name or initials under the picture. During the course of therapy, each "layer" of the child's brain, representing various levels of emotional and cognitive expression, is colored in. For example, the outermost layer, the "green" layer, reflects the presenting problem. The parents, guardians, and/or agency workers refer the child with a single problem or array of problems, such as acting-out behaviors, various types of phobias, problems in concentration, and depression (in general, some array of undesirable behaviors, thoughts, or feelings). Early in therapy, the child and therapist discuss their understanding of the presenting problem(s). This usually occurs somewhere during the bonding process, which takes on average five or six weeks. When the child and therapist are able to agree mutually on these presenting problems, they color in the outermost band on the child's brain chart using the color green.

As therapy proceeds, the therapist uses a variety of active play therapy techniques (Berger and Tyler 1994) to attempt to help the child reach progressively deeper layers of emotional awareness and disclosure. Frequently, for example, a child who tends to act out discloses that he or she feels angry for some reason and may in fact cite the reason. The therapist will congratulate the child for having been able to make some sense of his or her feelings and together the two will fill in the next band on the brain chart, the orange layer.

As the child continues to explore thoughts and feelings through play, more vulnerability tends to appear, and feelings relating to isolation and abandonment, such as sadness and fear, may come to the surface. (It is important to note that the feelings at various layers will vary depending on the child's emotional history, personality style, and current degree of accessibility. For some children, "mad" belongs in a relatively early layer, while for other children, "mad" is very much unavailable at first and belongs to a deeper layer.) These feelings are seen as belonging to the next layer on the brain chart, the blue layer. (Note that the determination as to whether or not successively deeper layers of disclosure have been achieved rests on good, professional clinical judgment.) As the child continues to describe feelings, the purple layer is colored in. This represents a deeper understanding of these feelings which have come to the child's awareness. The child may begin to experience the hurt which can accompany the sadness. The yellow layer represents cognitive insight, at which point the child can verbalize feelings and how these feelings ultimately affect behavior. The final achievement, the black layer, indicates that a working-through process has occurred, and implies that the child is expressing genuine, accurate feelings and has reasonably good age-appropriate cognitive insight into the nature of his or her problems. The child is no longer overpowered by the feelings and has more choice related to action.

The model allows room for regression to a less disclosing level as well. If the child regresses in this way, the therapist has the option of coloring in another band of a color that has been used previously. Finally, periods of strong resistance or conflict can be noted by a red band on the chart. A visual representation of the model is supplied in Berger and Tyler (1994). In general, the Color-Emotive Brain model shows parallels to the progressive steps involved in psychodynamic therapy. The model is a visual representation of levels of disclosure and insight.

APPLICATIONS

In our practice, we have worked with children in both inpatient and outpatient settings. We have found the model to be effective in both types of settings with a wide range of ages. The technique has been tested on children ages 3 through 10. It has been used with severely behaviorally disturbed children in residential placement as well as in outpatient settings for presenting problems including fear of the dark, temper tantrums and other acting-out problems, and separation anxiety. The model has not been tested with psychotic individuals. It may be limited to children with at least borderline intelligence who have the capacity to use rational thinking. We have found that children up to the age of 10 respond quite positively to the model, but this does not preclude using it on other children or adults to facilitate therapy.

As the child visualizes his or her level of emotional insight and disclosure, it becomes possible for both therapist and child to determine how much progress has been made and how much additional progress needs to be made. The parents can also be informed of the amount of progress made using the visual model. Children appear to like the idea of the different colors representing successive goals in therapy. Once they begin coloring in layers of the brain, they will typically ask when they can color in an additional layer; this often provides the "hook" for additional, ongoing therapy. Needless to say, imagination and creativity are important in devising methods of getting the child involved in therapy at a given level of disclosure. This model serves as an aid in assisting the therapy process but certainly cannot take the place of a competent therapist.

Reference

Berger, S. N., and Tyler, J. L. (1994). The color-emotive brain: gone a long journey. *International Journal of Play Therapy* 3(1): 57–70.

34

Scribble Art

Leslie Hartley Lowe

INTRODUCTION

This is an art therapy tool that can be used in many ways. I first saw it used in a school counselor's group of some eight boys aged 7–11. As an ice-breaker, the focus on creative imagination and respectful team work was a quick way to get the children to have fun and learn to work together in a new setting rather than be self-conscious about art or social skills. But it has also been used diagnostically and therapeutically in many settings, from hospitals to private practice, with both individuals and families.

RATIONALE

Scribble Art has always been a useful process in the therapeutic context. Sometimes the picture that is produced is just a fun experience for everyone. Sometimes it can be a teaching tool for social skills, patience, self-esteem, and so on. Sometimes the processing of the experience is a learning opportunity for the client and/or the family about each other that leads to growth within each individual. As a family therapist, helping families find fun, respectful, creative opportunities to be together in a supportive way is a major goal. This activity meets that goal.

DESCRIPTION

Appropriate age group: 4 years and up; this can be played with just the therapist and client or with the whole family.

Time: 15–30 minutes depending on processing time.

Materials: crayons, coloring pens, felt markers, and such, and paper and a hard surface upon which to draw that all players can sit around (I use a board placed on the floor).

I use this activity after I have developed fairly good rapport with the client and his or her family. The younger the child, the earlier I involve the family in play therapy with the client, if in fact I have not involved them from the beginning. However, on a few occasions, I have used this as a rapport-building tool with latency-aged clients.

Step 1: I begin by asking the client if he or she would be willing to play a drawing game. I explain that we will be helping each other make a picture from scribbles. Since almost everyone feels comfortable with scribbles, even a very young child can see a way to fit in to this activity comfortably. It is not about talent or competence in handling drawing materials.

Step 2: I put a piece of paper on a hard surface and invite everyone on to the floor. This puts all of us on equal footing. I ask each person to pick one color only, and no two people can have the same color.

Step 3: I ask the client or a family member to make a quick scribble on the paper. If they appear reluctant, I will make the scribble. Note: In all of my scribbles and additions, I try to take a back seat to whatever the client or family members have in mind. I will only shape the process after we have done this numerous times, and I have a definite goal in mind for the outcome of the picture.

Step 4: The next person in turn looks at the scribble and adds something to it, based on what he or she thinks it might become. The person has the right to turn the paper in any direction and make the scribble into anything. Make sure that each person only adds a small something, as the idea of the project is that everyone will get several turns before the picture is complete.

Step 5: Each person continues to take turns in this manner until each person decides that he or she has nothing else to add to the picture.

As the picture begins to take on a life of its own, people can begin to appreciate each contribution, frequently with humor. Occasionally the picture will be violent or ghoulish. It is very important to respect each person's contribution without any negative comments. It is also important that no person wipe out any other person's contribution. It is OK; however, to change it into something else by adding to it.

Step 6: When the picture is complete, the therapist has a choice either to just appreciate and reinforce the positive aspects of the process thus far accomplished or to take it a step further. The next step is to ask people to share what they had in mind as the picture was created. This processing discussion can reveal a good deal about how people think and interact. The therapist can model acceptance and respectful opinion-sharing. Some things to note and discuss are:

a) whether any particular color dominates the picture, thus indicating a possible dominance in the family role that can be modified,

b) whether any particular theme comes out in the picture that parallels events or feelings in family members' lives,

c) particular contributions from younger family members that influenced the direction of the picture, playing up the positive contribution and encouraging the family to seek other opportunities to allow such contributions.

Step 7: (Use this as an alternative to Step 6 or as additions to it.) Ask one member to think about what might happen next in this picture and start a story that round-robins to each player until everyone agrees the story is over. Ask what the moral of the story would be.

Ask what happened just before this picture and let the story start from that point. Ask someone to start a story based on this picture.

If people are stuck or reluctant, I will start the story and send it to the next person when I think he/she can pick it up. Suggestion: Sometimes I have the Scribble Art for the client/family so that we can see if patterns develop and change. Sometimes I just make a copy and give the original to the client/family if they want it. The themes that arise in this format have been every bit as informational and useful as in sand tray therapy.

APPLICATIONS

DISORDERS: ADHD; family dysfunctions that reveal a lack of respect for each other and a difficulty in working together in a respectful way; PTSD or other trauma-related disorders.

TREATMENT GOALS:

1) increase self-esteem
2) increase ability to focus attention
3) increase respectful and appreciative behaviors towards others
4) increase ability to take turns and be patient when not client's turn
5) enhance ability to enjoy quiet activities
6) provide opportunity for family to do an enjoyable and creative activity together.

35

The Feelings Tree

Joyce Meagher

INTRODUCTION

In 1979, I was a play therapy student at the Children's Mental Health Center in Fairborn, Ohio. While using clay with a young, reluctant adolescent boy, I worked with him to design a nature scene, per his request. As I made a tree, I thought of ways to encourage him to talk about his feelings regarding a parental divorce. It occurred to me that the four basic clay colors included in the clay box (yellow, blue, red, and green) could be identified with four basic feeling ("sunny" yellow or happy feelings, "blue" or sad feelings, "red hot" or angry feelings, and "green with envy" or jealous feelings). I began making small "fruit" balls of the four colors and placing them on my fruit "feelings tree." The client asked to help, and soon the tree was full of the four differently colored balls. He said that sometimes he had all those different feelings. I thought that there must be a way to encourage him to elaborate. I asked the client if he would like to "pick" a fruit or feeling, and tell me a time he recalled having it.

RATIONALE

The child is a participant in the process and decides how many "feelings" of each color to add to the tree. He has control of which feelings he wishes to discuss initially by picking off the colored fruit of his choice. The therapist can also play and model that any of these feelings are acceptable to have. The child gains encouragement to discuss his more uncomfortable feelings by choosing from the final "fruits" on the tree.

Children who come to therapy rarely understand that having and discussing feelings is acceptable; they confuse acting on the feelings and just having them. This technique helps them sort out the right to have and own a feeling. The therapist can later work with the child to identify acceptable ways to deal with various feelings.

DESCRIPTION

I usually take gray clay to make a rather flat tree on a styrofoam tray, with a full foliage top so that the "fruits" can fit on it, and a plain trunk. For more sophisticated children, a trunk made with roots can symbolize "getting to the roots" of feelings (i. e., causes). I have found that about four of each color fruit is adequate to discuss basic feelings and nonthreatening enough to keep the discussion fairly time-limited (about ten minutes). There is a sense of completion when all the fruit has been picked.

APPLICATIONS

I have used this technique with children as young as 3½, depending on how proficient the child is with language and concepts. Most children can at least discuss feelings of happiness, anger, and sadness. Jealousy sometimes needs to be explained as a concept, but the clients then readily ascribe it to situations with peers and siblings.

Children with issues of anxiety, aggression, depression, and peer conflict do very well in beginning to understand their feelings by using this technique. Issues can be clarified and concentrated on afterwards, once this basic concept of expressing simple feelings freely is learned.

I have used the Feelings Tree with over fifty children and it has always been met with enthusiasm (some children will even ask to put more of one colored "fruit" back on the tree to be picked again because they recalled more examples of having that particular feeling). Many children have later asked a parent to buy them some clay so that the game can be played at home with their family.

I start my initial play therapy sessions in a client-centered modality, so usually I do not introduce this technique for a few sessions. It can be used sooner, if the therapist wishes to be more directive in his approach.

Recently, a child whose Dad is in jail worked on a feelings tree with me. One range of four colors of feelings included: "I'm happy that my Dad called me yesterday . . . I'm sad that I can't see my Dad . . . I'm angry that my Dad has been gone so long . . . I'm jealous that my friends have a Dad at home." (We then proceeded to deal with ways to work through each feeling. The theme of abandonment by Dad is central to this child's therapy.)

36

Design-A-Dad

Stazan K. Sina

INTRODUCTION

The current body of research literature is replete with evidence illustrating the predominantly adverse effects of father absence (or perceived unavailability) on children. Father absence specifically has been observed to adversely affect: ego strength in relation to social alienation and self-centeredness (Fry and Scher 1984); self-esteem (Miller 1989); scholastic abilities such as spelling and arithmetic skills (Bain et al. 1983); and overall conduct (Goldstein 1984).

RATIONALE

Working with father-unavailable children in play therapy can be an arduous process. They will be unwilling to discuss their fathers for any number of reasons. They may harbor anger toward their fathers for the absence and thus display oppositionality; they may possess little or no knowledge of their fathers and thus feel unable to discuss them; or they may have difficulty expressing their feelings and thoughts for reasons relating to the psychotherapeutic process itself, such as a difficulty establishing the transference. Design-A-Dad was thus created to act as a bridge between therapists and clients by stimulating children's recollections of their fathers. This tool has great potential therapeutic utility in that it allows children to project thoughts and feelings onto the figures, which subsequently provides therapists with opportunities to explore issues surrounding fathers.

As in toy-centered pretend play with miniatures, the stimuli for the play activity are not the toys themselves. In this form of play the children's thoughts and feelings serve as the stimuli. This play, sometimes called fantasy play, creates a framework in which children can discharge emotions, thoughts, and gestures in an acceptable, therapeutic fashion. This type of play "allows gratification of impulses that would not be allowed [or would not be possible in the case of deceased father] in reality" (O'Connor 1991, p.5). Here I am specifically referring to such behaviors as screaming at the father, striking the father, or crying in front of the father.

Design-A-Dad also provides children opportunities to create idealized or devalued representations of their fathers. This also provides therapists opportunities ripe for interpretation while providing the children opportunities for corrective emotional experiences. Over the course of sessions, therapists may also address changes and/or consistencies in the representations of fathers as the treatment itself progresses.

DESCRIPTION

Several materials are required in order to make the items used in the Design-A-Dad technique. These materials may be purchased (rather inexpensively) at most arts and crafts stores. Several colored pieces of felt can be used to clothe the dads. Therapists can choose either to prepare a variety of clothing styles ahead of time, or to make them with the children for rapport purposes. Here, therapists may also create clothing that enables the child to portray more athletic, portly, or slim builds. The felt can also be used to make several different styles of hair, eyes, moustaches, noses, and mouths. Eye and hair color can also be accounted for in this regard. The actual bodies can be cut from many materials, such as felt, posterboard, or foam rubber. Additional materials may also be incorporated such as adhesive eyes, moustaches, and so on. Since these materials are usually available in many shades of colors, therapists will also be able to be culturally sensitive.

Child clients will also adhere "feeling pieces" to their father representations. As in the Color-Your-Life Technique (O'Connor 1983), particular feelings are paired with certain representative colors (i. e., yellow=happy, blue=sad, black=scared, brown=lonely, orange=excited, green=worried, red=mad, and purple=whatever feeling they choose it to represent (Ammen 1994). Therapists should feel free to add to the list of feelings as needed. These pieces may be made out of a variety of materials as well. I have found that the foam rubber works well because it comes in all of the above colors, and is flexible and soft. These pieces can be cut into a shape that visually represents the feelings it is associated with (i. e., happy=a smile shape, sad=a frown shape, scared=a small circle, lonely=a thin, long shape resembling the number one, excited=the shape of an exclamation point, worried=the shape of a question mark, red=a square, and purple=an oval). This may make feelings appear less abstract to younger children. Once the feeling pieces are cut out, therapists are to mark the colored pieces with the corresponding color names.

The process begins with clients choosing particular bodies for their dads. They may begin in any manner they see fit. They may first either design the face or dress them (provided all clothing and facial pieces have been prepared by therapists beforehand or by therapists and clients together). Along the way, therapists should facilitate the children's discussions of their fathers as opportunities arise to do so.

What makes the process most therapeutic however, is the incorporation of the feeling pieces. Here, children choose particular feelings to ascribe to their fathers based on how they see their dad's emotions (part real, part projection). This is done by placing the feeling pieces underneath the dad's shorts, in the places where feelings come from—the chest and belly. Metaphorically, therapists may refer to feelings as being "on the inside and needing to come out." A potential therapist verbalization could be, "Wow, your dad's shirt has trouble fitting over all those feelings. I bet it would fit and feel better if those feelings were able to come out sometime." Over time, as the child explores and processes these various emotions, the relevant feeling pieces can be literally brought to the outside of the figure.

APPLICATIONS

Design-A-Dad is to be used by child clients in the third level of development (ages 6–11). At this stage, children have generated conservation skills. The ability to conserve allows children to use their thought processes "to override experiential input in order to make their perceptions more consistent with reality . . . [they] can compare and contrast information based not just on their experience of it but on what they "know" to be true (O'Connor 1991, p. 78). Once conservation is mastered, children are then able to internally generate a whole host of emotions that they had previously been unable to generate. They are "beginning to be able to categorize affects not only by the internal sensations that are generated but by the situations in which they occur" (O'Connor 1991, p. 81). Children are thus offered opportunities to effectively process the dads whom they have just designed.

Design-A-Dad is appropriate for children of virtually all diagnoses with two possible exceptions: children who are actively psychotic and children who have been sexually abused. Because this process requires children to dress and undress the figures, therapists should be careful to consider the potential impact upon the sexually abused child before proceeding with this activity.

EXAMPLE

CW is an 8-year-old child client whose father's work necessitated their separation for up to periods of three months. CW was subsequently referred to treatment for separation anxiety. During the fourth session, upon the child's brief mention of his dad, the therapist suggested that he design his dad: "You know, I'd like to know more about your dad. Here are some things we can use to do that. You can make him so I can have a picture of him in my head." CW proceeded to design his father's face, giving the therapist ample opportunity to discuss with the child various qualities the father possessed.

As the child became more at ease and as the discussion progressed, the therapist instructed the child to use some of the feeling pieces to show how the "dad" feels at times. The therapist further instructed the child to place the feeling pieces under the dad's shirt "in the feeling place." CW then began to discuss each feeling over the course of the next few sessions. As each feeling was discussed, the child placed that feeling to the side, illustrating how the feeling was "now out." As the process evolved, the therapist facilitated the child's age-appropriate understanding of the various feelings associated with the father's unavailability. The child was further able to differentiate which feelings were his and which may be his father's.

After approximately six sessions, the child felt comfortable inviting his dad into the sessions. Before Design-A-Dad was implemented, the child was both unwilling and unable to invite his dad in. As a result, the use of Design-A-Dad facilitated the child's ability to incorporate his father into the sessions, where he then proceeded to express his thoughts and feelings to his father about the separation.

References

Ammen, S. A. (1994). Standardization of colors for the Color-Your-Life Technique (O'Connor 1983). Unpublished personal communication.

Bain, H. C., Boersma, F. J., and Chapman, J. W. (1983). Academic achievement and locus-of-control in father-absent elementary school children. *School Psychology International* 4: 69–78.

Fry, P. S., and Scher, A. (1984). The effects of father absence on children's achievement motivation, ego-strength, and locus-of-control orientation: a five-year longitudinal assessment. *British Journal of Developmental Psychology* 2: 167–178.

Goldstein, H. S. (1984). Parental composition, supervision, and conduct problems in youths 12 to 17 years old. *Journal of the American Academy of Child Psychiatry* 23: 679–684.

Miller, T. (1984). Paternal absence and its effect on adolescent self-esteem. *International Journal of Social Psychology* 30: 293–296.

O'Connor, K. J. (1983). The color-your-life technique. In *Handbook of Play Therapy*, C. E. Schaefer and K. J. O'Connor, pp. 251–258. New York: Wiley.

——— (1991). *The Play Therapy Primer*. New York: Wiley.

37

Synthetic Clay in Play Therapy

Martha D. Young

INTRODUCTION

The use of this medium in play therapy has many advantages. The material is very malleable, does not stiffen like Play-doh™, behaves more cooperatively than plasticene, and appeals to children aged 3 through 11. It appears to have an oil base, which makes it easy to clean off wooden surfaces with a standard wood cleaning liquid. The product is sold by Constructive Playthings as "color dough," and by Hoover's as "playpat."

Children appear to enjoy play with this special clay for several reasons. It is very tactually pleasant to use. They can shape it into almost any form, alter it, and destroy it whenever they please. Rolling and carving seem to be outlets for aggressive feelings. Working with the clay tends to facilitate their expression of feelings and concerns. Many have seemed to be quite engrossed in their activities. Interpretation of their creations is generally simple and accepted by the children. Obviously the complexity of the play is somewhat circumscribed, but I do not think that detracts from the efficacy of the technique.

DESCRIPTION

Children choose only one color of clay to use at a time, in order to avoid contaminating the colors. They are given a small rolling pin and a letter opener. On the cover of the sandtray table they can play with the clay in any manner they desire. They are cautioned, however, that stabbing the table top isn't great for it. Although I have been asked by some children to provide them with cookie cutters, I have not, in order to facilitate their original expression.

My clients have used the clay to resemble food and have tea parties or meals with it. Some have cut it into representations of themselves or of experiences they have had and told stories about what they have created. Others have simply manipulated the clay into various forms.

APPLICATIONS

Children of several diagnostic categories have productively used the clay. Specifically, my child clients have included children with ADD (some who have been sexually molested), children with oppositional–defiant disorders, and depressed children.

Most recently a bright, restless 8-year-old boy who has acted out oppositionally in school and at home, and is being evaluated by the school psychologist and a local psychiatrist to differentiate between ADD and bipolar disorder, played with the clay. He divided it into two balls, which he molded into humanlike figures. Taking some toothpicks, he armed each figure, and named them according to the configuration of the toothpicks. Holding one figure in each hand, he made them engage in a battle to the death. A frequent outcome was that one figure would engulf the other. He took great delight in his play, and provided a narration as the figures were fighting. At the end of our session he was more relaxed and had a brighter affect than he had had when he entered the room.

Section Four

Game Play Techniques

38

Checkers: Rules or No Rules

L. G. Agre

INTRODUCTION

In many client-centered approaches the therapy involves the role of choice for the child. When a child is in the playroom, there are many times that one might choose checkers. When this is done, we work with issues of trust, consistency, and control. Is life predictable? Can I have an impact on my life? In this life, what are the rules we go by to keep ourselves in school, to keep ourselves out of harm's way?

RATIONALE

In many ways checkers can provide a unique medium to teach the child various things. Depending upon what is needed, the rules of the game can be chosen for the benefit of the child to build ego strength with having a child follow rules or have self-control. If, however, a child is fearful, withdrawn, or has difficulty taking a lead role, the child can be the one who makes the rules to the game. In this technique, the rules provide the focal point.

DESCRIPTION

This technique involves having the child follow all the rules. Their therapist says, "Do you want to play by the real rules or do you want to make up a game?" If the child wants to go by the rules, the therapist can say, "The way I play, you must always take your jumps and you tell me where to move. If your checker gets too close to mine, the natural consequence will be for my checker to jump yours. That is the only way I play."

Often, we will have a discussion about how in life there are rules whether we like them or not, and that there are consequences to our actions: one thing does lead to another in life in general, as well as in the classroom. The therapist continues, "In this room, when we play checkers, we always take our jumps."

APPLICATIONS

This technique works well with children who choose checkers. Children seem to be delighted by winning. I have had only one child lose and that child wanted to lose. This technique allows children to be risk-takers, to correct their mistakes, to plan ahead, and to play with an adult in a way that is predictable and safe.

39

Beat the Clock

Heidi Gerard Kaduson

INTRODUCTION

Many children with impulse control problems find it difficult to maintain good self-esteem. Throughout their lives, these children are told "Stop," "Don't," and so on. They rarely finish tasks that they start, and therefore they do not receive the good feelings related to completion and productivity. Over years this may prove to increase a child's negative self-worth and acting-out behavior. I have noted that many children with impulse control problems seem to be able to show more self-control when they are motivated. The *Beat the Clock* game was created by me in order to help motivate these children to exhibit self-control and receive the rewards of productivity that they were missing.

RATIONALE

One of the therapeutic powers of play is mastery. It is the basis from which I created this game. When a child is engaged in an enjoyable activity, they tend to persist at it longer. This persistence quite likely will produce success in mastering the task, staying on task, and earning the reward. The impulsive child can see the success obtained when a task is completed, and the reward is both the task and the sense of competence.

DESCRIPTION

In order to implement this technique, the therapist needs a kitchen timer, poker chips, drawing materials, blocks, and some easy reading books. The child is introduced to the task at hand (building a tower out of blocks, drawing a picture, coloring in stencils, or reading a book).

Therapist: We are going to play the game Beat the Clock. First I will give you ten poker chips. Here are some blocks. I will set the timer for ten minutes. During that time, you are to build with the blocks and make a tower without being distracted by anything around you. If you look up from your project, you will have to pay me one chip. Each time you get distracted or ask questions or do anything except build the tower, you will give me another chip. If you are able to stay on task, without being distracted for the entire ten minutes, then I will give you another ten chips. After you have fifty chips, you can pick anything you want from the Treasure Bag [a bag of small toys purchased in advance]. Any questions?

Child: When I am finished with the tower, do I stop?

Therapist: That's a good question. You must continue until the timer stops. You will hear a bell [therapist demonstrates the sound of the bell]. If the tower is finished, build something else. You will only receive the chips when the timer goes off. On your mark, get set, go.

The therapist remains unintrusive for the first few minutes, and then creates some distractions. The goal is to train the child to stay on task no matter what is happening in the room, out the door, or in the hall. In the beginning, the child will be distracted by the therapist dropping things, cleaning up, and so on. As the game continues over several sessions, the child will be very motivated to earn the fifty poker chips and pick a prize. The next step is to increase the time by five minutes each time a fifty poker-chip prize is attained. Many children are able to stay on task for an entire session over time.

APPLICATIONS

The game is very useful for children with attention deficit hyperactivity disorder or any other impulse control problem. Providing a positive environment, where fun is the main objective, allows the child to explore his or her own possibilities of completion and competency. The reward system becomes the motivator, but the result of success becomes the real reason they continue to play. Just the look on the child's face as he or she receives the ten chips for being totally on task for the entire ten minutes reflects the goal of this technique.

40

Pounding Away Bad Feelings

Donna Cangelosi

INTRODUCTION

This technique was designed to help children communicate about problematic feelings and situations and to help them develop options and skills for approaching similar situations in the future.

RATIONALE

The mechanisms through which play serves as a modality for therapeutic change have been outlined by Schaefer (1993). This play technique provides the therapist with a tool to promote several of these mechanisms or curative powers. Among these are: overcoming resistance, communication, creative thinking, catharsis, abreaction, relationship enhancement, enjoyment, understanding and empathy, mastery, and game play.

The game "Don't Break the Ice" is very appealing to youngsters and is seen as fun, challenging, and exciting. As such, it is a helpful addition in the play room. The game has set rules, such as taking turns and tolerating the frustration of losing, and therefore promotes socialization. Used as a therapeutic tool, "Don't Break the Ice" can provide a vehicle for communication, catharsis, and abreaction as well as an opportunity for the therapist to promote creative thinking and mastery (i. e., through direct statements, metaphorical teaching, or modeling).

DESCRIPTION

Materials Needed:

"Don't Break the Ice"™ by the Milton Bradley Company.

Directions:

The child is asked to discuss a situation which caused him or her to feel angry, frustrated, hurt, bad, sad, or mad. She or he then taps out a block of ice with the plastic mallet (provided in the game) to "get rid of the feeling." The therapist then prompts the child to think about ways for effectively handling the situation in the future. Options and ideas are offered for anticipating similar situations, preventing them, and/or dealing with them when they arise. The therapist then takes a turn and builds upon the child's example in order to highlight certain points and to role model effective coping and problem solving. The child and therapist continue taking turns in this manner until all of the ice pieces have been tapped away.

When used for group or family therapy, individuals can ask each other how they would handle the situation, or each person can offer options. (In some cases it may be helpful to start the game talking about less threatening feelings to ease the child into the game and to gather information about his or her pleasures, coping, etc.)

APPLICATIONS

This technique can be used in individual, group, or family therapy. When used with a group of children or with family members, ideas for effective coping are solicited from all participants. The exercise promotes open communication, cooperative efforts toward problem resolution, catharsis of negative or other overwhelming feelings, and understanding of self and others. It is therefore useful for a wide variety of clinical populations.

References

Milton Bradley Company. *Don't Break the Ice.*

Schaefer, C. E. (1993). *The Therapeutic Powers of Play.* Northvale, NJ: Jason Aronson.

41

The Pick-Up-Sticks Game

Barbara McDowell

INTRODUCTION

Many play therapists emphasize the importance of assisting their child clients in recognizing, expressing, and managing their affective states (Allen 1988, Gill 1991, Jernberg 1979, Oaklander 1969). In order to manage his affect, the child must develop several skills. For instance, the child must develop an awareness of a variety of affective states, the ability to relate those affects to their environmental events, and the ability to verbally express the affects in an appropriate manner (O'Connor 1983).

Play has been used as a way to communicate with children and to help them express their feelings. Anna Freud (1928) conceptualized play as a mechanism to build relationships with children who will then become increasingly verbal. Realizing the importance of encouraging verbalization in children as they cognitively mature (Harter 1983), therapists strive to create activities that will be playful while increasing the child's verbalizations. O'Connor (1983) achieved this goal when he developed the Color-Your-Life Technique, an activity that pairs colors with affective states. The technique allows the child to express his feelings through coloring, and subsequent discussion of the activity encourages the child's verbalizations.

RATIONALE

The Pick-Up-Sticks Game was adapted by this student to facilitate affective expression in children. The activity assumes the child has previous knowledge of color–affect pairs, introduced by an activity such as the Color-Your-Life Technique (O'Connor 1983). This adapted version of the Pick-Up-Sticks Game uses a familiar format to assist children in pairing affect with situations in their lives and verbally expressing those affects. Since children typically enjoy the original version of the Pick-Up-Sticks Game, they should find this adapted version relatively nonthreatening.

DESCRIPTION

Therapist Variables

This technique may be used by any therapist who wishes to help his or her child clients express their feelings and pair affective states with environmental events in a game format. Since this technique is used after the child has developed the ability to recognize primary affective states, interpretations may be used frequently. They will help create awareness within the child and encourage participation. An accepting and empathic attitude by the therapist will be most conducive for the desired goal of affective expression.

Child Variables

This technique was designed for children who have developed an awareness of color–affect pairs and the ability to recognize primary affective states. It requires the child to have adequate verbal skills and concentration to focus on the activity. It is contraindicated for children who have concentration or attention difficulties, as it would create a situation for the child to fail, limiting the opportunities for self-expression. This activity may be particularly beneficial for competitive children whose desire to win the game will drive them to pick up sticks with a color/affect they would normally avoid.

Materials

The only material required for this activity is one of the commercially available Pick-Up-Sticks Games. For those not familiar with the game it consists of a number of plastic or wooden sticks, each about one quarter the diameter of a pencil and one of several colors.

Technique

This activity should be presented to the child in a playful, enjoyable manner. Children are typically familiar with the Pick-Up-Sticks Game. However, if this game has not been played previously, the therapist must explain it to the child. Either the therapist or the child may hold the sticks in their fist and drop them in a pile on the floor or table. The object of the original game is to remove a stick without moving any of the other sticks. The therapist and the child take turns removing sticks. If, when a stick is being removed, other sticks are moved, the player must leave the stick and end the turn. Whoever has the most sticks at the end of the game wins. The game can be made more elaborate by assigning different point values to each of the colors.

For this adapted version of the Pick-Up-Sticks Game, the therapist should first review the color–affect pairs learned in previous sessions. This may be done by using the Color-Your-Life Technique or by verbally reviewing this information. The color–affect pairs in the Color-Your-Life Technique are: yellow–happy, blue–sad, black–very sad, red–angry, purple–rage, green–jealous, brown–bored, and orange–excited. The therapist should then introduce the Pick-Up-Sticks Game in his or her usual fashion. The therapist will explain the rules of the game to the child, adding the new rule. Each time a stick is successfully removed, the player must describe a time when he or she felt the feeling associated with the color of the stick.

Both the child and the therapist will follow this rule. Rather than disclosing personal information, the therapist may wish to tailor his or her responses to the particular needs of the child. In addition, the therapist may wish to allow the child to pass a specified number of times during the game. If the therapist chooses this option, the child should be told prior to the start of the game how many passes will be allowed. This will allow the child some control over the information and feelings he or she expresses. However, only a small number of passes should be allowed during a game so the child is less able to entirely avoid uncomfortable affects. As the game is being played, the therapist will recognize many opportunities for interpretation. For example, the therapist may interpret the child's choice of stick he or she picks up, what color stick the child wants to pass on, as well as the child's affect and behavior throughout the game.

APPLICATIONS

The above technique is used in the following session with a 12-year-old male client. The child has a history of neglect and alleged abuse. He is currently in foster care and one of his primary treatment goals is to recognize and express a variety of affective states. It is a challenge to introduce activities that will not be perceived as "babyish" by this young man, while still eliciting affective expression. His competitive nature makes him open to this adapted version of the Pick-Up-Sticks Game.

The session began with the Color-Your-Life Technique. This had been played in previous sessions and was familiar to the client. Rather than coloring the feelings he has felt throughout his life, he colored his feelings during the past week. After the therapist reviewed the color–affect pairs and explained the instructions to the adapted version of the Pick-Up-Sticks Game, he appeared excited to play the game, stating, "I'm good at this, I'm going to beat you!" The first few turns of the game were completed with very little anxiety created by the expression of his feelings about certain live events. My disclosures during the game were tailored to the needs of this particular client. I did not disclose personal information, rather information that pulled for similar affects–experiences in the client's life. There are typically lone sticks that were able to be removed quite easily during the initial phase of the game. As the game progressed, however, he began to realize that in order to successfully remove a stick he would have to choose blue (sad) or black (very sad) or purple (rage) sticks that symbolized affects that were uncomfortable to express. He initially tried to pick sticks with more comfortable affects but that were more difficult to remove from the pile. This resulted in his failure to successfully remove the stick. These attempts to avoid discussing anxiety provoking affective states were interpreted. His competitive instincts soon became stronger than his desire to avoid certain stick colors and subsequent affective states. He then began to choose the most strategically beneficial sticks, even though they were blue, black, and purple. Again this behavior was interpreted. At the end of this game, I had the most sticks and won the game, most likely due to the client's choice of sticks that symbolized fairly neutral affect. He quickly claimed that we needed to play again and this time he would beat me! We played a second game, following the same rules. During this game, the client's motivation to choose a certain stick was based entirely on his desire to win the game, which he did. He continued to experience some anxiety when pairing uncomfortable affects with environmental events, however, he was more willing to do so. Subsequently his expression of affect was reinforced by winning the game.

This activity was received well by this client because of his competitive nature and his ability to concentrate on the game. It utilized an enjoyable game format to encourage the pairing of affects with environmental events as well as the verbal expression of those affects. In addition, interpretations were made throughout the game. Interpretations were not only directed at issues of affect but also at his competitiveness. There were many opportunities to relate-in-session behavior with out-of-session behavior. This adapted version of the Pick-Up-Sticks Game turned a relatively silent activity into a playful verbal exchange. This activity was successful in creating a playful environment while addressing a critical treatment goal: affective recognition and expression.

References

Allan, J. (1988). *Inscapes of the Child's World.* Dallas, TX: Spring Publications.

Freud, A. (1928). *Introduction to the Technique of Child Analysis.* New York: Nervous and Mental Disease Publishing.

Gil, E. (1991). *The Healing Power of Play.* New York: Guilford.

Harter, S. (1983). Cognitive-developmental considerations in the conduct of play therapy. In *Handbook of Play Therapy,* ed. C. E. Schaefer and K. J. O'Connor, pp. 95-127. New York: Wiley.

Jernberg, A. M. (1979). *Theraplay.* San Francisco: Jossey-Bass.

Oaklander, V. (1969). *Windows to our Children.* New York: Center for Gestalt Development.

O'Connor, K. J. (1983). The color-your-life technique. In *Handbook of Play Therapy,* ed. C. E. Schaefer and K. J. O'Connor, pp. 251-258. New York: Wiley.

42

The Stealing Game

Steve Harvey

INTRODUCTION

A common behavioral difficulty shown by many preschool and elementary-aged children is stealing. The play therapist encounters this difficulty particularly in family-oriented psychotherapy. Stealing behavior is exasperating and frustrating for parents as they are powerless to stop their child, particularly as children grow older and their stealing techniques become more polished. In this way, the child's stealing and the family's response to it become self-reinforcing, in that children gain significant feelings of power and control over their parents as their parents continue to express increasing amounts of behavioral controls, thereby making stealing an ever more attractive behavior for their children.

This form of stealing and family frustration seems to occur particularly among children for whom there have been significant family disruptions: among stepfamilies, in adoptions of high-risk children, and among children who have experienced significant early trauma. Winnicott (1971) suggested that such stealing in the family context might be related to the child's attempt to obtain original and primary maternal love and attention that was missing from a child's early development. Whether or not all child stealing is an attempt to "steal" or receive primary attachment and acceptance could be further discussed. However, it is clear that stealing within a family context has a strong relational component in which children develop a dramatic role and the actual act of stealing becomes very meaningful within the family context far and above the actual concrete act of taking something. Further, it is true for any therapist who has heard a parent's frustration that adults are quite often unaware of the larger dramatic significance because of their frustration and strong desire to have the child's behavior controlled.

In this situation, the family-oriented play therapist is in a unique position to help parents and children significantly enhance their relationships, gain further understanding of the relational significance and meaning inherent in the act of stealing, and possibly begin to reshape their emotional experience with each other.

RATIONALE

The primary reason for using the Stealing Game is for the therapist to help the family put all of the drama surrounding the stealing behavior into a playful, interactive context. Once the therapist and family are able to develop a "game" of stealing, the parents and child can begin to gain some distance from their family tension, develop some mutual strategies from playful enactments to be used at home or better address the stealing episodes, begin to address any relational tension produced from the roles of stealer and stealee, and begin to gain some understanding of the core-related emotional significance of the stealing. The therapeutic use of a stealing game to make a playful, interactive context developed from more superficial home behavior to address deeper emotional issues follows the therapeutic rationale in Dynamic Play Therapy (Harvey 1990, 1991, 1993, 1994, 1995).

In general, Dynamic Play Therapy is an integrated expressive play therapy approach in which family members are encouraged to engage in creative and expressive movement, drama, art, and video play together as the therapist helps to identify and coach family members to actively create playful metaphors between them that address significant relational issues, particularly those related to attachment, loss, and trauma. Dynamic Play Therapy proceeds as the therapist, and later therapist and family, begin simple and concrete interactive playful interactions involving various expressive mediums, observe how the creative play process breaks down, and later find ways to incorporate or change a family's cooperative expression with each other so that family members can develop a freer sense of playful improvisation.

DESCRIPTION

The Stealing Game is best applied with families of children aged 6 to 12. The therapist usually sets up the game after a relationship with the family is well established and the stealing behavior is reported. This usually occurs after the initial intake and evaluation process (one to two months). After the parent reports ongoing stealing behavior and the therapist is able to engage both parent and child in describing what usually occurs by gathering such information as what has been stolen and what usually happens, the therapist sets up an initial activity which is called the Stealing Game.

In this activity, all the play props are placed on one side of the room. A line is drawn and the parent is given the role of guarding the props, and the child is given the role of stealing them. The game proceeds with the rule that if the stealer is able to take a play prop across the line, he or she is able to tell the protector to immobilize a body part, and the game is restarted until the stealer is able to steal another prop. At this point, he or she is able to tell the protector another body part to immobilize. The game continues until the protector gives up.

Usually the play props include several scarves, large pillows, stuffed animals, and so on, and the line across the room is a ribbon or rope and is quite clear. Often, a parent or therapist needs to be the judge as to when a prop is actually taken from the protector's side of the room to the stealer's side across the line. A judge's decision saves a continuing argument as to whether a prop has been stolen or not. Typically, immobilization of a body part occurs with the stealer asking the protector to place an arm behind the back, lift a leg up, or close an eye (or place a blindfold over the eyes to take away eyesight). Finally, a stealer may also ask a protector to stop talking, thereby preventing verbal commands. During the playing of the game, the therapist needs to coach both stealer and protector to be more playful in their role enactments.

Once the protector gives up, or when all the props are stolen, the roles are reversed so that the child becomes the protector, and the adult becomes the stealer. The parent has the same rules as the stealer, and asks the child to immobilize a body part when something is stolen. The Stealing Game is played back and forth with different participants until there are clear breaks, shifts in affect, or the game changes through the interactive process. At this point, the Dynamic Play Therapist makes adjustments in the game to better account for such play shifts. The therapist can also ask both parent and child to draw the most important scenes of the Stealing Game, or a videotape can be made and reviewed. The general goal of these activities is to have both parent and child begin to understand and more playfully engage in the relational aspect expressed in the Stealing Game. Typically, the most important aspect of the therapeutic work occurs in these second scenes following the game itself, in which the therapist helps the parent and child begin to build a new and more personally relevant interactive game based on how the Stealing Game was initially played.

Typical examples of the development of such game extensions involve what happens to the props during the stealing play. Often, the parent will take the scarves or some other small props and hide them on his or her person, or otherwise hold on to them quite tightly to keep something and thereby frustrate the stealing child. A typical response to this is to develop even more interest in the scarf that is not freely given. A therapeutic response at this moment would be to have the parent and child engage in some verbal negotiation concerning the remaining scarves while attempting to use verbal directions to allow the metaphorical significance of what the last scarf may actually mean in the emotional give-and-take of the parent–child relationship. Some examples of this deeper meaning might include for the parent the last moments of personal identity, and for the child love and attention from a parenting figure that has been withheld. Given the potential for such metaphorical significance, the negotiations between parent and child concerning the last props can become quite powerful and have personal significance for the players.

APPLICATIONS

The Stealing Game is perhaps used best among elementary-aged children who show conduct disorder and/or attachment-related problems in their family situation. Typically, such children are extremely hard to engage in any mode of treatment, particularly the more traditional verbal or behavioral forms of psychotherapy. Such children are typically over-represented in the populations of foster care and adopted children for whom the development of trust and generation of spontaneous expression of feelings is very difficult.

Interesting and productive extensions of the Stealing Game have been used with adult family members, adult siblings, or adults with their parents, as well as in marital therapy to explore relational difficulties. In these cases, the props are openly acknowledged to be metaphors for the emotional significance of the relationship being explored, and the Stealing Game is less overtly about "stealing" than it is about relational issues in general. However, as in the Stealing Game with young children, the initial activity becomes a very convenient, concrete context from which to begin exploring the meaning of emotional exchange in long-time, intimate relationships.

References

Harvey, S. A. (1990). Dynamic play therapy: an integrated expressive arts approach to the family therapy of young children. *Arts in Psychotherapy,* 17:239–246.

——— (1991). Creating a family: an integrated expressive approach to adoption. *Arts in Psychotherapy* 18: 213–222.

——— (1993). Ann: dynamic therapy response to ritual abuse. In *Play Therapy in Action: A Casebook for Practitioners,* ed. T. Kottman and C. Schaefer, pp. 371–415. New Jersey: Jason Aronson.

——— (1994). Dynamic play therapy: an expressive arts approach to family intervention. In *The Handbook of Play Therapy, Volume II,* pp. 85–110. New York: John Wiley and Sons.

——— (1995). Sandra: the case of an adopted, sexually abused child. In *Dance and Other Expressive Arts Therapies,* ed. F. Levy, pp. 36–46. New York: Rutledge.

Winnicott, D. W. (1971). *Therapeutic Consultations in Child Psychiatry.* New York: Basic Books.

43

Consequences: Reaching the Oppositional Defiant Adolescent

Neil Cabe

INTRODUCTION

One of the characteristics of children presenting with Oppositional Defiant and Conduct Disorder diagnoses is an apparent inability to recognize consequences for their actions. In some sense, they are unable to recognize that one action in a series results in unwanted outcomes. When a child is able to see that he or she can interrupt a behavioral process, he or she may also learn that outcome may be changed.

RATIONALE

My work with this population leads me to believe that locus of control is an issue in treatment. Most of the oppositional defiant children I have seen feel as if their lives are beyond their own control, and that their behavior is as well. They have adopted a decidedly *external* locus of control. Part of the aim of the therapeutic process is to help the child adapt an *internal* locus of control, which will improve control of his own behavior, increase the child's sense of self-efficacy, and mediate his defiant behaviors. The defiance and opposition themselves may be an attempt at developing this internal locus.

With younger children, I have had some success using a wireless remote control earth mover, pushing blocks around the playroom and bulldozing them into piles. I do not have a sand tray, but that medium might prove even more effective. In the process, I help the child describe his own effectual behavior, and note that he is in control of the play environment. Working with adolescents is more problematic. Some of them are still free enough to allow themselves to play with the earth mover. Many will not. In the latter cases, I have found the use of dominoes and a toy called the Domino Rally to be very effective.

DESCRIPTION

A simple set of dominoes is cheap and readily available. Many of the adolescents I have seen already know how to play the game, which allows us a second activity with the same toy. In playing the standard domino game, I continue to emphasize rules, which is developmentally important for the child.

In addition, we simply set the dominoes up—using two or three sets—in intricate patterns on a table in the play room, and topple them over. This is an activity many of my clients had not experienced and they enjoyed it greatly. Next, I set up a row of the topple-over dominoes, letting each piece represent one action in a series that led a negative outcome for the child. We then discuss which of the activities in the chain could have been changed or simply omitted in order to avoid the negative outcome.

For example, domino 1 represents walking into the school, 2 is hearing about a fight down the hall, 3 is going to see the fight, 4 is staying there, 5 is not dispersing when a teacher intervened, 6 is not leaving when the teacher addressed the client directly, 7 is disrespect directed toward the teacher, 8 is going to the office, and 9 is getting suspended. The child is easily able to identify a number of different strategies for avoiding the suspension. In the case in point, which is an actual one, eliminating or changing any one of numbers 3 through 7 would have altered the outcome from negative to neutral.

Be aware that the child will probably first say he should have just stayed home in bed. Even this can be a therapeutic moment for the therapist who is prepared to discuss the need for an education. I have also found it interesting that the children are much more able than I to remember exactly which domino represents which particular activity. It is important to pay attention to the sequence and process as you examine it with the child.

The Domino Rally is a clever little battery-operated machine that actually sets plastic domino-like blocks up for knocking over. Using it allows the child to direct the machine around a table, emphasizing again his control over his own environment. The explanatory process remains the same as when using standard dominos. Domino Rally is available at most toy stores.

In subsequent sessions, my clients have been able to remember the activity and to apply the process to other incidents in their lives. The learning of the process itself will help the child realize the beginning of the possibility of an internal locus of control for himself, and helps with the healing process. The activity is inexpensive, memorable, and effective.

44

Hide-and-Seek in Play Therapy

John Allan and Mary Anne Pare

INTRODUCTION

This approach is not actually a technique but rather therapeutic play that develops organically from both the needs of the child and the structure of the playroom. Our recognition of the importance of this game came as a result of observing certain children and how they played out this game in the therapy room. Even with no logical place to hide, they would pretend to disappear, albeit in full view of the therapist. Early on in our practice as play therapists, in a playroom with a curtained area that was used for storage, we found children time and again disappearing and reappearing from behind the curtain, in many variations of the peek-a-boo and hide-and-seek scenarios. This experience led us to research this game in greater detail and also, in future versions of the playroom, to construct a number of hidden spaces.

RATIONALE

There is a natural sequence in the emotional development of infants to toddlers to young children that includes the progression of the play of peek-a-boo, to chasing games, and finally to hide-and-seek. The developmental tasks that are accomplished through these games include the mastery of interpersonal anxiety and separation anxiety and the experience of separate identity and intimacy through reunion, leading to the development of emotional (or object) constancy. Peek-a-boo and hide-and-seek help children make the shift from needing the physical presence of adults to building an interior psychological life that enables them to successfully function when parents or primary caregivers are not physically present. These games are universal, appearing across cultures and through all ages of childhood. However, we find that children play these games in a repetitious way in play therapy when their has been a weak attachment bond or breaks in attachment and when they have not been able to master these developmental tasks. With the safe container of the therapeutic experience, hide-and-seek can provide the opportunity to readdress this developmental work in order to overcome anxiety, gain mastery and build a stronger sense of self.

DESCRIPTION

Unlike specific play therapy techniques, the therapist does not actively introduce this approach. Rather, in the arrangement and design of the playroom, every effort is made to create structures that facilitate this type of play. As well, the therapist maintains an analytical attitude, which involves awareness of the child's attachment issues and observation and response to any introduction of the peek-a-boo and hide-and-seek themes in play. For example, when a child purposefully disappears behind a chair or table, the therapist immediately responds with an exclamation: "Oh, no, I can't see Megan! Where did she go?" This response can help the child to move into the attachment work of this game. Though children will initiate this game in any space, we have found that purposefully designing the therapeutic playroom to include accessible hidden spaces greatly enhances the opportunity for this reparative work to emerge from the play. Some examples are: angling a bookshelf away from the wall, attaching a curtain at child height and placing blankets and pillows in the triangular space created; using full length drapes instead of curtains over windows; bringing in large cardboard boxes; or designing a carpeted, curtained cubbyhole in a corner of the room. Failing these possibilities, a simple piece of material attached with velcro over the space for a chair in an office desk will suffice.

Children might initiate this game by saying "Close your eyes for a minute," or "Pretend you can't see me." Often language isn't used, as when a child ducks under a desk or behind a door when the therapist's back is turned. These nonverbal communications are in fact an invitation to enter the game. In response to these overtures, the therapist joins the spirit of the game both verbally and nonverbally, and especially with emotional intensity. We have noticed that there is a range of feelings embedded in the drama of the game: there is the arousal of the child's body, the thrill of being wanted and sought, the pleasure of surprise, the power of controlling the interaction, the anxiety of loss, the pain over the loss of the loved one, the delight and relief of reunion, the fear of aloneness, the conquering of that fear, the great pleasure of confusing an adult, and ultimately the empowerment that comes with magic.

In the course of searching for and finding (losing and being reunited with) the child, the therapist verbalizes this wide range of emotions with intensity: "Oh, no, I can't find Megan! [with dismay] I wanted so much to play with her. [with disappointment] What if I can't ever find her again? [with apprehension] I'll be so sad if I can't see her soon. Oh, there you are Megan! [with great relief and delight]." Equally important is the reversal of roles, with the therapist the one who hides and the child the one who orchestrates the reunion and thus experiences mastery over loss.

APPLICATIONS

The use of this approach is helpful in the play therapy of children who have suffered a loss or multiple losses through emotional neglect, divorce, death, apprehension, or from many moves, hospitalization of themselves or a primary caregiver, or other forms of broken attachment where children do not experience feeling wanted or desired.

Depending on the individual child and the particulars of the attachment issue that the child is struggling with, there are a number of variations on the hide-and-seek theme that we have observed. There is the most primitive form of the game, that of peek-a-boo, which captures the anxiety of disappearance and the thrill of reconnection. There is impromptu vanishing and re-appearing, generally at the start or end of a session, which may reflect ambivalence or anxiety about the intimacy of therapy at the beginning and when ending, may be an indication of separation anxiety. There is the structured game of hide-and-seek, where we see more ego consciousness, an emphasis on adhering to rules, and often role reversal, with the child playing both passive and active parts (hider and seeker). There is hide-and-seek with props, such as symbolic play in the sand tray, and the use of puppets, studded animals, or disappearing creatures like turtles, snails, and baby kangaroos. Finally, there is transformational play, where the child uses hide-and-seek to explore and strengthen a new aspect of self, often using masks, costumes, and the introduction of new dramatic personae.

We have noticed a number of situations in hide-and-seek where the child may become fixated on one predominant response pattern. We describe these below, giving a possible hypothesis and a beginning interpretation the therapist might make to help the child understand the situation and move towards resolution:

Situation: the child who only wants to be the seeker.
Hypothesis: needing to be in control.
Interpretation: "You want to be the boss. . . . You like it best when you're in control."

Situation: the child who can't stand to stay hidden.
Hypothesis: not able to stay with the tension, the anxiety of aloneness.
Interpretation: "It's scary being all alone. . . . Maybe you're afraid no one will notice you... or find you."

Situation: the child who doesn't want to be found.
Hypothesis: avoidance of intimacy, ambivalent attachment, anger.
Interpretation: "You're so angry you won't let me see you. . . . You don't want anyone close."

Situation: the child who wants to play hide-and-seek endlessly.
Hypothesis: may not be able to internalize gratification.
Interpretation: "I wonder if it's hard to believe I/others really care about you."

When hide-and-seek is acted out in the play therapy room, the child is working on the important developmental task of emotional constancy (Mahler 1976). Through the play and the skillful involvement of the therapist, the child has the opportunity to rework attachment issues, to externalize the pain of broken or weak attachment bonds, to master the associated anxiety, and to introject the experience of being desired and of being reunited with the loved person. This process can lead to the internalization of a more secure sense of self and positive sense of self-worth.

References

Burton, C. (1986). Peekaboo to "all the all the outs in free": hide-and-seek as a creative structure in drama therapy. *Arts in Psychotherapy* 13: 129–136.

Frankiel, R. (1993). Hide-and-seek in the playroom: on object loss and transference in child treatment. *Psychological Review* 80: 341–359.

Mahler, M. (1976). Rapprochement subphase of the separation-individuation process. In *The Process of Child Development* ed. P. B. Neubauer, pp. 215–230. New York: New American Library.

45

The Spy and the Sneak

Bria Bartlett-Simpson

INTRODUCTION

The spy and the Sneak tends to be effective for families who are stuck in negative cycles of interaction. This game is especially useful for children who engage in sneaky, manipulative behavior. It is therapeutic because it helps change negative family patterns into positive ones, thereby increasing the members' enjoyment of each other and improving their self-esteem. When this game is continued with other rewards for good behavior and positive play experiences, the child learns that the benefits of positive behavior outweigh the negative attention of acting out. The parent, in turn, regains appreciation for her child and begins to understand how to elicit and maintain positive interactions.

DESCRIPTION

First, talk with the child, in the absence of the parent, about sneaky, positive activities she can do to surprise her parent.[1] Tell her she is the Sneak who will engage in some of these behaviors to see whether her parent, the Spy, can discover what they are. Brainstorm some ideas together and try to focus on ones related to the treatment goals. For instance, if sibling rivalry is a major conflict, you may suggest she think of ways to surprise her brother with kindness. Tell her to engage in 3–5 good behaviors and "Remember, be sneaky, and don't tell anyone!"

Then bring the parent into the session and explain her role as the Spy. She is to make a list over the week of all the Sneak's good behaviors. Ask them both not to discuss it until the next session. At that time, the parent brings her list and the three of you discuss what happened. Be sure to praise the child and process how both the parent and the child feel when she engages in these behaviors.

Continue the game for several sessions. The parent often notices more actions than the child had planned and starts to develop a routine of attending to and praising good behavior. The child, in turn, relishes in the positive attention as well as the opportunity to surprise her parent.

---

1. The basis for this game was presented at a workshop by Kenneth Moore, MSW, Laureate Hospital, Tulsa, OK, May 17, 1995.

46

Pool Play: Helping Children Get Out from Behind the Eight Ball

Stanley Kissel

INTRODUCTION

During the third session, Tom, an 11½-year-old who wore his DSM-IV moniker of Oppositional Defiant Disorder with considerable pride, asked if we could play with the pool table that was on open display in my office. After I had made a few poor shots, he proceeded to clear most of his balls off the table and made a number of derogatory comments about my skill as a pool player. In addition, he was quite boastful regarding his capabilities. This attitude is quite characteristic of children whose maladaptive behaviors have been characterized as "loose" (Kissel 1990). Loose children have considerable difficulty controlling their impulsive and behavioral expression of thoughts or feelings. They seem to lack concern regarding the feelings of others, have difficulty anticipating the effects or consequences of their behaviors, and have been reinforced in the past for excessive nonverbal expressions. After he missed a shot, I had a mercurial run and won the game. He commented, "I think I've been hustled!" As we ended our session, I suggested that pool is quite similar to life in that "it isn't over until it's over."

Pool has been a staple recreational activity found in most residential and inpatient programs. Often such programs have a recreation room where child care workers and residents can play with each other. Occasionally therapists will use the pool table, especially while working with resistant children or adolescents. Recently, there have been a proliferation of miniature pool tables constructed to scale, from portable to table-top pool tables. This has made it possible for some play therapists to include pool tables as a staple item in the playroom. Although pool has not been included in major anthologies on play and game therapy (Schaefer and O'Connor 1983, Schaefer and Reid 1976), the game embraces a considerable number of characteristics that play therapists feel are significant: expression of feelings, relationship, socialization, and symbolism.

In contrast to many board games, pool requires considerably less attention to the game, thus permitting more attention to the child's feelings, attitudes, and style of play.

Like other tools available to the play therapist, pool provides an opportunity for the child to evidence his or her distinct style and manner of relating in the playroom. The loose, nonattentive, oppositional type of youngster behaves distinctly differently while playing a game of pool than the uptight, anxious, worrisome child. Some resistive children will be helped when they see the pool table as an available game. It tends to discount the "don't treat me like a baby" syndrome, which at times can impede therapy with late latency and early adolescent children. Difficulties with verbalizations some children experience can also be broken when playing the game of pool. The modification discussed in the following section makes pool especially helpful for getting children to experience and express feelings. Presently, considerably more girls are in therapy than in the past. Mid-latency-aged girls have similar interests in playing pool as do boys. When young latency-age children are seen, pool can be played with them despite their inability to handle the sticks. We dispense with the pool sticks, and the white ball is thrown into the balls in place of the cue stick.

RATIONALE

During a game of pool the therapist has multiple opportunities to communicate a wish to be of help and acceptance, while providing safety and empathy. Pool provides an interesting distraction from anxiety, making it easier for the child to talk about issues that brought him or her into treatment. If the child is unwilling or unable to talk, pool can be used therapeutically, as such issues as rule violations, cheating, and limit testing and setting quickly rise to the surface. This is a more productive use of time, in contrast to sitting quietly and waiting the child out. The positive relationship that is generated and the comments that are directed to the specific actions of the child during the game help the child to begin to change his subjective perceptions of the world, of authority figures, and hence of his or her self-concept.

Modifying the traditional game of pool can also help children to recognize, express, and better manage their affective states. This is particularly useful for the early to mid-latency-aged child. O'Connor (1983) developed the Color-Your-Life Technique, an activity that has children pair colors with affective states. Kissel (1988) modified the technique so that children who struggle with ambivalence can be helped to feel more comfortable with expressing and accepting dual feelings towards the same person, or similar feelings to different people. After teaching the child the color–affect association segment, the child colors in a circle and is helped to perceive that the different colors coexist and do not change each other. After the child is clear about this segment we shift to a discussion of how the same thing happens with different feelings. The pairing concept of O'Connor is readily extended to pool, so that children who have difficulty experiencing or expressing feelings can develop an awareness of a variety of affective states, learn how to relate these affects to environmental effects, and develop the ability to verbally express their feelings in an appropriate manner.

DESCRIPTION

For the unmodified version, the rules of pool apply. The child decides which game of pool—eight ball, solids and stripes, straight pool, or any variation—will be played. For the modified version, use only the seven colored balls and inform the child that this is a special type of pool game. Review the color–affect pairing by laying out the seven balls in front of the child and then discussing how different colors are sometimes associated with feelings. The child is encouraged to provide a feeling for five of the seven colored balls. Five feelings are sufficient, and it is helpful to have two neutral balls.

Active discussion between child and therapist is encouraged. O'Connor suggests that the therapist begin by asking children if they can pair an affect with a particular color:

Therapist: "Can you tell me what feeling might go with the color red?"

Child: "Uhm, I don't know."

Therapist: "Can you think of a time when people get very red in the face? Think about cartoons you have seen. When do the characters scrunch up their faces and get red?"

Child: "When they are mad!"

Therapist: "That's right. Most people think that the color red goes along with being angry." [O'Connor 1983, p. 254]

The child and therapist continue this type of discussion until each color is related to a specific affect. The following are some suggested pairings which are consistent with art therapy interpretations: black–sadness; red–anger; yellow–happiness; brown–boredom; green–jealousy, envy.

The child is then informed that the one who gets the most balls is the winner. The rules are the same as regular pool with one exception: each time a ball is successfully pocketed, the players must describe a time when they felt the feeling associated with the color of the ball in order to keep the ball. They can choose not to discuss a feeling but then the ball goes back and the other player has a turn.

The therapist can tailor his or her responses to the particular needs of the child rather than unnecessarily disclose personal information. Should a child become particularly resistive and pass a significant number of times, when the next game is played the passing rule can be modified, allowing just one or two passes in a game. Should a specific color cause a child to repeatedly pass or become extremely uncomfortable, block, or evidence play disruption, then the therapist can confront and provide an interpretation.

APPLICATIONS

James, a 10-year-old ADHD youngster, was being seen in therapy because of his inattentiveness and impulsiveness. As might be expected, his social behavior was significantly below what would be expected for someone of his age, and his parents reported that he had difficulty interacting with peers because of his aggressiveness and impulsivity. He had a great deal of difficulty in game playing because he was unable to tolerate losing, and would either disrupt the game or quit. He expressed much interest in the pool table and we played quite often. During the early part of our pool play he would take his turn and then would either walk around the room, play with some other objects in the room, or punch the punching bag when he was upset about missing or after I made a shot. I would pause as I watched him without comment. He would ask whether I made a ball or whether it was his turn. My response, which became rather stylized, was that I was waiting for him before taking my turn. Slowly, over time, he began playing more interactively and his play moved from a parallel type of play to a more social and less egocentric type of play. Parallel changes were reported by his parents in his peer interactions. As he played more interactively his level of skill improved, thus giving me opportunities to reflect on his mastering the game. I was also able to highlight the benefits of taking turns, practicing, and being more involved. Thus Jim was able to discover some of the benefits of being attentive, practicing being more involved and less impulsive.

Frank, a 12-year-old youngster, who was extremely anxious and had considerable fears of failing, played quite tentatively. He commented that he had a table at home, and he asked if I would play. He was quite insistent that I take the first shot to break the balls open. When I suggested that we flip to see who would go first, he was quite uncomfortable. While he had been rather fair and relatively open in other games, he became considerably ill at ease and gave a great sign of relief when I won the flip. During the play, when it was his turn to break, he suggested we flip again, and he would cheat to avoid having to break. He was uncomfortable because he was afraid that he would not hit the balls with sufficient force. His avoidance of taking the first shot symbolized his concerns about aggression and retaliation. After I commented how uncomfortable he was with breaking the balls (taking the first shot) though he had little difficulty shooting during the game, I was able to lead the discussion to his concerns about the balls breaking and how mad he felt I would become. The ambivalence around aggression and retaliation, as well as his own feelings of lack of control, were all easily discernible as I spoke with him about what happens to the pool balls when they are hit. Talk about the pool balls helped diffuse some of his anxiety, so we could discuss his worries and fears, which were related to his out-of-therapy behavior (i. e., aggression at home with siblings and in school with peers).

References

Kissel, S. (1990). *Play Therapy: A Strategic Approach.* Springfield, IL: Charles Thomas.

O'Connor, K. J. (1983). The color-your-life technique. In *Handbook of Play Therapy,* ed. C. E. Schaefer and K. J. O'Connor, pp. 251–259. New York: Wiley-Interscience.

Schaefer, C. E., and Millman, H. (1977). *Therapies For Children: A Handbook of Effective Treatment for Problematic Behaviors.* San Francisco: Jossey-Bass.

Schaefer, C. E., and O'Connor K. J. (1983). *Handbook of Play Therapy.* New York: Wiley-Interscience.

47

Tumbling Feelings: Easing Children into the Counseling Relationship

Christina Mattise

INTRODUCTION

Easing children from the arena of playground drama or academic struggle into the very different world of the counseling relationship can be a challenging task for the school counselor. Counseling within the school setting exists as a sphere within a sphere, each possessing separate and distinct expectations, language, and rituals. By combining a popular commercial game with affective expression skills, the child is able to unwind from the school setting and engage in his or her counseling tasks in a gradual, relaxed fashion.

RATIONALE

The Tumbling Feelings game serves a dual purpose. Early in the school counseling relationship, the game, with its emphasis on mutual disclosure and discussion of feelings, quickly helps the child realize the uniqueness of the counseling adventure. The counselor is not concerned with spelling or arithmetic errors. The counselor is neither disciplinarian nor parent. The focus may be a new and different experience to the child not used to attentive listening or one-to-one relationships with a supportive adult. Secondly, the playing of the game allows the counselor the opportunity to model important skills that will enable the child to express him or herself, maximizing the counseling experience.

DESCRIPTION

The counselor must locate and purchase a variation of a children's block game which is easily available in most discount or toy stores. (It may be known as "Jenga" or "Tumbling Towers.") The game consists of 50+ rectangular blocks, approximately 3"× ¾". Plain unfinished wood is best, as the counselor will be writing a "feeling word" on the broadest, long side of the block. The counselor should select words that correspond to the developmental state of the targeted caseload (words like ecstatic or furious would be less appropriate than happy or mad for an elementary population of less sophisticated readers). A second set of blocks affords the flexibility of adding or subtracting feeling words to make the game more issue-specific for a particular child.

Setting up the game with the child.

After the words have been written on the blocks, the game is played according to the manufacturer's directions, with the following exception: blocks are always placed with the words facing down, therefore no words are visible while playing the game. As found on the directions on the outside of the box, place three blocks side by side on a sturdy surface, leaving a small space between each block. The next layer of three blocks are placed on top of the first, but perpendicular to them, again always leaving a small space between them. Three-block layers are continually placed on top of one another (alternating layers lengthwise, then crosswise) until all the blocks have been used, forming about an 18" tower.

The setting up of the game provides a rich opportunity for observation of the child. Does the child wait for help, request it, or discourage it? Is the child bold and confident or cautious and tentative? Is eye–hand coordination crude or polished? Does the child talk happily of playing this game and others with friends or family or is the concept of a "game" stiff and foreign? Is the child a confident reader or hesitant and avoidant?

Playing the game.

Once the tower is completed, play begins. The player attempts to select a loose block and remove it from the tower without causing it to collapse. Children have a highly effective method of tapping the blocks to determine which block, if removed, will place the tower in the least jeopardy. This technique can be mastered by adults after considerable practice. (Let the children model the behavior for you!) Once a block has been removed, the player who selected it reads the "feeling" and tells of a situation where he or she remembers experiencing that feeling. Players may respond to each other with questions or comments. The counselor may want to reflect a child's feelings or check for clarity of understanding if the feelings or events are somewhat complicated. The counselor may want to tailor his or her own responses to model appropriate disclosure or draw the child closer to more meaningful issues. This should be done with care and with the consideration that the novice child player sees this as very much of a game, at least until a trusting relationship has been built with the counselor. A more seasoned player may use the blocks as a safe, less directive way of letting the counselor know of significant emotional events that may have occurred since they were together last.

Once the player has described the feeling block, the block is placed on the top of the tower continuing in the lengthwise, crosswise pattern. Players may not remove blocks from the top layer, so that they are always pulling a block from underneath other blocks. The player who topples the tower loses the game, although the focus should remain as much as possible on the content of the feeling blocks and the spirit of companionship while playing: "Gee, do you think I should try to take this block? What would you suggest?" Reflective, process-oriented comments on the child's ongoing behavior are most effective: "You looked unsure of taking that block, but you were oh so careful and look, you did it!"

Again, the playing of the game offers the counselor many opportunities to view the child in action. Much can be learned about the child's sense of fair play, competition vs. cooperation, game etiquette, willingness to comply or need to "adjust" game rules in his or her favor, and generosity or frugality of spirit.

APPLICATIONS

Most children enjoy games, especially in the school setting where they feel they are somehow escaping the fate of their fellow classmates.

This game is an equal mix of physical dexterity and verbal expression, so it is comforting to the less verbal child. Feeling responses can be brief and follow the basic format (name the feeling and tell when you once felt that way), limiting the need for self-confidence in one's verbal creativity. A child can easily progress from simple, primitive responses to more complex descriptions as practice increases trust and skill level. The counselor always has the capability of modeling a desired direction when it is his or her turn. Therefore, though the game is an excellent icebreaker, it also possesses the intrinsic ability to grow along with the therapeutic relationship.

48

Make Your Own Board Game

Sandy Carter

INTRODUCTION

I am a teacher in an adaptive behavior self-contained classroom. I work with junior and senior high school students who have been classified emotionally and behaviorally disturbed. Frequently they also display learning disabilities. A common behavior is defiant/oppositional, which means they refuse to do anything they are asked to do. When presented a task, they may blow up, throw things, use profane language, or, on the contrary, put their heads down and go to sleep. In short, they don't like to do school work. My job is to teach them anyway, as well as help them develop more functional coping skills and socially appropriate behavior.

One semester I had a student who would not pick up a pencil. The school counselor continually challenged me to get a "product" from the student, some extension of his ability to read, write, and do arithmetic. To meet this challenge, this game came into being. As the student became intrigued by the prospect of "making a pile of candy," he also got caught up in the game, and, becoming impatient with trying to explain to me what he wanted me to write down for him, he took the pencil away from me and filled his own square. After that we passed the one pencil back and forth as he demonstrated that he could put his thoughts on paper, work basic math problems, and create strategies for stumping the other player, me!

RATIONALE

The technique succeeded in meeting its first goal, that of engaging the student in a reading, writing, and arithmetic lesson. Surprisingly, it also evolved to be a device for obtaining valuable family pattern history and self-concept ideation, as the storyboard revealed many of the child's dreams, hopes, despairs, traumas, and aspirations. The facilitator could then employ therapeutic techniques—reflective listening and projection of possible outcomes—based on the information provided through the metaphor of the game.

DESCRIPTION

Begin with a large sheet of paper, such as a large newsprint tablet or a sheet of posterboard. I like a newsprint tablet because I can keep several games on it as in a book, and as students return to their game, they can decide whose game to play. (Remember I am working in a classroom group setting. The game is also helpful in a one-on-one setting, in which much more intimate information will be revealed.) With a yardstick, draw a 2½ inch border around the edge of the paper. Mark this border off in rectangles, similar to a Monopoly board. Designate one corner square as the starting point by writing "GO" in it.

Have a supply of individually wrapped candy on hand to use as player's markers. Place a piece of candy for each player on the GO square. Roll the dice; high roller goes first. The play passes to the left, clockwise. Player One moves his or her candy according to the roll of the dice. If the player lands in a blank square, he or she fills in the square with instructions, whatever he or she chooses. Thus choice and creativity become important components of the game. Sometimes students will write in a skill challenge, such as a spelling task or a math task; sometimes it will be a life challenge, such as, "You have a flat tire; go back three spaces." Be cautious of children who write tasks that will cause humiliation to others or cause others to lose heart, such as, "A hurricane hits your house; give back all your candy." These are not appropriate choices. The child can be redirected to select a task that will have a positive outcome or be affirming in some beneficial way.

The play continues, passing from player to player, until all the squares are filled in. The player follows the instructions of the square he or she lands on. If the square is blank, he or she fills it in. Each time a player passes GO, he or she receives a fresh piece of candy. It is suggested that the candy not be consumed until the game is over. If time is a factor, the facilitator may begin the game by saying, "We will play until __ [such and such a time, by the clock, which should be visible to all]; we may continue the game at another time if you wish."

APPLICATIONS

This game has proven itself to be particularly useful with children who are withdrawn, and with children who are defiant/oppositional. It holds the attention of ADD and ADHD children. It enhances skill development in children who are reluctant to reveal their inadequacies and learning disabilities.

I also used it with a child who had regressions. One day he would be a lively, inquisitive 15-year-old, struggling with his textbooks and math dyslexia; the next he would be stuck somewhere around age 5, wanting to build race cars with Legos, spin the library chairs, run screaming through the halls. In a one-on-one game session with him, he revealed some parts of his family history and his projected life plan that enlightened the facilitator considerably as to the whys and wherefores of his refusal to grow up and perpetual desire to return to a simpler, less confining and demanding time in his life. The facilitator was then able to convey this understanding to his counselor, who confirmed many of the facilitator's suppositions, and some progress was made in helping the family identify and acknowledge the key issues in the child's life.

49

Chess Playing as a Metaphor for Life Choices

Leslie Hartley Lowe

INTRODUCTION

This technique developed by accident, combining the latency-aged child's desire for competition with a growing desire to understand cause and effect and use it to achieve the child's goals. Almost any game can be used to assist a child to learn strategic thinking that can then generalize to life experiences, but chess seemed particularly useful in this regard. Chess can be learned relatively quickly, but it can be as complex as the individuals who play it, thus matching and challenging simultaneously.

RATIONALE

If therapy is an opportunity to have an experience that allows the individual to consciously master himself and make changes in behavior and attitude that affect the quality of his life, then the use of this game is therapeutic. Children are able to internalize the thinking learned in the process of playing the game, use the metaphor of chess as a way of seeing the world, transfer their learning to the world outside the therapist's office, and have fun in the process.

DESCRIPTION

Appropriate age group: 8–12-year-olds

Time: 45 minutes (each game takes from 15–40 minutes, but processing occurs both during and after the game). Best used in 5–6 sessions in a row

Materials: chess board and pieces

I will encourage an interest in learning how to play chess, but usually just having the game visible on my shelf is enough to encourage a request to play.

Session 1: I begin by teaching the basics of chess and encouraging the learning process. There is something about chess that intrigues this age group, and I have found that even the most hyperactive child will sit for twenty minutes and focus on learning and playing chess. Initially, my goal is just to teach the game and encourage my client to enjoy learning.

Session 2: After 3–4 games, most children have a rudimentary knowledge of how each piece moves and understand the purpose of moving chess pieces. I clarify that all of their moves are focused on one of two purposes: either self-protection of the king or getting into a position to take the opponent's king.

I now begin the process of helping them see consequences to their moves. I use a questioning strategy to stimulate their thinking processes, using such questions as:

1) What will happen to that piece if you move it there?
2) Will that move help you protect your king or get you in position to take my king? Every move should count for something.
3) What other choices do you have for that piece to move? Look at *all* the choices before you move.
4) What other moves might help you more?
5) If you make that move, what do you think I will do?

Initially, I encourage them to think only one move ahead. I always give the child the opportunity to change his or her mind after rethinking a move for the first 5–6 games we play. As the child becomes more proficient, I shape behavior toward long-range planning and strategizing. I will ask these same questions many times during a game, and we sometimes play two games in a session so that the child is hearing these questions often.

Session 3: I start requiring him or her to think before a move or take the consequences. I will ask the child to verbalize his or her thinking about why a certain move was made. We begin to discuss options for moves and I share what moves I am likely to make in response to the child's move so that the child can see the game from my point of view also. I try to help the child begin to predict what moves I might make in response to his or her moves.

Session 4: I begin to draw parallels between the choices and thought processes used in chess playing to the child's thought processes, choices, and behaviors in real life. Using the same questioning strategy as in Session 2, we talk more about life choices regarding behavior in certain problem situations and try to predict outcomes, so that the child leaves my office with a different way of seeing his life and exerting control over his behavior.

In subsequent sessions, we do more talking than playing, although we continue to play chess as the child desires. Once the child catches hold of the metaphor that life is a big chess game, he or she begins to take some pride and delight in sharing how he or she was able to think ahead and avoid being "taken" by a teacher or a parent or an aggressive peer because of the new ability to think of choices and outcomes before making a decision.

Session 5: I encourage parents to play with their children and frequently, with the child's permission, invite them into the session to observe how I use the tool. I then encourage them to play with the child in session and I help them learn a questioning strategy for shaping behavior that they can then use at home more effectively than screaming and/or punishing. It gives me an opportunity to discuss a choices–consequences model with parents and allows me to help them change their relationship with the child by opening up their choices for disciplining their children more respectfully and effectively.

APPLICATIONS

DISORDERS: Oppositional defiant disorder, conduct disorder, ADHD, Tourette's disorder

TREATMENT GOALS:

1) increase self esteem
2) increase ability to focus attention

3) increase ability to connect choices with consequences
4) increase ability to foresee consequences given certain choices
5) increase ability to plan and execute appropriate choices
6) increase ability to exhibit good sportsmanship
7) increase ability to verbalize thinking process
8) enhance ability to enjoy quiet activities

Section Five

Puppet Play Techniques

50

Battaro and the Puppet House

Martha J. Harkin

INTRODUCTION

A creative therapy technique is often born from necessity and/or desperation. Battaro and The Puppet House emerged initially to meet the expressive needs of children, and evolved as powerful catalysts to communication between child and therapist. In response to children often wishing to be on television, the Puppet House was created as a decorative canvas theater that hung from a wide shelf. After a 7-year-old boy in treatment for terrorizing adults and children destroyed three inflatable punching bags in three sessions, Battaro was created: a 54" durable fabric bag filled with shredded polyfoam, sewn and hand-painted with a nonaggressive human figure.

RATIONALE

The therapeutic value of these tools became immediately apparent. First, they needed no introduction. Children (and adults) responded to them as unique features of the office, an instant attraction that provided client-initiated activity. The 7-year-old exhausted himself on Battaro during the fourth session. By the fifth and sixth sessions his aggressive response weakened. He began to demonstrate issues through play in the Puppet House, revealing his fear of and concern for the imprisoned father who had abused him. Parent and teachers immediately noted positive behavior changes.

Importantly, the Puppet House offers a safe retreat during an intense session. The child can regroup his or her energies while observing the therapist through peepholes in the doorknob and flower prints in the canvas. (Adults have also used the screen while discussing painful material.) Children often participate more actively in the initial interview process when they take refuge in the Puppet House. This enables them to add their reactions and comments through puppets. In observation situations, parents can be seated behind the screen while therapist and child pretend that no one else is present. This is a very useful avenue when working with small children where a one-way mirror is not available, or when the child is having difficulty separating from the parent.

DESCRIPTION

Technique within the framework of these useful tools evolves from the therapist's ability to allow the child to lead self-initiated activity in a safe place with unpressured time. The therapist adheres to Virginia Axline's (1969) guidelines that the child leads the action or conversation, and that the therapist maintains the relationship through acceptance and permission for the child to express feelings completely, and reflects the child's words or behavior in ways that help the child understand the feelings expressed. As the child interacts with the therapist through Battaro and the Puppet House, he or she has the opportunity to develop a feelings vocabulary and to experiment with ways of solving problems. The therapist can role-play a bumbler, and ask, "What do I say [or do] now?" If the child's directions are something the therapist cannot or will not do, then the two can negotiate what will be acceptable. This kind of interchange provides the child with a feeling of empowerment.

APPLICATIONS

Since work with Battaro and the Puppet House is initiated by the client, they are useful tools with a variety of problems. In addition to use with the aggressive child, the withdrawn and/or neglected child is also served. He or she seeks the comfort of hugging Battaro, often taking Battaro into the Puppet House where he or she talks with him, observes the therapist through peepholes, and can move outward at a self-selected place. Usually the withdrawn child is eventually able to express suppressed anger through Battaro.

The most common sequence in interactions with Battaro begins with expressions of aggression and anger that move toward demonstrations of frustration and need for power. Battaro is battered, knocked down, trampled, and bounced against the wall. This phase may end after one or two sessions, or the child may develop a ritual around his or her interaction with Battaro, as illustrated in the case study to follow. The second phase often reflects client insight into his or her feelings, and a move to incorporate Battaro as an ally. As the child heals, he or she begins to separate from Battaro, using it less and turning to developmental games and talk with the therapist as a way to develop adequate coping skills. As therapy progresses through its ups and downs, the client can always return to Battaro and/or the Puppet House to dramatize a current stress and work through the problem.

Battaro and the Puppet House are useful for helping the therapist assess the child's progress through the content and affect of the material presented. During the termination phase of therapy, often difficult for many children, Battaro and the Puppet House can be incorporated into termination ceremonies, allowing the child to express him or herself through a familiar medium.

EXAMPLE

The following example demonstrates some of the possibilities these tools offer. All names are fictitious and identifying detail has been omitted.

Peter is a 5-year-old boy who had been in therapy for one year and was transferred to me when Peter's therapist left the agency. When Peter was four years old he climbed onto a bed where his father had laid a loaded gun when he left the room for a few moments. The gun discharged and killed the younger brother, a toddler. Peter has been a difficult child from early childhood and the younger brother, an easy child, was clearly the favorite. The parents had also been in therapy for year but had not yet cleared the toddler's room or let go of their grief and anger. Marital tensions present before death were also exacerbated.

Peter uses the first two sessions to explore the therapy room, test the therapist, and spend a great deal of time venting his feelings on Battaro. At the opening of the third session, Peter throws Battaro head first into the Puppet House again and again.

Peter: [shouts] Arrest that man.

Therapist: You want me to arrest that man?

Peter: Yeah! He's a robber! He drives fast—and one bad thing—he shot someone.

Therapist: He shot someone.

Peter devises a scenario where I am a sheriff asleep in the office. He takes Battaro into the Puppet House and hides himself behind Battaro. He then shoots a rubber dart out into the office.

Therapist: [awakens] What did I hear?

Peter: [shoots gun again]

Therapist: Fee Fi Fo Fum—I smell a robber with a gun. [looks into Puppet House] Who are you?

Peter: I'm the landlord.

Therapist: I'm looking for a robber with a gun.

Peter: He's not here.

Therapist: [aside] What should I do?

Peter: Keep looking for the robber.

Therapist: [Searches high and low around the office, pretending the file and bookcases are buildings. Returns to Puppet House door and pretends to knock.]

Peter: [falsetto] Who's there?

Therapist: It's the sheriff. I'm looking for a robber with a gun.

Peter: [falsetto] He's not here, keep looking.

I search all over the office, returning to the Puppet House, bumbling, unable to see behind Battaro, much to Peter's glee. This scenario is repeated week after week with Peter developing a gentler affect as we work on the idea that maybe the robber isn't really a robber and maybe he isn't bad. The funeral anniversary stirs up a strong aggressive reaction and Peter comes to the next session threatening to hit me and giving me orders that I shoot the robber. I set limits, diverting aggressive demonstration to Battaro and assuring Peter that I do not shoot robbers.

In the next few sessions he continues the scenario, introducing a lion and a tiger mask; Peter wears the lion (a symbol of power), I wear the tiger. Soon after he announces at school that he had shot his brother. This is reported to the parents who, in turn, discuss the event with the therapy team. After two more sessions of ritual play, Peter comes to the next session looking very quiet. He initiates our Fee Fi Fo Fum ritual and I am sent high and low in the office looking for the origin of the "shots." On the third return to the Puppet House:

Therapist: [knocks on door] Hello! Is anyone here?

Peter: [normal voice] Yes.

Therapist: [opens Puppet Theater, speaks to Battaro] Who are you?

Peter: [normal voice] Peter. [Peter is hiding behind Battaro]

Therapist: May I come in?

Peter: [normal voice] Yes.

Therapist: [putting arms around Battaro, holding tenderly] Oh Peter, I've been wanting to talk with you about your brother. How sad that there was such a terrible accident. I have wanted to hug you. [hugs Battaro] "I've wanted to tell you that you couldn't know the gun would shoot. You were a little boy, 4 years old, who wasn't protected from a gun. [then holds Battaro, tenderly patting head and back while Peter watches intently. I invite Battaro out into the office and carry him to stand near my chair where I quietly sit. In a few moments Peter emerges, lays his hand on Battaro for a few seconds. He then brings out the "Don't Break the Ice" game, which he has used often after our weekly sessions. Usually he has dashed the blocks out of the frame before the game is finished but this time he carefully and skillfully takes out

> blocks so that the final block to drop the "ice" is mine, and he wins.]

After this session, his use of Battaro and The Puppet House diminished, and as Peter moved into first grade, he initiated play with sand and clay. He was eventually able to tolerate board games with rules, play on a T-ball team, and manage his behavior more productively at school.

A year later we were able to use Battaro and the Puppet House in a difficult termination experience. When I told Peter that I was leaving the agency to work in a treatment center, he struck Battaro viciously several times, then entered the Puppet House and snapped the thick dowel in the lower edge of the theater opening over his knee. We were able to talk about his anger over my leaving and the feelings each of us was having. The broken dowel symbolized the break in our relationship, so we talked about making change without breaking the meaning of our relationship. We planned how we would spend our final session the following week, which included his helping me install a new dowel in the Puppet House and planning which games we would play before meeting his new therapist.

Note: Battaro and the Puppet House are made and sold by Harkin & David Designs, Inc., 5601 Mapleleaf Dr., Austin, TX 78723 (512) 929-8611.

Reference

Axline, V. (1969). *Play Therapy*. New York: Ballantine.

51

The Dowel Finger Puppet Technique

Jo Ann L. Cook

INTRODUCTION

The initial application for making and using dowel finger puppets began with the need to provide children with an opportunity to create a personal representation when using finger puppets. Children in middle childhood seemed especially apt to become invested in the process of portraying and describing themselves, often developing puppets dressed in their current or favorite clothing or sports uniforms, usually based on how they viewed themselves at their best. Some created themselves as they wished they appeared, as a type of "ideal me," which was also therapeutically useful. The technique continued to develop with the children's leads and became quite versatile as they began to expand to depict themselves in transition, for example, the "old and new me" and other dichotomies, including "scared and brave," or to change the original puppet, for example, to add arms and legs to depict power and strength, physical or personal growth, or changes in identifications. Others requested to be able to configure their families, friends, teachers, or other important figures in their worlds and to bring these to life in their play. Over time, children involved the puppets in many different processes and were increasingly able to identify the focus of the process as being on themselves and their issues.

RATIONALE

Children who are within pre-operational or concrete operational cognitive stages of development have difficulty grasping and applying experiences and understandings to their current and future situations. When the situation or analogy closely matches their own they are most apt to identify with the person and issue and relate to it through their own perspective. This technique uses a puppet that they have devised to represent, introduce, and describe themselves, their concerns, and desires. There is increased opportunity that the experiences, associations, and understandings will contain a greater element of ownership from which they can concurrently benefit as well as carry forward to meet new situations.

DESCRIPTION

The technique is presented as an opportunity to make a wooden dowel puppet of oneself and, after completed, to describe and introduce it. The therapist and child begin with access to a variety of materials including cloth, markers, clay, pipe cleaners, ribbons, lace, and glue. The dowels are presented as unfinished wooden figures that appear as heads with cone-shaped bodies. They are quite versatile, as they have been found to fit on any finger and remain securely during movement and puppetry. In addition, they also stand independently and can be used in other activities, such as markers for game boards. Thus they can be moved about and then left free-standing and at eye level with the other dowel figures. This has been helpful in observing a child's placement of his figures in relationship to others by spatial dimensions as well as being associated or dissociated from the group that they have configured. This information can be tracked and saved by tracing the location of the bases on paper and marking them by the name of the figure and situation that had been described. For example, children may place their puppet in the "audience" watching their family puppets, as narrators or directors who are producing or controlling the play, or as central figures in the story.

Involving oneself in constructing a personal puppet often engages the child in the process and allows for additional communication as well as through the puppets during the construction process. This also leads to the child placing the therapist's puppet at the distance he prefers in relation to his own or designating it to play an active or passive role. The use of the puppets may then involve the initial two in interaction, in communication with manufactured finger puppets, or with additional child-made dowel puppets when his issues and interest in the process unfold to require additional characters.

APPLICATIONS

As previously noted, the applications and variations with this technique have been numerous. In individual child work the puppets have been useful in addressing self-esteem issues, by working through puppetry to identify areas that the child would like to strengthen or develop, delineating strengths, and enacting the process. Similar use has been made for problem solving and planning by drawing a backdrop, maze, road, or board game that represents different choices and outcomes. Goal-setting activities have included drawing the process, steps, or moves toward a specified goal and creating an ongoing game in which the puppet advances with the child's progress. Similar anticipatory process work has been enabled for children who need assistance to prepare for new or difficult situations and to envision how they may cope with and overcome it. Puppets allow for personal and metaphorical storytelling with different "stages" or "acts" denoting changes in time, place, or perspective. Preparing and introducing the puppets through personal descriptions, wishes, and/or goals has successfully been used with individuals, groups, and families including group and family sculptures in miniature, current dynamics, and "instant replays" for processing or sculpting demarcations or changes. Since the puppet figures themselves do not actually physically identify the children, they are allowed to place them in the area of their choice from week to week, for example, in an elevated portion of a bookcase or in a private secure child-made container, between visits. Most request to keep them when the work is completed.

Note: the cone-shaped wooden dowels are 2½" tall with a 1" base. They are available from various craft stores and through the HearthSong Company (6519 N. Galena Rd., PO Box 1773, Peoria, IL 61656-1773).

52

Create-A-Puppet

Anne Blackwell

INTRODUCTION

Often in play therapy sessions children wish to create situations that are similar to the ones they have experienced. For example, if a child is playing with a dog family, he or she will often use the same configuration of ages, genders, and personalities that represent her or his own living arrangement, such as a baby brother puppy, a grandmother dog, and so on. While using commercial puppets in the playroom I often observed that children were unable to personalize them in the manner they sometimes wished to do. This led me to develop the Create-A-Puppet technique that I have used successfully for several years.

RATIONALE

Most people trained in the use of play therapy are well aware of the positive aspects of using puppets in therapeutic work. It is usually easier for children to express emotions such as fear, anger, confusion, and sadness by acting them out. Children will also use puppets to portray what they wish and hope would occur in their lives. Puppets often provide an opportunity for the play therapist to interact with the child, and also to add and solicit material as appropriate.

DESCRIPTION

Create-A-Puppet is an inexpensive and simple technique. Once the basic puppets have been made they are available for the play therapist to use spontaneously as appropriate in a session. Use the following pattern to cut 15–20 puppets out of inexpensive neutral-colored cotton material. Stitch the puppets with wrong sides together. If you don't sew, ask a friend or volunteer to help. As a last resort, the puppets may be stapled together. Color them with regular crayons (not markers, which bleed through the material) to make a variety of people that differ in gender, age, race, and facial expression.

APPLICATIONS

Children are encouraged to use the puppets to help them identify and express emotions as well as act out a variety of scenarios relevant to their lives. The following examples illustrate a few of the numerous ways these puppets may be utilized:

Ask the child to pick or color a puppet that shows how he or she is feeling that day. Ask the puppet to talk about that feeling.

Ask the child to pick or color a puppet that shows how he or she would feel if someone called her or him ugly, stupid, nice, and so on.

Taking turns, first the child picks a puppet and the therapist tells what might have happened to make the puppet feel that way. Example: the grandmother is crying because her dog died. Switch roles.

The child is asked to identify how other people might feel. Example: pick or color a puppet that shows how you think your mother feels when you wet the bed. Have the puppet talk about that.

The child is asked to identify how she or he wished other people would feel and act. Example: pick or color a puppet that shows how you wish your sister felt when she found out Uncle Jack was hurting you. Have the puppet say what you would like to hear.

The puppets may also be used to role-play situations that are important in the child's life. For example:

Ask the child to pick or color two puppets to be sister and brother and have them talk about their mom and dad getting divorced.

Ask the child to pick or color a puppet to be dad and one to be mom. Have the parent puppets talk about the child's abuse.

Ask the child to pick or color a puppet for you and one for him or herself to talk about the child's choice of subjects. Switch roles.

Therapist picks or colors a puppet to be the child and child picks or colors a puppet to role-play the therapist.

When I begin working with a new client, I make new puppets that correlate with his or her situation and appearance. (Example: glasses, braids, freckles, a gray-haired mom, etc.)

I keep a supply of blank puppets in the playroom for clients to use as they wish. Sometimes they want to make themselves, a family member, me, someone or something frightening, and so on. They may take home the puppets they make if they wish. I have used Create-A-Puppet with clients ages 2½ through adult with great success.

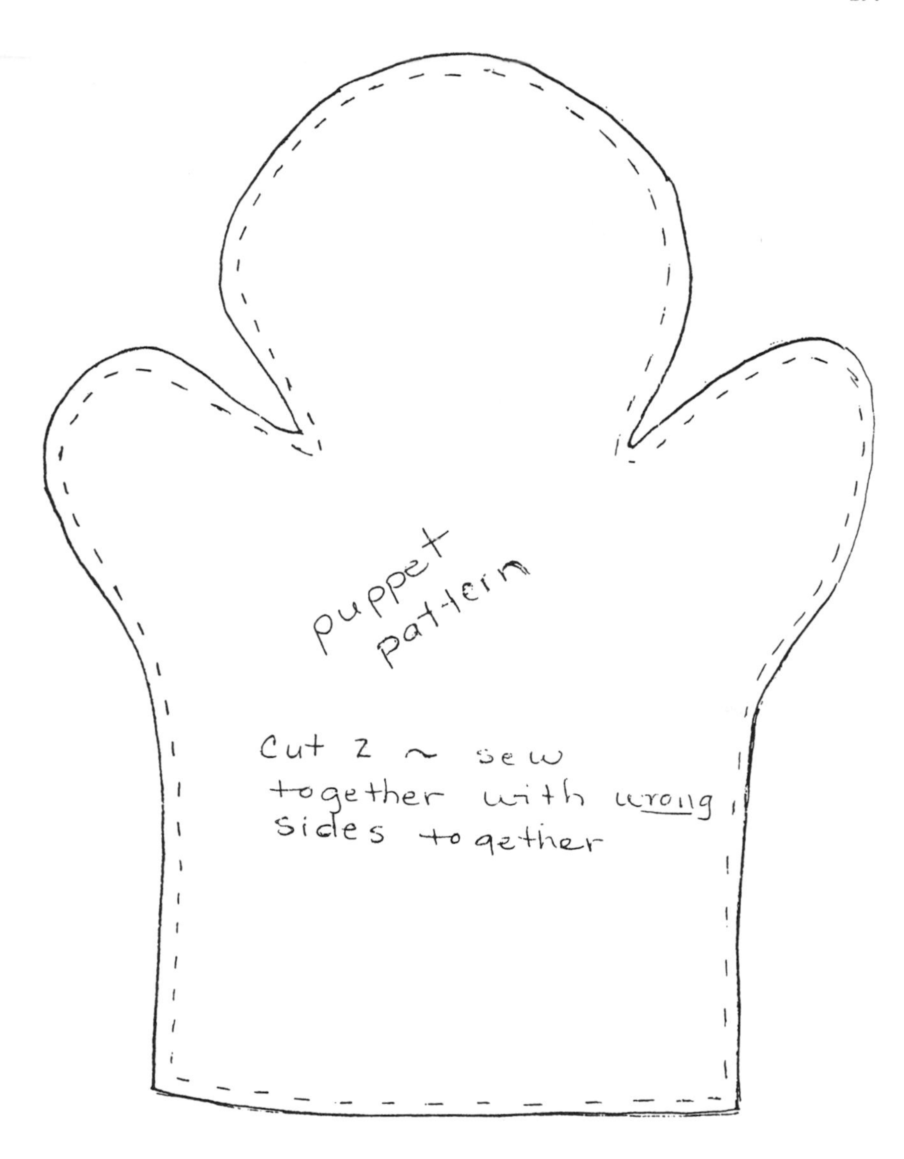

Puppet Pattern

Sample Puppet

53

Using a Puppet to Create a Symbolic Client

Carolyn J. Narcavage

RATIONALE

The use of puppets in therapeutic work with children was introduced by Woltmann (1940). Woltmann found puppets to be useful because they provide opportunities for spontaneity, are easily manipulated, and lend themselves naturally to a symbolic process of self-expression. Puppet play creates an atmosphere of fantasy that is absorbing to the child, while at the same time being nonthreatening (Haworth 1968). Children tend to identify with the characters involved in puppet play and to project their feelings and interpersonal conflicts onto them. In this way, children are able to communicate their distress without having to directly claim traumatic experiences and painful emotions as their own (Webb 1991). The therapist, in turn, can use puppets to reflect understanding and provide corrective emotional experiences in response to the child's play.

DESCRIPTION

Although many children naturally gravitate toward puppets and begin the process of projective expression on their own, some children are so withdraw, fearful, and self-conscious in the beginning stages of therapy that they strongly resist expression and interaction. These children often sit stiffly in the playroom, avoid eye contact with the therapist, and become increasingly reticent with every direct yet reassuring comment the therapist makes. Severely withdrawn children often avoid joining the therapist even when she models play behavior and invites the child to participate. Bow (1993) describes one means of overcoming child resistance with the use of puppets called the "hidden puppet technique." In this technique, the therapist hides a puppet in a sack and encourages the child to help coax the "resistant" puppet out.

Another way that the therapist can remove the focus from a withdrawn child and stimulate productive work in therapy is to *facilitate* projection of the child's feelings onto a puppet. For instance, if the therapist experiences the child as being frightened, she might take out a puppet, present it as being scared, acknowledge its fear, and reassure it of its safety. The next step is to enlist the child's help in attending to the puppet's needs. For example, the therapist might ask the child to hold and comfort the "frightened" puppet. By facilitating projection and enlisting the child's help in caring for the puppet, the therapist is able to achieve three important goals: (1) she is able to respond to the child's feelings in a nonthreatening manner. (2) she is able to mobilize the child's participation in therapy, and (3) she is able to begin fostering a positive, collaborative relationship with the child. As therapy proceeds, the puppet often becomes a safety object and is used by the child as a primary means of affective expression and interaction with the therapist.

APPLICATIONS

Puppets are useful in therapy with children because these play materials tend to naturally elicit affective projection. In work with extremely withdrawn children, however, the therapist may need to facilitate this projective process by creating a "symbolic client" out of a puppet. Creating a symbolic client removes the focus from the withdrawn child, increases her comfort level, and enables her to explore feelings from a safe distance. The therapist engages the child in helping to care for the symbolic client. This initiates the process of relationship building between the child and the therapist and allows them to metaphorically attend to the child's needs.

Bethany was a four-year-old, selectively mute child who presented as withdrawn, depressed, and fearful. At the time of her referral to play therapy, Bethany had been in preschool for several months and had not made even the slightest utterance in that setting. Her teachers described her as "emotionally dead" because she never smiled or registered typically expected affect in response to circumstances in her environment. In contrast to her behavior at school, Bethany reportedly talked with great fervor at home.

Bethany was the third of four children. When she was 3½, her parents, Rick and Kelly, divorced. Kelly had a long history of severe alcoholism and mental illness. She would drink continuously throughout most mornings and afternoons and would fly into rages in the evenings—screaming at the family, smashing furniture and dishes, and physically attacking Rick. The children frequently overheard Kelly threaten to kill Rick. Kelly was arrested a half-dozen times for public drunkenness and disorderly conduct and for physically attacking her siblings and her husband. Rick was awarded custody of the children after the divorce. Although supervised visitation was initially granted to Kelly, it was suspended after she showed up intoxicated to several visits with Bethany and her siblings.

Bethany began play therapy early in her second year of preschool. During our first session, she refused to explore the toys, resisted eye contact with me, hid her eyes when I spoke to her, sat motionless in the middle of the floor, and said nothing. My attempts to reassure her of my safety and to give her permission to play anything she wished only prompted her to become increasingly self-conscious and withdrawn.

During the second session, I decided to approach Bethany's fear in a less threatening manner. I took a cuddly bear puppet off the shelf and made him cover his eyes fearfully. I talked gently to Mr. Bear, acknowledging how scary it is to come to a new place and play with a grown-up he didn't know. I reassured Mr. Bear that we were in a safe place, that I was a safe person, and that I would not let anything bad happen to him or to Bethany while we played together.

Next, I used the bear puppet to convey a sense of unconditional acceptance toward Bethany and to give her permission to do whatever she wanted in therapy, including remaining silent. I made Mr. Bear say in a frightened voice, "I don't feel like talking. Talking seems scary sometimes." I responded to Mr. Bear by validating this feeling and telling him that it was all right with me if he chose not to talk when he didn't feel like it. I told him that I enjoyed being with him and that he didn't have to do anything in the playroom he didn't want to do. I gave Mr. Bear permission to communicate with me in other ways, such as pointing to the toys he wanted.

In the third session, Bethany appeared less frightened but remained inhibited. I repeated the interaction with Mr. Bear in which I responded to his fear. I invited Mr. Bear and/or Bethany to choose what we would play that day. Bethany sat motionless so I made Mr. Bear point to some dishes. Bethany watched as Mr. Bear made some food. Toward the end of the session, I talked to Bethany about how scared Mr. Bear was and invited her to help comfort him, a symbolic way of helping her to begin accepting comfort. Mr. Bear indicated that he wanted to hear a story. I framed this to Bethany as "helping Mr. Bear to feel better and less scared" and invited her to hold him while I read. She held the puppet and gave it several gentle hugs during the story. I commented on how good Bethany was at helping Mr. Bear to feel safe.

In the fourth session, Bethany entered the room and went immediately to Mr. Bear, giving him an affectionate look and a hug. I told Bethany that Mr. Bear was glad to see her and that he liked the things she did to make him fee safe, like holding him gently and hugging him. The puppet had become Bethany's safety object, and for several weeks after this point she incorporated it into every activity we did together. At the end of session four, Bethany placed Mr. Bear on her own hand. I said, "Mr Bear, you felt really scared when you first started to come here and play. Are you starting to feel better inside?" Bethany made the puppet nod his head affirmatively.

Bethany's early life experiences prevented her from accepting any type of physical nurturance from me in the early stages of therapy. She would not allow me to make even simple nurturing gestures, like helping her put on her shoes or caring for her when she played baby. However, Mr. Bear became our means of showing affection toward one another. Bethany allowed Mr. Bear to hug her and care for her during "baby play." She began to use the bear puppet to give me hugs.

As therapy continued, I used the bear puppet to explore Bethany's past traumatic experiences. During session eleven, Bethany presented Mr. Bear with a variety of new puppets to meet. I made him cover his eyes and shake with fear. After several repetitions of this, I said gently, "A long time ago, someone used to be very mean to Mr. Bear. Now he gets scared of people sometimes and doesn't know who is safe and who isn't."

Bethany demonstrated that the new puppets were safe by having them display gentle behavior, like hugging Mr. Bear. Also in this session, I used the puppet to demonstrate a way Bethany could practice communicating with people while feeling "in control" (e.g., without people she didn't want to hear her being privy to what she was saying). I had the puppet whisper to me and to Bethany throughout the session. To my amazement, Bethany began whispering to her preschool teachers the following week and to me several weeks later.

The bear puppet became less central as therapy progressed and as Bethany began using other puppets and dolls as a means of symbolic communication. However, before therapy ended, Bethany and I had spent a great deal of time doctoring Mr. Bear and fixing his wounds so that he was strong and felt good inside. Mr. Bear, the symbolic client, was an invaluable tool in Bethany's process of healing.

References

Bow, J. N. (1993). Overcoming resistance. In *The Therapeutic Powers of Play*, ed. C. E. Schaefer, pp. 17–40. Northvale, NJ: Jason Aronson.

Haworth, M. R. (1968). Doll play and puppetry. In *Projective Techniques in Personality Assessment*, ed. A. I. Rabin, pp. 327–365. New York: Springer.

Webb, N. B., (1991). *Playing for their Lives: Helping Troubled Children through Play Therapy.* New York: Free Press.

Woltmann, A. G. (1940). The use of puppetry in understanding children. *Mental Hygiene* 24:445–458.

54

Puppetry

Marie Boultinghouse

INTRODUCTION

Play is a natural activity of childhood and possibly the most effective means of learning. Play is really practice for real life and provides sufficient elasticity for accommodating any number of events, people, and situations. While the child knows that play isn't real, in some ways it assumes real-life proportions. It provides for the safe practice of behaviors with possible built-in consequences by which the child learns. It provides for the development of empathy through role playing and behavior rehearsal. The many shades and colors of play provide an infinite number of possibilities for practice and learning that would be unlikely through other modalities.

Puppetry is a potent form of play and one that readily adapts to an endless variety of combinations and possibilities. The child is readily able to identify with animal or people puppets and their problems and is thus able to suggest and think through appropriate problem-solving strategies. Puppetry lends itself naturally to storytelling, with its own endless variety of possibilities. The child is able to "act" through the puppets and is able to vicariously try out different behaviors and problem-solving strategies and then to consider resulting consequences to himself or herself and others in his or her environment.

RATIONALE

I have become interested in the use of puppetry due to the lasting consequences of its use. Although I have rarely had a child remember very long what was said through discussion, I have discovered that they remember many months later the lessons that Fritz, the firehouse dog puppet, learned. These are always real-life lessons such as consequences of violating family rules by running in the doghouse or climbing on the doghouse roof. After the puppet has finished its story, the child is readily able to apply it to his or her own life circumstances. Puppetry can also be effectively used to help the child deal with anxiety and what the puppet has learned about facing the source of fears, coping with anxiety, and ultimately reducing anxiety to a manageable level. Fritz, of course, has had some school experiences of early life so he is able to identify with the child's fears and problems pertaining to getting along with his or her teacher and peers, coping with academic demands, and cultivating the ability to delay gratification. The use of puppetry is readily adaptable to empathizing with the child who has inattentional/hyperactivity/impulsive characteristics; this provides for the introduction of procedures that Fritz has found effective and that provide for teachers and parents therapeutic procedures for their own use.

DESCRIPTION

It is helpful to have a variety of puppets and allow the child to choose which one he or she wishes to use. The writer has Fritz, the firehouse dog (red fireman's hat, white and black spots, and long pink tongue), a yellow "banana" kangaroo with baby in its pouch, and an orange monkey. Although children like all of them, they seem to prefer puppets that open their mouths, whether or not they have teeth. Children find it pleasant to have Fritz bite their ears or give them a kiss (sometimes as a reward). The kangaroo with a baby in its pouch lends itself to the subject of siblings as well as single parent families. In one instance, the orange monkey's mother left the jungle to work in a people-making factory while the yellow kangaroo baby's father left home because he often drank too much "rotted coconut juice" (alcohol). Children as well as their parents have to learn to cope with changed circumstances.

One use of puppets is the creation of stories similar to those of the child but slightly removed in time, place, or circumstances. The therapist begins the story by introducing characters with their own contexts (parents were fighting, parent left home, parent became unemployed), each child adds to the story spontaneously without coaching, and the therapist adds a component that gives the children something to think about or suggestions for problem solving (similar procedures were described by Richard A. Gardner). Children are asked to draw a picture about what might happen next or to use clay to make something pertaining to the story theme. At the next session, the drawings or clay activities are reviewed; the story is then reviewed briefly (the therapist having previously recorded the main ideas and events of the story) and the session begins with a new story segment with use of the puppets. When appropriate, allowing the parent to remain in the session is often quite fruitful. Careful observation of puppet choice and role played in developing the story is quite productive.

Another wrinkle in the use of puppetry is to have each of the puppets share its own story and impact of events beyond its ability to control following the setting created by the therapist. Each puppet may be encouraged to share what came before, what is happening now, and what may happen in the future (as is used in projective storytelling strategies). Ask the child specifically what the puppet can do about the situation, regardless of what parental or caretaker figures do.

It is both easy and fun to create a group story drawn on flipchart-sized paper, with all children sharing in the story drawing the later in describing what is happening. It is important to see that each child contributes through use of the puppet drawing.

Another possibility is to have children write the puppet's journal through use of the puppet or memory of the puppet. From nonhardening clay, create something the puppet may have created to represent the events of the puppet's day; store the clay in zipper plastic bags for use in another session. Bring journals and drawings or what was created to the next session; discuss what each child thought and felt about the journal writing, clay creation, and drawing.

Another very productive possibility includes the use of Fritz or a similar puppet to address racial issues. Fritz, a Dalmatian by inheritance, can readily identify with children who are faced with biracial issues. It is very simple for him to talk about his grandfather dog who had more black spots than white spots and unkind remarks with which he had to cope.

He can also help, through role playing, to teach the child how to remove fun from name-calling (such as smiling, shrugging his dog shoulders, talking about how the remark thrilled him, etc). Beyond that, it is very easy to provide homework assignments that the child "research" (through imagination) other figures on his family tree—to the grandfather's grandfather. This is great fun but it also provides for considering issues of loss, family changes, and many kinds of unexpected (perhaps undesirable) events.

APPLICATIONS

Many applications were referred to above and others are possible. I find it helpful to use puppetry with other compatible strategies in dealing with phobias, aggression, family problems, bullying, biracial issues, peer problems, anxiety (including fear of the dark), taking the fun out of name-calling, and sibling rivalry. Doubtless there are many other applications. Puppetry and associated procedures can be used successfully with children at least through the fourth grade.

A recent new wrinkle which the writer has used dealt with biracial issues. The biracial child (caucasian mother and African-American father were college students) was adopted at birth by an African-American couple whose own child was born a few months later. Parents attempted to share the adoption realities with the child. After being told that he was adopted, he went to school and told his teacher that he was a doctor. He was referred to his adoptive mother and himself as orange and his adoptive father and sister as black. He decided that he didn't want to be black; he is a most attractive child with light brown skin and curly brown hair. It was very easy to have Fritz talk about his own wise grandfather dog's experiences, since he had more black than white spots. It was easy to turn this into drawings and ultimately a family tree. The family tree was very timely and provided for discussion of losses, since his own adoptive grandfather died only a few months previously. His adoptive sister and his mother were included in the session; sister contributed and mother observed. Mother also read and discussed with children at home stories related to the main theme. The children both loved the activities. When the child hadn't been seen for a few months, his first question at next contact was "Where is Fritz?" At other times, there was practice in conflict resolution, removing the fun of name-calling, and dealing with bullying by others. According to the mother's report, the child has become much more self-confident, his crying has almost disappeared, and he does extremely well in school.

References

Gardner, R. (1971). *Therapeutic Communication with Children: The Mutual Storytelling Technique.* New York: Science House.

Irwin, E. (1993). Using puppets for assessment. In *Play Therapy Techniques,* ed. C. E. Schaefer and D. Cangelosi, pp. 69–81. Northvale, NJ: Jason Aronson.

55

On the One Hand . . . and Then on the Other

Christina Mattise

INTRODUCTION

In the school setting, one of the advantages of teaching school-wide classroom guidance to elementary school children is the opportunity to expose *all* children to the use of therapeutic tools for self-expression. Many children will directly benefit and use techniques learned in classroom guidance for the expression of feelings in their daily lives whether on the bus, on the playground, or at home with their families. For others with deeper, less accessible needs, the primary benefit will be found in the indirect exposure to the potential and "magic" of play therapy. Children who have previously experienced the satisfaction of recognition and expression of problematic feelings with their peers in classroom guidance (even if they have only *observed* more functional students model those skills) arrive for individual sessions with a degree of familiarity, investment, and often a personal attachment to some of the therapeutic tools, especially the puppets. Puppets can be used to help children recognize, identify, and begin to cope with dilemmas that create conflicting emotions within them.

RATIONALE

Children who are preoccupied with conflicting feelings surrounding difficult issues in their lives are often gripped by a sort of paralysis, rendering them unable to cope with the emotional, social, and academic demands of the typical school day. The issue at hand can vary in dimension (by *adult* standards) from mother demanding that the child wear the "wrong" color sneakers to the trauma associated with divorce. Until the grip of the emotional tug-of-war inside the child is loosened, the child's efforts to cooperate (either with peers or adults) or to concentrate on learning are rendered useless. Often, the ability to identify and accept the existence of conflicting feelings provides the child with an immediate sense of relief. Obviously, additional work is required in either an individual or group setting for resolution of complex issues, but mastery of the skills necessary to recognize and express the existence of mixed affect can provide enough of an emotional Band-Aid to get the child through the day. For less traumatic issues, the reduction of anxiety, combined with increased awareness and communication skills, is highly effective in removing the child's emotional roadblock.

DESCRIPTION

A pair of puppets may be used to teach children how to identify and assimilate conflicting feelings surrounding a problematic issue in their lives. Names the "On the One Hand . . . and Then on the Other" puppets, these puppets are actually children's mittens that have animal faces painted on them. Available in many children's clothing departments, any whimsical mittens may be used as long as they are identical (representing the two facets of the same problem). These puppets are presented in the classroom as aids in discussing conflicting feelings and ideas.

The counselor may use the puppets, an excellent aid for the beginning of the school year, to discuss conflicting feelings about leaving home. For example, "Let's talk about the way you felt right before you climbed onto the school bus on the very first day of school." Typically, children will describe a wide range of emotions, from excited anticipation of seeing classmates whom they have missed over the summer to real terror of leaving Mother and facing the unknown. The puppets "agree" enthusiastically with the child's statements with, "Do you know, that's just the way that I feel!" The counselor queries, "Are there other children that had some of these same feelings about getting on the bus on the first day of school?"

While the children are sharing their emotions, the counselor actively reflects their feelings with one hand reflecting positive emotions (excitement, confidence, anticipation, fond memories) and the other hand addressing negative issues (fear, anxiety, loneliness). After several examples from the children, the puppet discloses in amazement, "You know, right now I think I am feeling frightened and excited at the same time! It's like I'm getting pushed and pulled at the same time. Let's call these different-feelings-at-the-same-time our push/pull feelings. Has anyone else ever felt that way?" Invariably, many hands shoot high in the air and the discussion turns to expressing those feelings which are puzzling because they seem to be opposite one another. "Let's talk about those feelings with our puppets. The puppet on the right hand can talk about all the happy, easy feelings. We'll have the puppet on the left hand talk about the more difficult feelings like feeling sad or mad."

The counselor frames the experience for the children by asking for a volunteer to list "all of the different feelings you might have had when, for example, you heard that Mom and Dad were going to separate." The children decide which hand (right - happy or left - sad/mad) should talk about each feeling. "So I think I heard you say that on the left hand you are really sad and frightened that Daddy is leaving because you are afraid that you are really going to miss him. But on the right hand, part of you is a little relieved because the yelling is scary and you want it to stop. Did I get that straight?"

After the counselor has modeled several examples, children are encouraged to put on the puppets and describe their feelings about a situation that they may be experiencing. For the purpose of generalizing these new skills, the counselor may state, "You know, we can use the idea of talking about our push/pull feelings even when we don't have the puppets on our hands. We can use our heads to think about the different feelings we are having and decide if we should count each feeling on our right (happy, glad) or left (sad, mad, or bad) hand." The counselor may also discuss:

What kinds of different feelings might we feel at the same time?

What can we do if these feelings are very strong?

What can we do if we are feeling confused about these feelings?

What can we do if thinking or worrying about these feelings takes lots of our time, attention, and/or energy?

What can we do if these feelings leave us feeling sad or mad most of the time?

Once the children become accustomed to thinking about conflicting emotions, the puppets are readily called upon in the classroom setting whenever the children or counselor recognizes these themes as occurring. "Does this sound like push/pull feelings to you? Let's get out the On the One Hand... and Then on the Other puppets and talk about it!"

APPLICATIONS

The On the One Hand . . . and Then on the Other puppets can be used for any situation wherein a child's healthy functioning is impaired by ambivalent or conflicted feelings. Issues may range from normal developmental issues such as sharing friends, feeling popular, or facing puberty to the situational adjustment necessary to accept the arrival of a new sibling, moving, or loss of a loved one who had suffered a long illness. Children dealing with anxiety and/or depression from psychologically threatening events such as suicide, alcoholism, divorce, and sexual abuse benefit greatly from this technique.

Section Six

Play Toys and Objects Techniques

56

BodySox

Kimberly Dye

INTRODUCTION

BodySox, winner of the 1993 Early Childhood Director's Choice Award, is a Lycra stretch sack with Velcro opening that enwraps the whole body. It was designed to facilitate a corrective body image, body boundary, and imaginative play for attention deficit children and eating disordered adults. Its four-way Lycra stretch fabric provides tactile feedback that can be reminiscent of early mother–infant bonding, a necessary step in body image formation.

It creates an experience of "I can see you but you can't see me," which increases a sense of personal safety, loosens inhibition, and stimulates a spirit of play, the backdrop for therapeutic interaction between client and therapist. Children freely enter the imaginal space inside BodySox's protection and dance images such as rolling rocks, hatching eggs, moving puzzle pieces, or birds of flight. Relationship mover and observer can develop spontaneously through storytelling or shape naming.

RATIONALE

Material of a developmental nature often arises during sessions. Inside a BodySox is akin to Winicott's "holding environment" (Winnicott 1982).

The containing, wrapped feeling can satisfy those with inadequate early bonding by recreating an in utero or symbiotic experience. Slow rocking or rolling movements can also be soothing to hyperactive or depressed children.

Mahler's phases of separation can also be simulated and moved through accordingly (Mahler, Pine & Bergman, 1975). The fabric can be pushed, pulled, and pressed away from the body as a way of enlarging the personal kinesphere and separating from the "status quo." Individual body parts, an arm, a leg, or head, can begin to emerge from the confines of the walls by extending through the Velcro opening. This exercise can bring up issues of body shame, feeling exposed, or separating from the familiar. As the client works through negative feelings and spends as much time inside the sack as feels comfortable, they can gradually be encouraged to emerge at a pace that feels right. Emerging can than evoke feelings of freedom, excitement, and/or readiness to become separate.

APPLICATIONS

An adolescent struggling with anorexia liked to hide from Mother in the house at various times throughout the day. Mother was not amused by the game and would often become fearful of the adolescent's intention. We began working and playing with the BodySox as a way of meeting the client where she was, simulating the hiding experience, and exploring how it might fulfill an unmet need. The BodySox became a hated object, symbolic of the pressured, entrapping quality she experienced in relation to her mother. She pushed and pulled and expanded the walls of the BodySox. Upon encouragement to dialogue with the walls of the BodySox, the client began to access and express aggression towards her mother. Her hiding behavior decreased as she began to verbalize her feelings towards Mother. The BodySox experience helped her to create healthy boundaries that began to replace her refusal to eat.

References

Mahler, M., Pine, F., and Bergman A. (1975). *The Psychological Birth of the Human Infant*. New York: Basic Books.

Winnicott, D. W. (1982). *Playing and Reality*. London: Routledge, Chapman, and Hall.

57

The Me Doll

Jessica Stone-Phennicie

INTRODUCTION

As a project, many grammar school students have lain down on butcher paper and had their bodies traced. The tracing is then colored and taken home to parents. When I was in fourth grade, this was my assignment. Even then I thought it was fascinating to see a tracing that outlined my own fingers, arms, head, and so on. There I was, one dimensional, on butcher paper.

While learning about techniques used in play therapy, I began to think about the tracings and how I could apply them therapeutically. I modified the tracing assignment to create a three-dimensional representation of a client. The ability to create and examine a symbolic representation of oneself can be very therapeutic. The Me Doll is a simple, inexpensive way a therapist and child can discover self-expression and representation. This technique can be used with clients of various cultures, races, and ethnicities.

RATIONALE

The Me Doll allows the client self-expression and identification. Through this self-knowledge, the child and therapist can gain insight into a particular situation, into who the client is, or how she or he sees her/or himself. The ability to identify symbolic representations of the client's affect and/or memories is a foundation on which to build further self-knowledge. Further self-knowledge can lead to personal growth throughout life.

The creation of the doll can be fun and engaging process for both the client and the therapist. Therapeutic issues can be discussed and articulated in a creative way, consistent with the tradition of play therapy. The creation can be an ongoing process, or merely an observational assessment of self-expression and identification. The product is a tangible, three-dimensional self-representation that can be a vehicle for growth and change.

DESCRIPTION

Supplies:

1. a large roll of paper in colors that reflect the ethnicities of your clientele (butcher paper works well; however, the color assortment is limited)
2. staples
3. crayons, colored pencils, and/or markers
4. items gathered to fill the Me Doll; these can be gathered together or the therapist can provide a varied selection of items to choose from

Additional Materials:

1. sequins, ribbon, yarn for hair, etc.—basically anything you would like to supply the child with to adorn her or his Me Doll
2. cotton, polyfil, or newspaper

Creating the Me Doll is a very individualistic process. The therapist may determine the sequence of steps when creating the doll according to her or his theoretical framework. I will recommend a sequence based on my personal preference, experience, and framework.

I recommend tracing the child as an initial step. This engages the child in the activity and introduces the activity as something fun and creative. The tracing of the child should be done on two layers of paper preferably in a paper color closest to their own skin color or one they are comfortable with. Once the tracing is completed, the figure should be cut out through both layers of the paper, leaving approximately 1½ to 2 inches beyond the pattern edge to allow for stapling.

The child can then draw in the figure as he sees fit. The therapist may guide the child with an appropriate therapeutic theme, for example, "Draw how you see yourself" or "How do you feel about yourself/your life/your situation?" It is important that the therapist use specific information obtained from the previous sessions to formulate appropriate themes for the creation of the doll. The therapist may provide as few or as many items for decorating the exterior of the doll as deemed appropriate.

The next sessions the therapist and child go on a gathering trip. This could be around the office or building, or even a nature walk. I recommend a nature walk; however, not all facilities can accommodate this. The child should identify items that signify feelings, thoughts, memories, and so on. For example, a rock can signify anger or a leaf can remind her or him of a family trip. If the child feels strongly about an item or items that signify significant themes, a substantial quantity of these items should be gathered. For those in a brief therapy setting, the therapist may want to supply an adequate variety and supply of items from which to choose.

It is during the gathering sessions that most of the therapeutic discussions take place. I recommend having multiple gathering sessions. The therapist should facilitate and encourage the child's participation. The more items gathered, the more likely one is to have significant events, affect, and memories, represented. This also increases the likelihood of a proper representation of the child as she or he sees her- or himself.

Once you have gathered the items, the project will be to fill the Me Doll. All the items should be included: the good and the bad, the memories and the emotions, anything which makes her or him unique, special, or just like everyone else. Depending on the age, cognitive level, and/or maturity level of the child, she or he can even attempt to identify where they feel certain emotions in their bodies and place the item in the appropriate place in their doll. Any additional space can be filled with cotton, polyfil, or newspapers.

The doll should then be "sewn up" with staples. Arm and leg joints can be created for a realistic look. As the sessions continue, the child may even choose to remove items, as if to signify a lack of current importance. The child may also add items to signify new issues or accomplishments. The gathering of new items may occur spontaneously or per the therapist's direction, or be brought in by the child between sessions. When the chosen therapeutic theme has been sufficiently worked through, the doll can be sent home as a tangible reminder of the work that was done.

APPLICATIONS

Variations of the uses of the doll are restricted only by the imagination. If a facility does not have storage space for the dolls between sessions, the doll can be created on a smaller scale. This technique can be used for children (individually or in group), adults, and even families.

Stephen is a 6-year-old Hispanic male who was sexually abused by a 12-year-old male cousin. One incident has been reported by Stephen. He presented having difficulty leaving his home and being left alone with people other than his parents. He was experiencing nightly night terrors since the incidents. Stephen had difficulty expressing anything and rapport was difficult to establish.

After obtaining parental consent, Stephen and I began the Me Doll creation process. "How do you see yourself?" was our therapeutic theme. Stephen eagerly participated in the gathering session. We went on nature walks and with each item he identified and gathered, we discussed the affect or memory. A notepad was used to identify each item and what it symbolized. When we finished our initial gathering sessions, we had accumulated many rocks, bugs, leaves, feathers, and an old sock.

We filled his doll with the items. He had identified anger in his abdominal region, so we placed his anger rocks in a large bag and Velcroed the bag in place. The arms, legs, and head were lightly filled with crumpled newspapers. We placed the other items in randomly. After sewing up the doll, Stephen picked it up and remarked how "heavy the stomach area was, just like mine."

Throughout the sessions Stephen and I referred back to the doll. We used the doll in role plays. Over time, he began removing some of the anger rocks. He brought in some small toys and items that made him happy. During our last month of sessions, he took out the unidentified old sock and threw it away. His parents completed an updated assessment form routinely used with clients every twelve weeks. They reported an improvement in his ability to leave the home, and he will again stay with a lifelong babysitter. He had had two night terrors since therapy began. The doll was sent home with Stephen with the understanding that he could return with the doll during any future sessions.

This technique can be applied to various therapeutic issues. The therapist can modify the technique to her or his theoretical framework. This is a useful, fun, creative and versatile play therapy technique.

58

Tearing Paper

Kathy Daves

INTRODUCTION

This is a fun activity that also has therapeutic value. It develops teamwork, offers alternatives to fighting, allows children that are very intense to loosen up, extends boundaries of those violated, gives children an opportunity to make a promise and fulfill it, and provides bonding between the therapist and clients.

DESCRIPTION

I have used this with a variety of clients from 5–12 years of age. The number in each group has ranged from two to five clients, and should be limited if the clients have poor impulse control or are extremely active.

This activity requires one phone book, and several Sunday papers or other discarded paper. The group begins by having the children raise their right hands and promising to help clean up when the activity is over. I explain that we are going to release negative feelings by doing an activity that requires lots of energy. We spend a few minutes discussing various feelings and a variety of situations that may have created the different emotions.

Next I tear out pages of the phone book and show the children how to tear them into smaller pieces. Usually I tear them once down the middle, then tear those strips into smaller pieces. The size of the torn paper is not important.

We put the small pieces in the middle of the room. When we have a large pile, all group members (including myself) start throwing the paper into the air. The pieces of paper fly all over the room. The kids love it! The children who have perfectionistic tendencies tend to be more cautious at first but generally they will participate with increasing freedom. The children enjoy piling up the paper and then jumping into it or burying each other. Mostly they enjoy throwing handfuls into the air repeatedly.

I usually let the activity continue as long as time will allow. Then comes the cleanup! As we work together, I acknowledge how they fulfilled their promise. Then after all is straightened up, we process how it felt for them to release all that energy and emotion and discuss how this could be adapted for home or other situations. I have used this many times and it has proven to be an easy, fun, productive activity that requires little preparation.

APPLICATIONS

I have used this technique with a variety of clients, including a group of ADHD boys, family therapy with siblings who fought much of the time, sexually abused children, inner-city kids, children with behavior problems, and children with perfectionistic characteristics.

59

The Mad Game

Patricia Davidson

INTRODUCTION

Many children seen in play therapy have issues of anger, and most deal with their anger in inappropriate ways (i. e., by acting out at school or home, or by violence against others, self, and/or property. If the child is allowed to be angry in the play therapy setting, and he is given acceptance and positive regard by the therapist, he can then learn acceptable, appropriate ways to express his anger (as well as other feelings) outside the play setting.

RATIONALE

The rationale for using this technique is twofold. First, it normalizes and generalizes that "people get angry and that's okay." It allows for verbal expression of the child's anger as well as kinesthetic expression at the end of the game. Thus, the child learns two acceptable ways to express anger appropriately.

DESCRIPTION

The therapist uses cardboard bricks, or wooden or plastic blocks. The therapist then divides the blocks or bricks equally among the participants (including the therapist) with the instructions that each person will place a brick or block atop the previous one at his or her turn. (The game works best when each person has 5–8 turns).

At each person's turn, he or she makes a statement about something which angers him or her (or something that isn't fair). All statements are acceptable, from silly to serious. For example, "It's not fair that I can't eat dessert first," or "I get mad when my sister hits me and breaks my toys."

If the therapist is aware of specific issues of therapeutic concerns, he or she may introduce the issue, such as, "It makes me angry when adults hit children" (abuse), or "I get mad when grownups drink and fall asleep when their kids are hungry" (abuse/alcoholism).

Once all the bricks or blocks are stacked, the child (identified patient) is asked to think of something that *really* makes him or her angry, to make a "mad face," and invited to knock down the bricks or blocks in any manner the child chooses. The game is then over and may be repeated if the child desires. No processing is necessary.

APPLICATIONS

This technique works well with children (ages 3–13) seen individually, with parents and/or siblings, and in groups. It can also be used as a non-threatening way for expression of other feelings, such as sadness or injustice, by changing the wording to "It makes me sad when . . ." or "It's not fair when. . . ." It is applicable in cases of aggression, withdrawal, or depression, and may be tailored to meet the special needs of the specific child and family.

60

Sculpt-It

Michael Cascio

INTRODUCTION

This technique uses imagination, projection, and teamwork to facilitate psychological relief from conflicts and stress. Formulated to create a forum for sibling conflicts to be resolved, this activity encourages children to construct an image of how they perceive their world. There is only one rule, namely that they have to use all materials in the box in the time allowed. The therapist observes the level of communication, dominance, self-esteem, and conflict resolution as the children complete the project.

Eliciting information permits the children (and also the therapist) to discover a connection between them. By having a discussion at the completion of this project, the siblings are reinforced for their ability to complete the task and to work together to "beat the clock." Their explanation of the process toward completion allows the therapist to begin to understand the issues and differences the siblings bring to the session. Furthermore, the "story" behind the completed object (what it is doing, etc.) provides a wealth of metaphors that create understanding and insight.

RATIONALE

The main therapeutic value of this technique is that it allows siblings with conflict to find their own way of cooperating and connecting. However, the value goes far beyond that experience alone. It also:

1. Provides an opportunity for a sibling system to present itself in an honest, noncritical manner;
2. Allows the siblings to tell their story as they perceive it, revealing emotional issues and cognitive preoccupations;
3. Creates a sense of attunement or empathic understanding between the therapist and the siblings;
4. Offers an avenue of language and circumstances to introduce change and more productive coping mechanisms.

DESCRIPTION

The Sculpt-It technique utilizes rather simple items for self-expression. An ordinary shoebox is filled with general supplies found in most offices, for example, paper clips, string, paper cups, index cards, tin foil, Saran Wrap, glue, scotch tape, and crayons. The siblings ar told they have 15 minutes to create something using all the items in the box. I reflect on the process, but not to the point that it interferes with the dynamics occurring between the siblings. I announce the time remaining as a motivational intervention, interjecting when one or the other begins to lose interest. When the time expires (I usually fudge when they need a few more minutes) I ask the following questions:

1. What have you both created?
2. Where did it come from? How does it work? Is it fast, slow, happy, sad [elicit descriptive adjectives]?
3. Can you create a story using the finished object? I will usually let either of the siblings start the story, and interrupt them at various points in the dialogue to allow the other sibling to pick up the story. A variation on this would allow the children to have 5 minutes alone to develop a story and provide you with the narrative.

The story is a most useful exercise in revealing the problems and conflicts between the siblings, as well as within the family. It creates a playful avenue to express self-perceptions, doubts, anxiety, and anger. Fearful inner thoughts and feelings are expressed through creation and dramatization. In the case of sibling conflicts, there begins to be a means to find compromise and industry.

APPLICATIONS

This technique was formulated as a team building and bonding activity for siblings in conflict with each other. However, Sculpt-It has also had value as a tool for depressed children, ADHD children, children of divorce, and for family therapy activities (either the entire family or just a child with the parents). The process and outcome allows for success in attaining a goal, ingenuity, a spirit of cooperation, and the importance of the metaphorical value to expressing cognitions and emotions in a non-threatening avenue of activity.

Judy, age 9 was described by her mother as an angry child who focused her rage on her 13-year-old sister, Susan, and her mother, Deborah. Deborah noted that Susan was a very controlling and demanding person. As Susan entered puberty, her thoughts and interests were becoming more external to the family. The father's commitment to his profession kept him preoccupied and he was described as aloof with the family and overinvolved at work. The mother saw herself as the main disciplinarian, but found herself unable to keep the peace between Judy and Susan.

At the time of intake, Judy had been both verbally and physically abusive toward Susan and her mother. The intensity of these conflicts usually instigated the father's intervention, which consisted of separating any physical conflicts. However, a majority of the time, he would leave the home and drive through the neighborhood to allow time for the fracas to subside. Deborah, on the other hand, would lock herself in the bedroom, leaving the two girls to handle the situation. Judy was labeled the instigator and troublemaker.

Most significant throughout individual and family therapy was the Sculpt-It session. Both girls vacillated between cooperative and independent approaches to the project. Judy needed to guarantee the individuality of her contribution in order to draw attention to herself. However, the whole project was always addressed by the co-therapists, not individual parts of the assignment.

The finished project was described as a monster from another planet. The monster would gain energy from conflict and disagreement. However, the monster was tired of this way of life and moved to Earth, where everyone was thoughtful and cooperative. The monster soon discovered its need to re-energize, but couldn't find any conflicts on Earth. The monster then thought that inflicting violence on itself would generate energy. The monster shot itself in the head, and killed itself. It couldn't find a way to coexist in this world.

The metaphoric communication in the project depicted children who knew no other means to exist within their family. And, in fact, the termination in the story paralleled the growing discontent between the parents and their thoughts of divorce.

Homework assignments for these girls focused on cooperative coordination of tasks to be presented in future therapy sessions. The co-therapists, rolemodeling parents, provided equal praise and encouragement. Soon, the children's "energy" was supplied through cooperation and agreement with each other.

The Sculpt-It session in an important tool to initiate sibling teamwork. Follow-up assignments are homework-based, and are presented by the siblings in future therapy sessions. This may include: (1) develop your own game and teach your therapist how to play; (2) devise a "skit" or dramatization to present in therapy.

61

The Magic Carpet Technique

Dolores M. Conyers

INTRODUCTION

The Magic Carpet technique is recommended in play therapy with children as an available selection among the toy collection in the playroom, as a transition tool with children having difficulty at the beginning of the therapy hour, and as an at-home resource for parents to employ with children having attention and control issues.

DESCRIPTION

Along with the collection of toys in the playroom is a colorful, fringed carpet. Many children pay no attention, but others put it to full use as a magic carpet. The carpet among the toys is for children to make use of or not, as they desire. As a magic carpet it takes them to places, allows them to escape from places, or simply allows a place of peace and solitude. Sometimes it is not a magic carpet at all, but another means of transportation, such as a car, a room in a house, an isolated and lonely island, or a fortressed castle surrounded by a moat full of alligators. The carpet tucked among the toys is naturally appealing to children in the "let's play house, build a fort, or make a tent from a blanket" years.

A number of differently colored or designed carpets can be made available to children in the playroom. They can be rolled and stacked in a magazine rack or another storage container. A child may use several carpets to represent different places, such as a house, daycare center, school, or hospital. In the case of a divorce situation, one carpet can represent the mother's home and a second carpet the father's home. Children will sometimes construct a house with carpets representing each of the different rooms. They often will use play dishes and other toys to furnish these rooms. One child used a carpet to represent the grandfather's home. A blue carpet that was placed next to it represented the body of water located near the home. (One safety caution originates from the fact that when a child sets up several carpets, movement from one to another usually occurs. The danger of slipping or tripping increases. Therefore, ensure that the carpets are nonskid.)

The Magic Carpet technique can involve another carpet at hand for the therapist to spread just inside the playroom door. Here it becomes a tool to aid transition into the playroom and the therapy hour. For the most hyperactive or anxious of children a 5–10 minute "ride" on the carpet can transport a child into the session with the therapist. Having a simple snack or participating in a brief and fun activity on the carpet is usually part of this "ride."

APPLICATIONS

The Magic Carpet technique in another form can be taught to parents for use at home. It is recommended for use with ADD or ADHD children. One to three times a day, the parent spreads the special magic carpet for a special time. With very young children the parent can participate on the carpet with the child. Activities may include reading to the child or having the child select a book and pillows to pile on the carpet for a time to read to himself or herself. This type of activity lends itself to timing with a kitchen timer for 5 to 15 minutes, depending on the age of the child. Other activities are making a puzzle or frosting cupcakes with or without the parent on the carpet to help, depending on the age of the child. Such activities are not timed in minutes but continue until the task is complete (i.e., all the cupcakes are frosted). For these at-home times using the Magic Carpet technique the rules are simple: the magic carpet is used for no other purpose in the home; the activity is constructive and pleasing to the child; the activities are geared for successful completion in the 5–15 minute time period; the carpet "rides" are no more than 3 times a day and 5–15 minutes per ride; the child and parent, if taking the ride, do not leave the carpet until the time is up or the task is complete; the technique of the "ride" or the activities involved are never used as punishment in any way, but are always a positive experience.

62

The Snake

Alan Lobaugh

INTRODUCTION

Since the beginning of human history there have been images of the snake or serpent that continue to weave their way into story, myth, and culture. In ancient Near Eastern cultures the serpent is defeated in order for creation to begin. In the Ugaritic myth of creation, Baal destroys Lotan, the coiled snake. Isaiah 27:1 records how Yahweh will punish Leviathan, the fleeing, twisting serpent. "He will kill the sea dragon" (pg. 618). The snake also takes on the voice of temptation in the garden of Eden (Genesis 3:1). At times the snake represents disorder and chaos. In other instances, the snake is evil, seeking to destroy what is good. Since it has such power to evoke these concepts, it is important for a snake to be included in the playroom.

DESCRIPTION

As children explore the playroom, it is fascinating to note the frequency with which they choose the snake for play. Many children focus several minutes of their play time with the snake, often burying it in the sand, sometimes using it to attack "innocent" bystanders. What are the thought and feelings that go along with this snake play?

There appear to be two main metaphors emerging through the snake. First, some children see it as representing some terrible force in their lives. They want to hide it, cover it over, even stack things on top to keep it away. "There, that'll fix him!" At times though, the children bring the snake out from under the heavy stack, revealing its power and the force that continues to threaten their lives. No matter how big the pile, no matter how many things they add, the snake finds a way out and wreaks havoc with the characters surrounding the story. At times, when the snake is buried, the sand will be smoothed over, and a peaceful scene will be created. This parallels the "elephant in the living room" concept, where everyone knows it is there but no one will talk about it. "Don't wake the sleeping giant." Other times, children pretend that no one knows it is there. Then it is truly a surprise (at least to the characters) when it appears.

How many soldiers, rockets, and bombs does it take to subdue this beast? Can it ever be fully destroyed? Many times in the playroom, children kill the snake over and over again, only to have it revive when they are breathing a sigh of relief. For these children, issues of power and control are vital. They are searching for tools that will enable them to overcome the evil they face. Fear, anger, and hate are often wrapped around this play. In adequacy and insecurity are expressions of children who feel helpless to win the battle.

A second theme is presented when the snake doesn't want to be found. Children sometimes try to hide the snake *from* something. While issues of fear and insecurity are expressed as in the previous play description, these children show the snake as helpless. They hide the snake in hopes that no one will come looking. Hopefully, the snake will remain unfound, safe in its hiding place in the sand. Various expressions come through when the snake is discovered. Some characters will try to hurt it while others sympathize and try to defend this frightened snake (similar to "The Reluctant Dragon").

APPLICATIONS

Both of these play experiences are expressed by children. Many who have experienced trauma and/or abuse are more likely to return to this theme again and again. Children who deal with an unknown or unconscious event can project it onto the snake. Other children who face the divorce of parents, ongoing alcoholism in the family, or a sense of inferiority may also benefit through this play. While some children focus on an uncontrollable force always on the attack, others center their attention on the helplessness of the victim. The issues and feelings surrounding these play events are similar in both cases.

The number one task of the therapist is to let children know they are not alone as they face the traumas played out in the playroom. Seeing and feeling as the children see and feel helps them through some difficult situations. Even though the trial may seem unbearable, the children have someone who will go with them through the trouble. As a therapist or parent, one can reflect the range of feelings expressed when the children are dealing with the snake. The therapist can focus on moments of insight, clever strategy, and success to help the children learn coping methods. Exploring the nuances of each option presented is another way to work through the problem with the children.

When children break free from old patterns, when they create new ways of dealing with the snake, progress is being made. It may take every ounce of "good" to overcome this "evil," but that is a sign of hope. When they can subdue, even defeat the snake, when they show fewer signs of fear, more power, a stronger spirit, and rekindled confidence, one can believe that the play is having a therapeutic effect in the children. (Isaiah 27:1 Revised Standard Version, 1952).

63

The Baby Bottle Technique

Diane Murray

INTRODUCTION

An enduring toy in the playroom is the baby bottle. Virginia Axline (1947) and Clark Moustakas (1953) were credited with initially recommending the baby bottle for the play therapy room. The baby bottle has more recently been determined by Charles Schaefer (1981) to be in the top ten list of toys that produce a high number of verbal responses that are also revealing in content.

The baby bottle is a universal object that can easily be brought into the playroom. It is truly a part of every child's past experience. It is not a toy yet can be utilized in the therapeutic playroom to bring out inner needs and emotions.

This chapter discusses my observations of the baby bottle's usefulness in play therapy sessions over the course of seventeen years. I have noted some commonalities among the children who use or do not use it and how they respond to it.

RATIONALE

I have found the baby bottle to be a useful tool in play therapy. It is a familiar object that arouses emotions and provides a way for a child to communicate feelings. More specifically, it provides a way to communicate feelings about, and needs for , nurturance and soothing.

DESCRIPTION

It is essential, I have found, to use a genuine baby bottle found in a pharmacy or supermarket, rather than a pretend baby bottle found in the toy store. Children seem to react more profoundly to the genuine article. It is something real from their own actual life experience, whether they consciously remember it or not.

The therapist plays a nondirective role during the process of play with the bottle. The bottle is simply placed with the toys and the child will determine if it becomes a part of the therapy process. The therapist follows the child's lead. Water should be available for the child to fill up the bottle with and to suck out.

Children seem to be draw to the baby bottle. They look at it initially with wide eyes, as if they can't believe seeing a real baby bottle sitting along with the toys. They study it, associating to it. It elicits associations to their own experiences with it. It appears the outcome of that stirring of thoughts and emotions determines the child's subsequent interaction with it. Some children put it aside and come back to it later. Some put it aside, come back to it later to touch it, take the cap off, and put it away again and do nothing more with it. Some become very involved with it.

APPLICATIONS

From my own observations, children who have suffered parental neglect, abandonment, or abuse are the ones who become most involved with the baby bottle. Children who are in treatment for adjustment reactions, even if severe, such as divorce, loss through death, or other traumatic event, don't appear to become as involved with the bottle. These are children who, even though stressed and exhibiting problems, appear to have received relatively healthy nurturing prior to the trauma. In many ways they seem less needy.

Children who become involved with the bottle like to fill it with water and then enjoy sucking it through the nipple. There is a look of pleasure on their faces. My observation is that this activity serves one of two purposes, depending on the child. One goal it serves it to soothe and comfort the child through regression to an infantile state. These children lie down and suck and smile. The smile is one of pleasure and seems also one of secret collaboration, as if they're thinking, "I know I'm too old for this but it's fun and I'm glad you're letting me do this." When they've had enough soothing they return to another activity, going back to the bottle periodically, especially when feeling stressed by emotions brought out through another activity or conversation we are having.

Another purpose of this activity is to provide a way of interacting with the therapist. For example, one untrusting, distancing, abused 5-year-old girl interacted with me by having me hold the bottle for her while she sucked, picking it up for her when she dropped it, and so on. It was a way of being in control but receiving nurturance at the same time, a potentially corrective emotional experience. One disturbed boy initially would rarely answer me when I spoke to him, but would suck water out of the bottle. It was the only way he took away from the sessions any good feelings for a while. It seemed to serve as a bridge between us.

References

Axline, V. M. (1947). *Play Therapy.* New York: Houghton-Mifflin.

Moustakas, C. E. (1953). *Children in Play Therapy.* New York: McGraw-Hill.

Schaefer, C. (1981). *The Therapeutic Use of Child's Play.* New York: Jason Aronson.

64

The T-Shirt Technique

Nancy H. Cochran

INTRODUCTION

Ongoing participation and support by a primary caretaker is an important and necessary component in the effective therapeutic process for sexually abused children. The therapist must find ways to help the caretaker cope with personal distress, while at the same time helping the caretaker (who many times is the nonoffending parent) be as supportive as possible in helping his or her child through difficulties related to the sexual abuse. The technique of making a special T-shirt or nightshirt may be used to enhance the relationship between the primary caretaker and the child, while helping both of them develop communication skills and coping strategies to deal with stressful issues.

RATIONALE

Some common stress-related reactions for sexually abused children include: generalized fear and anxiety, sleep-related problems (insomnia, nightmares, bedwetting), a sense of the body as "damaged" or "different," self-injurous impulses, and somatic complaints. The technique of making a special T-shirt or nightshirt with his or her caretaker offers a creative, nonthreatening activity wherein the child is encouraged to identify specific stressful issues and talk openly with his or her caretaker about fears, worries, and concerns that may have seemed too overwhelming or frightening previously. By enhancing communication and the relationship between the caretaker and the child, it is hoped that therapy becomes concurrent with system change, and that the child will be better able to discuss worries and concerns about body image and developing sexuality with his or her caretakers. For children with sleep-related problems, the technique is used to address negative associations with bedtime and sleep, and to help the caretaker and the child develop a bedtime routine that includes positive sleep associations and soothing activities for the child. The therapist assists by listening and helping the child and caretaker communicate. In doing so, the therapist affirms his or her trust in and genuine regard for both the child's and the caretaker's abilities to communicate with each other and work through stressful issues.

DESCRIPTION

Cotton T-shirts and a variety of colors of fabric paints are the only materials needed. Prior to making a special T-shirt or nightshirt, the child's specific stressful issues are discussed with both the child and primary caretakers. The caretakers may be encouraged to read and discuss with the child age-appropriate books (or portions of books) that are specifically written to address worries or concerns of the sexually abused child. Books about body changes and feelings during early adolescence may also be used for older children and their caretakers. Books such as *It's My Body* by Lory Freeman, *My Body is Private* by Linda Girard, and portions of *It Happens to Boys, Too* by Jane Satullo, Roberta Russell, and Pat Bradway have been used by this author to facilitate discussion with the child and caretakers. Lynda Madaras's books, *"What's Happening to my Body?" Book for Boys*, and *Growing Up Guide for Girls* are also helpful in addressing concerns about sexual development with older children and their caretakers. *Moonbeam: Meditations for Children* by Maureen Garth is a helpful book for children who are experiencing sleep problems. It offers simple visualizations and affirmations to help a child relax and quiet fears before bedtime.

During sessions with the caretakers, the therapist may want to help the child verbalize feelings about stressful issues by using open-ended sentences such as: "My body is . . ."; "When I'm frightened, I . . ."; People I trust are . . ."; "At bedtime, I . . ."; "When I'm angry, I . . ."; "I feel most peaceful when . . ."; and so on. Internalized behaviors (sleep disturbances, self-injurous impulses) and externalized behaviors (aggressive acting out, sexual acting out) may be addressed, and a plan may be devised for how the caretakers can help, and how the child can let others know how he or she is feeling or what he or she needs to feel better or safe. The therapist may then suggest, "A good way to remember how special your body is, and how to let trusted adults know how you are feeling, is to make a special T-shirt that has pictures and words that can be like reminders." The therapist, caretakers, and child then work together to paint a T-shirt that the child can wear in the daytime or a nightshirt, depending on the needs and wishes of the child. The caretakers may choose to draw a special picture or write a special message to the child, but for the most part the child is encouraged to design the T-shirt and choose the special drawings or messages that he or she wants on the shirt. The therapist may want to include a special message or a pictorial or written reminder of relaxation techniques or cognitive behavioral methods that have worked best for the child. Often the child will choose to make both a T-shirt for wearing to school and a nightshirt. Some children like to make T-shirts for their caretakers and siblings as well.

APPLICATIONS

This technique may be used in a variety of situations wherein the therapist wants to help a child better express fears and concerns about body image and/or difficulties feeling safe and relaxed at bedtime. It is also very helpful in encouraging children to take pride in and develop a healthy attitude toward their bodies. I have found the technique most applicable in working with sexually abused children and their caretakers. It offers a creative, nonthreatening activity wherein the caretaker and the child feel supported and safe bringing up and discussing stressful issues related to the sexual abuse. It allows for a meaningful time wherein the caretaker may express through thoughts and actions that the child is loved and believed and that the child's abuse was completely the fault of the offender. For the sexually abused child experiencing sleep-related problems, it allows for a plan to be devised and written out through symbols and words on a special nightshirt.

This technique was originally implemented with a 10-year-old female who was working through a number of issues related to neglect by her parents and sexual abuse by her stepfather, which continued from 4 through 9 years. Her mother reported that the girl would not sleep in pajamas, but insisted on being fully clothed. Clinical symptoms included touch phobia, insomnia, and academic failure. The mother expressed that the girl had been a straight A student and had no problems sleeping prior to disclosing sexual abuse. The mother had difficulty speaking openly with her daughter about the sexual abuse, and just wanted her daughter "back to normal."

Initial client-centered therapy sessions revealed a bright, creative girl who chose to draw, paint, and write poetry during sessions. Many of her poems expressed concern and sadness for her stepfather who was in jail and anger towards her mother for "loving my baby brother more" and "crying all the time." Many times this girl would also express extreme hatred for her baby brother, and would admit to wanting to hurt him. This girl often spoke in baby talk while in sessions with the therapist, and during these sessions began to express a need for nurturing (wishing she could be the baby) and being cared for by her mother.

The T-shirt technique was suggested after the girl had asked that her mother come into sessions for part of the time. The mother and daughter had read the book *My Body is Private* as a homework exercise, and had been working on a special workbook together. They had devised a schedule of special bedtime activities (reading, giving each other backrubs) that had begun to help them establish a better relationship and help the girl go to sleep. During the session the girl made matching T-shirts for her mother, baby brother, and herself that had pictures and words about all the different "favorite things" they liked to do together as a family. She and her mother then worked together on a nightshirt for her to wear to bed. This shirt listed ways the girl could try to relax and feel safe (saying a prayer, turning on the nightlight, asking Mom for a backrub, asking Mom to sing some songs with me) as well as special messages and pictures from her mother (You are my special, beautiful daughter, I will always take care of you, I'm sorry you were hurt . . . it wasn't your fault). Additionally, the girl included some statements such as "Private . . . keep out!" and "Do not touch without permission from owner!" to express her need for privacy and her right to say when she did and did not want to be touched.

This technique provided a nonthreatening, creative activity for the mother and child that lasted three sessions. During these sessions this mother and daughter were able to say some important and meaningful things to each other. Additionally, they found out that they both enjoyed doing creative things together, and they planned other arts and crafts activities to do together at home. Shortly after these sessions, the mother shared that she was sexually abused as a child, and became involved in a group for adult survivors of childhood sexual abuse.

References

Freeman, L. (1983). *It's My Body*. Seattle: Parenting Press.

Garth, M. (1992). *Moonbeam: Meditations for Children*. New York: HarperCollins.

Girard, L. W. (1984). *My Body is Private*. Martin Grove, IL: A. Whitman.

Madaras, L. (1988). *The What's Happening to My Body? Book for Boys: A Growing Up Guide for Parents and Sons*. New York: Newmarket Press.

Madaras, L. (1988). *The What's Happening to My Body? Book for Girls: A Growing Up Guide for Parents and Daughters*. New York: Newmarket Press.

Satullo, J., Russell, R., Bradway, P. (1987). *It Happens to Boys too*. Pittsfield, MA: Rape Crisis Center of the Berkshires Press.

65

The Photo Album Technique

Sueanne Brown

INTRODUCTION

Many children seen in a therapeutic setting are unable to adequately express their thoughts and feelings. This is increasingly true when children are confronted with issues of bereavement. Their ability to distinguish and decipher their feelings and then to sufficiently verbalize these thoughts is a difficult task.

RATIONALE

The photo album technique is a nonthreatening activity that allows a child to safely elicit thoughts and feelings through photographs. Utilizing pictures allows the child to take the focus from him- or herself and will elicit remarks such as, "I remember . . .", "At that house . . .", "I don't like . . .", "My mom . . .", and so on. A myriad of feelings generally surfaces.

DESCRIPTION

A request is made of the primary caretaker to collect an assortment of photographs that cover the life span of the child. Instruct the caretaker to include a large variety of photos including, but not limited to, different homes the child had lived in, vacation photos, pets, friends, holiday snapshots, school performances, vehicles they owned, and so on. The goal is to gather a diverse number of photographs to cover the many avenues of the child's life.

In selecting an album, the child should be included in the decision-making process. The following choices can be given: the therapist can select an album, the child can buy a new one with his caretaker, or the child can choose an older one from photo albums at home.

During the following session, the play therapy project can be initiated. The materials needed include: a photo album, photographs, scissors, markers, and self-sticking labels (¾" × 5¼"). The photos should be spread out over the floor so that they can easily be seen and inserted in chronological order. Throughout this process, a multitude of thoughts and feelings can be released: discussion of family, processing memories, feelings in relation to the life of the deceased, the process of life, feelings towards losses, and feelings associated with grief, such as anger, sadness, and confusion.

Once the pictures are in chronological order, they can be placed in the photo album. The child can then adhere a label beneath each picture to describe each individual photo. The therapist then becomes the "secretary" and writes a description that the child dictates onto the label.

APPLICATIONS

This technique works well with bereavement, but can be expanded to deal with other losses that are inherent in a child's life. For example, in divorce situations, a child may feel the loss of one of his parents. Photos dealing with the past may bring these feelings to the surface. In addition, the loss felt when a family moves, the loss of a friendship, or the loss of an old school are cases where this technique could be applied.

66

The Angry Tower

Sheri Saxe

INTRODUCTION

This expressive play therapy technique was dubbed the Angry Tower by my 7-year-old client, Michael. It evolved out of my desire to provide this child with the opportunity to express angry feelings that I suspected he was denying.

I had recently read about a technique in which the expression of anger was facilitated by having the client throw a ball against a wall or against cardboard boxes. Inspired by that technique, I brought in a huge plastic bucket (meant for popcorn) that contains six smaller nesting buckets, and a soft fabric football. I told Michael he could build a tower out of the buckets and then knock it down with the football. I said that he could throw the ball as hard as he wanted and say things that made him mad while he was doing it. I mentioned that the harder he threw the ball, the louder a noise the buckets would make when they came crashing down.

RATIONALE

The appropriate expression of anger is difficult for many children, especially children who have experienced abuse, trauma, or loss

(Oaklander 1988). Clinically, I have observed these children to go to one of two extremes: either the anger overflows uncontrollably into all areas of their lives, or it is buried and hidden by depression, withdrawal, and/or low self-esteem.

According to Oaklander (1988), "What seems to be necessary is to allow the child to be *conscious* of the anger, to *know* anger. This is the first step in helping children feel strong and whole instead of fearfully running away from and avoiding angry feelings, or discharging them in indirect ways which might harm themselves or alienate others" (p. 211).

Physical expression of angry or aggressive feelings in the safe environment of play therapy can help children to "know" their anger, to release it, and to progress to appropriate anger expression in their lives (Landreth 1991, Namke 1995).

DESCRIPTION

This play therapy technique consists of placing a small fabric doll on the top of a "tower" of plastic containers and smashing the "tower" with a soft ball. The doll can represent anything, from a germ, to a teacher, to an event, to the client himself. The client should state what the doll represents and verbalize anger while throwing the ball. For example, he could say "I hate my teacher!" or "I'm so mad at myself for ———" or I'll never like ——— again!" The therapist reflects the child's content and feelings, saying for example, "You are *really* mad at your teacher."

Building the tower himself and having it stand as sturdily or as precariously as he wants seems to give the child a satisfying sense of control. The added element of the doll placed on top of the tower provides the child with even more control and flexibility.

One more element of this technique is the way these buckets nest into each other and then are sealed with a top. The child can place the doll, the ball, and the buckets inside of this compact space, and then seal the top on them. This seems to give the child a sense that his feelings are safely tucked away in the care of the therapist.

APPLICATIONS

This technique is useful with any children who have difficulty with anger expression. This includes children who suppress angry feelings, as well as those who are overly aggressive. Children who have experienced abuse, trauma, neglect, abandonment, or any other losses will probably be dealing with unresolved anger (Terr 1990).

The presentation and framing of the technique varies depending on the needs of the individual child. A timid, repressed child, for example, may require reassurance that it is permissible to knock down the tower and to yell. The therapist may be called upon to model the anger expression, and the child's beginnings may still be gentle and hesitant.

On the other hand, the aggressive child will need to understand that the purpose of the technique is to "get rid of" their anger safely *in order to help them be able to control themselves "out in the world."* A clear distinction must be made between smashing the Angry Tower for therapeutic purposes and smashing people or property outside of the playroom. They can also be taught that at home they can punch a pillow in their bedroom or throw a ball hard against a wall (where nothing can be damaged).

I used this technique with 7-year-old Michael, whose 2-year-old brother had died several months earlier from leukemia. His parents had recently initiated a lawsuit against the baby's doctors for improper treatment. Therefore, one might expect the typical angry feelings following a death to be exacerbated. However, Michael consistently (over six therapy sessions) denied feeling any anger, both verbally and in his play and drawings.

After more than a month of peaceful play therapy, I presented the tower of buckets as something that he could knock down. Michael, having been quiet and somewhat withdrawn, began hesitantly and awkwardly. With my encouragement, however, he soon began firing the ball into the buckets with great force. After one or two silent tries, he said, "I get mad at those germs that killed my brother!" and threw the ball. He continued doing this for three sessions, with slight variations, growing progressively louder and throwing more violently. It became the first thing he wanted to do when he came into the therapy room.

Eventually he took a soft 4" doll and placed it on top of the Angry Tower, saying, "This is the doctor who gave my brother the wrong medicine!" When he threw the ball at the tower, the "doctor" flew satisfyingly across the room, where Michael proceeded to stomp on him and twist his limbs.

As time went on, Michael became a more relaxed little boy. He was displaying a wider range of feelings at home and at school. It seemed as if a painful constriction within him had finally loosened.

The goal of this technique, as with other expressive therapy techniques, is to allow children to experience and label their anger, so that they can feel it when it arises and express it appropriately.

References

Landreth, G. L. (1991). *Play Therapy.* Muncie, IN: Accelerated Development.

Namka, L. (1995). Angry child but can't talk about it? *Association for Play Therapy Newsletter,* September, p. 14.

Oaklander, V. (1988). *Windows to our Children.* Highland, NY: Gestalt Journal Press.

Terr, L. (1990). *Too Scared to Cry.* New York: Basic Books.

67

Balloons of Anger

Tammy Horn

INTRODUCTION

During the last year, I worked with severely emotionally disturbed children, preschool through elementary school age. The biggest concern we had with these children was all the anger they had inside them, and how to help them work it out in an appropriate way. Throughout the year, in groups and individually, I struggled with how to help these children understand what anger is and what can happen if it is not released from the body properly. Part of the problem was that you can't see anger. The children were able to talk about what made them angry, but still did not seem to understand it. They identified the anger as the aggressive acts they used to release the anger. After trying many different techniques to help the children understand anger, I thought about how I could visually show them anger, and I came up with Balloons of Anger.

It is difficult to help children understand that it is OK to feel angry, but not OK to hit or hurt people or objects when they view anger as acts of aggression. By using balloons, I was able to identify the balloon as the body and the air inside the balloon as anger. This helped give the children a visual picture of anger.

RATIONALE

In this day and age, children of all ages and socioeconomic classes are angry. Children today have to witness and deal with violence, death, divorce, lack of parental involvement due to the need for more parents to be working outside the home, and a general lack of safety and security in their environment. While the feeling of anger is normal and acceptable, children have difficulty understanding and expressing it appropriately. I feel that part of my job as a therapist is to help my clients get in touch with their feelings, express them, and deal with them. Balloons of Anger not only provides a way for children to understand their anger, but through this exercise children are also allowed a way to release their anger in an appropriate way. Stomping and popping balloons enable children to see, hear, and feel their anger, thus allowing them to get in touch with it and express it.

DESCRIPTION

This is a directive anger technique designed to help children understand how anger can build up inside them, how it can explode and hurt themselves or someone else, and how they can release it slowly and safely. It is theory-based in Cognitive Behavior Modification. This technique can be used either individually or in a group setting.

Supplies: Balloons!

1. Have each child blow up a balloon. Then have them tie the balloon, or help them tie it.

    a. explain that the balloon represents the body, and the air inside the balloon represents anger.

    b. ask the children (after the balloon is tied), "Can air get in or out of the balloon?" Ask the children what they think would happen if this anger (air) was stuck inside them? Ask if the balloon was their brain and the anger (air) was inside their head, would there be room to think clearly?

2. Then have the children stomp on the balloon until it explodes and all the air comes out.

a. Ask children if this seems like a safe way to let their anger out. Why/why not? Some children might be afraid of exploding balloons. Talk about this fear.

b. Explain to the children that if the balloon was a person, the explosion of the balloon would be an aggressive act such as hitting a person or object. Ask them if this is a safe way to release anger.

3. Next, have the children blow up another balloon. This time don't tie it, but have them hold on to the end of the balloon so that the air stays inside the balloon. Explain that the balloon is the body, and the air inside represents anger.
4. Have them slowing release some of the air from the balloon and then pinch it closed.

   a. Ask them, "Is the balloon smaller? Did the balloon burst? Does this seem a safer way to let the anger out? Did the balloon stay safe while the anger came out?" Highlight the fact that the balloon stayed safe, and the people around the balloon stayed safe while the anger was released.

5. Have the children repeat this several times until all the air is released from the balloon.

Explain again that the air in the balloon represents anger. By talking about what makes us angry and finding ways to release it appropriately, it comes out slowly and safely. Remind them that if we let anger build up inside us, it can grow and explode like the balloons and we can end up hurting ourselves or someone else. Then go over different ways that they can appropriately and safely release their anger.

Variation: When done, draw a rainbow or have child draw one, and inside each part of the rainbow put a letter and have a child think of a way to safely release anger that starts with that letter.

6. Have them repeat the exercise if needed or until they demonstrate some understanding.

APPLICATIONS

This exercise has been used with aggressive children, ADHD children (due to their problems with impulsivity and aggression), and children who are having a difficult time controlling their tempers. It can also be used with withdrawn children who are having a difficult time expressing their anger and are internalizing it. Note: if withdrawn children won't participate and are in a group, you can have them watch first and participate during a repeat of the activity.

I used this technique with my kindergarten group during a series on anger control. This group on the whole was very aggressive, and this exercise was an attempt to help two of the children who were the most aggressive and the most resistive to talking about anger or participating in any anger control exercises. Everyone in the group chose to participate, and they enjoyed popping the balloons. They agreed it was unsafe when balloon pieces went flying everywhere, and were able to brainstorm different ways they could release their anger without hurting each other or objects in the room.

68

The Worry Can Technique

Debbie S. Jones

INTRODUCTION

Children have many worries that they keep inside themselves. These worries may be at the root of many negative behaviors, including temper tantrums, fears, separation anxiety, and peer conflicts. This activity invites children to identify and discuss their worries with an adult and/or other children.

RATIONALE

According to Strayhorn (1988), a child can learn the psychological skills necessary to become a competent individual. With his technique, Strayhorn identifies skills deficits, and then provides learning groups based on the targeted psychological skills. This learning group focuses on the following targeted psychological skills:

1. Closeness, trusting, relationship building
2. Cognitive processing through words, symbols, and images
3. Dealing with frustration and unfavorable events

4. An adaptive sense of direction and purpose.

Objectives include the patient demonstrating the ability to:

1. Utilize verbal skills
2. Recognize and verbalize one's own feeling
3. Empathize with others
4. Disclose and reveal oneself to another
5. Tolerate a wide range of other people's behaviors
6. Tolerate one's own feelings
7. Enjoy positive attention from others
8. Comply, obey, and submit to reasonable authority
9. Concentrate and attend to tasks
10. Aim towards making circumstances better
11. Initiate social contacts and engage in social conversation.

DESCRIPTION

Materials needed:

used powdered baby formula cans or any other reclosable can, washed and dried thoroughly to prevent rusting

construction paper and typing paper

markers

glue

scissors.

Directions:

1. Cut construction paper in a strip long enough and wide enough to cover the can. (Tip: you may want to prepare this ahead of time when working with a group.)

2. Have the child or children draw "scary things" on one side of the construction paper strip and color them with markers. If the children prefer, they can write down scary words instead.
3. When each child is finished drawing or writing, have him or her glue the strip to the can.
4. Put the lid on the can and make a slot in the top of it using the scissors. The slot should be large enough to put small, folded pieces of paper inside the can.
5. Cut small strips of the typing paper. Each strip must be big enough to write a few words on it.
6. On the strips of paper, have each child write down his or her worries with one worry to a piece of paper.
7. Each child should fold each worry and put it into the can he or she has made.
8. Take turns sharing one worry with his or her peers. Encourage the sharing of support and feedback.

APPLICATIONS

This technique can be used in a small group of 6–8 children or on an individual basis. It can be utilized with a variety of problems, including separation anxiety, explosive disorders, depression, and phobias. Sometimes children, and the adults who love them, don't realize the number of worries that children carry around with them. This concrete exercise can bring these hidden concerns out into the open so that they may be examined and discussed. It also assists the child to determine which worries he has control over and which worries are beyond his control. Once the worries are categorized in this manner, the adult can teach problem-solving skills for those worries the child can control.

Reference

Strayhorn, J. M. (1988). *The Competent Child: An Approach to Psychotherapy and Preventive Mental Health.* New York: Guilford.

69

The Cardboard City

Berrell Mallery and Randall Martin

INTRODUCTION

This chapter will describe the use of large cardboard boxes in the treatment of young children. The materials are inexpensive and easily available, many children find large cardboard boxes appealing and attractive, and boxes lend themselves well to imaginative play. This technique was introduced in a large play space in a school setting, but may be used in offices of various sizes. Dr. Mallery noted that the spontaneous use of boxes in the classroom and hallways by children suggested that these materials could stimulate therapeutic enactments. The boxes may be plain and undefined, encouraging self-generated definitions of the objects, or they may be painted and structured to resemble vehicles (buses, cars, trains, airplanes), dwellings and secret hiding places, costumes or clothing, helmets, monsters, and so on.

RATIONALE

After observing how preschool-aged children gravitate naturally to cardboard boxes as play materials, Dr. Mallery postulated that these boxes could be put to use in play therapy quite effectively. Children seem to turn these simple constructions into imaginative play objects. When the boxes are unadorned and unspecific in nature, they are ideal for children to project themes that are personally meaningful and relevant to their particular life circumstances. Children must summon their imaginative powers to define what the boxes are, allowing the therapist to assess the child's fantasy life, worries, and concerns. More directive therapeutic experiences may be elicited by painting the boxes so they resemble specific things, allowing assistance to less imaginative children, those who are concrete in their thinking, or those with particular phobias and/or apprehensions. For example, a cardboard "bus" was used by one child to "go home," and the "house" was used as if he were really at home. After this enactment, the child was sufficiently refueled to "return" to the therapy session.

The use of large boxes was found to be beneficial while treating children as young as age 2, some of whom did not have sufficient language to communicate existing rich intrapersonal dynamics. The materials may be used for children from preschool through latency age. The boxes provide an avenue for the expression of psychological barriers that interfere with the therapeutic process. Frequently children need to cut themselves off from the therapist and this need can be addressed metaphorically when a child climbs into a box and sets up a physical barrier. Fears can emerge and the child can implore the clinician to help her attain protection from a negative force (such as a monster). Children may then enlist the therapist's help to close the flaps when they are inside, to stand guard, and to negotiate with the "monster" or "bad guys."

For children who are less able to acknowledge their conflicts, either due to insufficient ego strength and/or cognitive limitations, the physical challenges and pleasures of negotiating the boxes is useful. The children are more likely to become engaged through their own initiative. The manipulation of boxes also provides an enjoyable means of gaining mastery over their motor skills and their expressiveness by successfully climbing into, crawling through, and organizing the boxes in their orientation and placement. Often the boxes are bigger than the children and this is a source of great pleasure for them.

DESCRIPTION

This technique is limited only by the range of the user's imagination. Simply having the boxes (or even one box) inspires usage as the children see fit. Boxes which housed large desks, tables, file cabinets, and other furniture are especially useful. For example, a box that was long and opened on one side was used to create a "house." With the opened side facing outwards, the "house" was created with windows strategically painted on the unopened ends and side. Another box with the opened side facing upwards was painted to resemble a bus into which the children would climb. A box with the open side resting on the floor resembled a car with the back end open and small openings cut into the sides representing windows. In addition, open-ended boxes can be used as "tunnels." Some children, especially in groups, like to crawl inside and stay there.

APPLICATIONS

The boxes enhance the therapeutic process especially with children exhibiting:

Learning Disabled, Mentally Retarded, Communication Disorders

Children who know how to play can gain therapeutic benefits from playing with big boxes. They enable expression that is often hindered when children have various limitations in cognitive abilities. These can include communication difficulties due to language disorders, learning disabilities, or global delays in cognitive functioning.

Pervasive Developmental Disorders and Autistic Disorder

This technique has been useful with autistic children. In their aimless wandering they are often drawn to the intrinsic motoric possibilities that each box affords. One boy who was seldom meaningfully engaged by his environment took pleasure in crawling into a box and then "popping out" in a "peek-a-boo" fashion that highlighted his efforts to become interpersonally related. This enactment naturally included a meaningful interaction. He also was often drawn into play with some other boys who were involved with running around the room crawling through one box, climbing in and out of another, and finding the one they wanted, over which they bartered with their peers. This led to an increase in the frequency of his meaningful interactions with the environment and his peers.

ADHD and Disruptive Behavior Disorders

As noted above, these boxes are effective in providing an outlet for active children while also providing structure. Children who easily become aggressive can be more manageable when the boxes are used, making therapeutic processes more available. The boxes are a beneficial tool in treating overly active and unfocused children. Creating "tunnels" and receptacles of various dimensions enables focused "chasing" or "being chased" scenarios. More focused and safer climbing and cathartic activities and common themes of play therapy intermingle well with these engaging primary enactments. One boy lay inside and kicked at the top and sides with full-blown anger and despair. This developed into a collapsed box into which he repeatedly crawled, kicked anew, and rolled around with agonizing moans until he rolled to a more peaceful resting place, after which he played happily and was noticeably "better" when he entered his classroom again.

Resistant and Defensive Attitudes

Young children who are resistant often choose to cut themselves off as literally as they can to make clear to the therapist their need to defend themselves and resist efforts at therapeutic intervention. The boxes allow them to play these themes out metaphorically, which may provide the clinician with an entree to interpret the purpose and meaning of the resistant play.

Separation Anxiety, Selective Mutism, and Anxiety Disorders (including Specific Phobias)

Children who are anxious about separating form significant family members may enact these fears by initially refusing to use the boxes, which would symbolically separate them from others. The clinician can, using successive approximation or modelling, encourage the child to move near to and eventually into the boxes. These changes in the child's stance with the boxes can later be generalized to other separation scenarios as the child becomes more comfortable with the notions of separateness and autonomy.

Children with specific phobias like claustrophobia and social phobia can similarly be encouraged to use the boxes to conquer their fears. Time-tested techniques like systematic desensitization can be undertaken using the boxes painted like the feared object (e. g., elevators, vehicles, etc.). The clinician may model cognitive processes and relaxation techniques while moving towards (and eventually inside) the feared object.

Socially phobic children who become anxious in interpersonal situations can enact their fears using the boxes. Children who are avoidant and do not want other children near them or "bothering" them can enact this. The cardboard barriers afforded by climbing into a box can provide an opportunity for supportively addressing and acknowledging the child's need to find a safe haven from social situations. It can also highlight the child's need to exclude others and isolate herself.

An especially bright but defiant boy (age 4 years, 9 months) initially presented with an inability to trust others and a need to cut himself off emotionally from people. His play with miniature human figures consisted of a little boy killing off all the other people, leaving himself alone. Two months later it was seen as the sign of a tentative attachment when he drew the therapist's room with a barely visible magic marker on black paper. A month after he drew this drawing, his involvement with the largest light-proof box indicated an atypical amount of engagement and trust in the therapist. He imaginatively and urgently enlisted the therapist's help in a dramatic, whispered voice asking the therapist to protect him from "them." He asked her to close the flap and whispered a multitude of instructions of what to tell "them" so "they" would go away. This enabled a meaningful dialogue about fears, threats, and ways of feeling protected.

70

Fortune Tellers

Judith Friedman Babcock

INTRODUCTION

Paper fortune tellers are a common toy that children have been making for at least thirty-five years. I don't know where or when they originated. They were popular when I was in grade school, and are still popular now that I have a grade-school child. When my son brought one home from school, anxious to tell me my fortune, I had the idea to use them in my sessions with the grade-school children I treat. I have found it to be a technique they enjoy.

RATIONALE

Fortune tellers may be useful in several ways. First of all, in the process of making the children acknowledge and express what their wishes, hopes, and sometimes, fears are. The therapist can write fortunes that suggest new wishes. For example, a therapist may include fortunes such as, "You will do well on your report card," or "You will make a new friend."

I believe that one of the reasons children enjoy playing with the fortune tellers is that they are somewhat superstitious. They partially believe that the fortunes they get are likely to come true. It gives them hope. I have found that children will usually continue to play with the fortune tellers outside of the session. This extends the benefit of the therapy hour.

DESCRIPTION

All that is needed to make a fortune teller is a piece of square paper, which is blank on both sides, and a pen or pencil. A piece of paper that is 8½" by 11" can easily be folded and cut or torn into a 8½" square (see figure 6-1). Start by folding the corners of the square piece of paper so that the four corners almost meet in the center of the page. It should look like four triangles fit together to make a square. Make sure that the triangles do not overlap each other. Now turn the paper over and do the same on the other side. Once again, make sure the triangles do not overlap each other. Now, turn the paper over. You should have four squares on the other side. Write a color on each square. Let the child pick his favorite colors to use. Turn the fortune teller over again. Write a small number of each flap of paper, one on both sides of each triangle, for a total of eight numbers. Now, under each of the eight numbers, you and the child can write a fortune. When everything is written on the fortune teller, fold and unfold it horizontally and vertically. Now insert your thumb and index finger under the squares that have the colors written on them. Ask the child to pick a color. Open and close the fortune teller one time for each letter in the color. Each time you open it, open it in a different direction, revealing different numbers. Now show the child the four numbers the fortune teller is open to. Ask her to choose one. Lift the flap under that number and read the fortune. (Some children might play that you open and close the fortune teller that many times again before choosing a fortune).

While choosing fortunes with the child, you can easily use this as a starting point to discuss what is possible and what isn't. In some cases you can discuss what the child may be able to do to make his wishes come true.

Some children, especially if they plan to use the fortune teller with their peers after the session, may want to write fortunes such as "You are ugly." This may be a good lead-in to discussions about social skills, and friendships. For therapists who see children in a school setting, you may want to ask the children not to use them during class. Teachers may find them distracting.

You may wish to instruct the child to use it at home with his family. This may be an easy way of improving communication between them and extending the therapy hour.

APPLICATIONS

I have found this technique useful with school-aged children, ages 6–11. It is most helpful with children who feel defeated and need encouragement to imagine that things can be better. It is useful in the early stages of therapy, to help in establishing rapport and in learning what the child's wishes and fears are. It may also be helpful to some children who need help making friends. They can use the fortune teller as an ice breaker at recess.

The fortune teller technique was used with Peter, an 11-year-old boy, during our fourth counseling session. Peter invited his friend, Jimmy, to come to the session with him. The counseling was school-based. Both boys were very angry that day at a teacher, Mrs. C., who kept them after school the day before. They beat a pillow that had a face drawn on it during the first part of the session. When they felt calmer, we discussed what had happened in class; then the three of us made a fortune teller together.

I introduced the fortune teller as something we would use in the session and that they could take with them. Peter and Jimmy made up the following fortunes, which provided me with insight into their fears:

> You are going to get beat up after school.
>
> You will get expelled.
>
> You won't go on the field trip.
>
> Somebody ugly likes you.

They then decided they needed some good fortunes. I suggested the following, which we used:

> You will get straight A's.

They added:

> Somebody pretty likes you.
>
> Mrs. C. will be nice.
>
> You will win the lottery.

Peter asked if these fortunes would really come true? I asked what he thought, and he said that he didn't think so.

I then told Peter's fortune. He got "Somebody ugly likes you." He laughed. I told Jimmy's fortune. He got "Somebody pretty likes you," and laughed. I told Peter's fortune again. He got "Mrs. C. will be nice." We ended the session on that note. They had come in furious at her and left with hope that things would get better between them. Both boys behaved much better for the next few weeks.

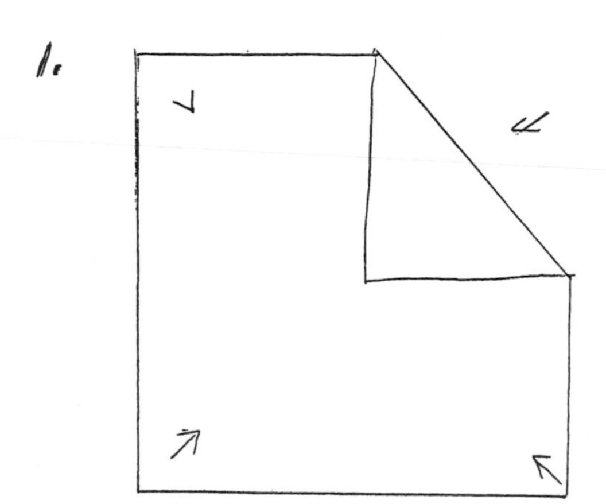

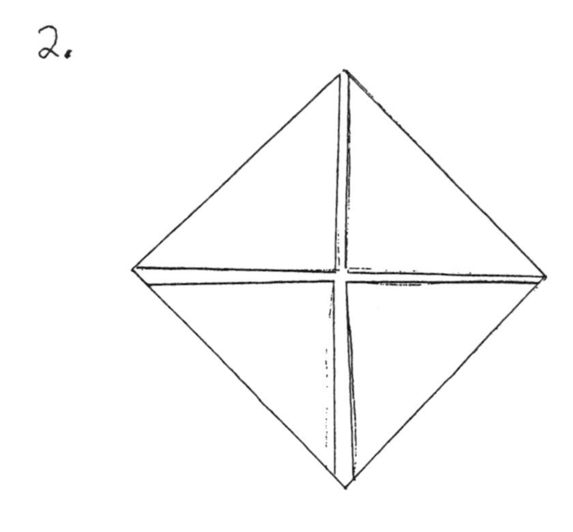

Figure 6–1

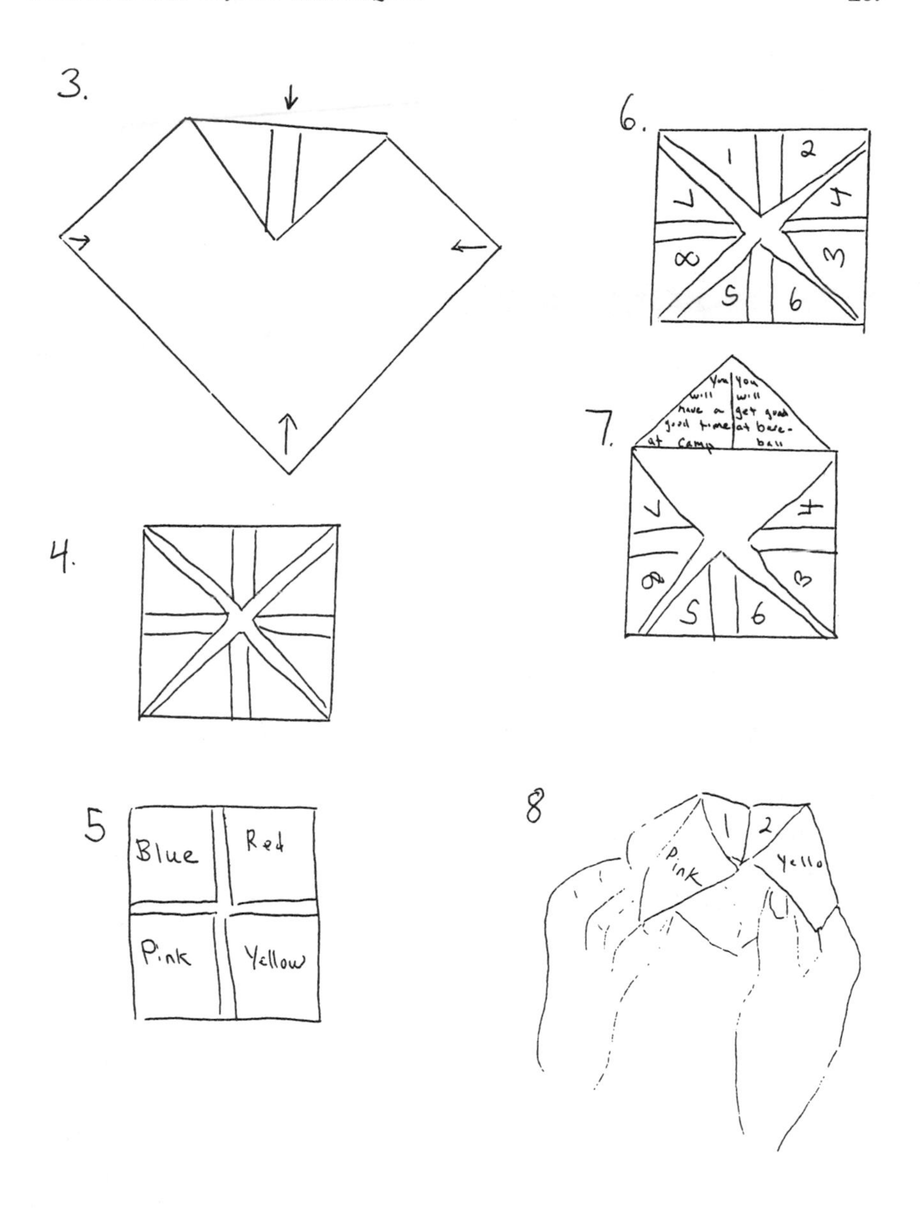

Figure 6–1 (continued)

71

Jenga and a Camera

Catherine G. Tierney

INTRODUCTION

The primary goal of a Special Education Day Program for emotionally disturbed children is to increase each child's cognitive, social, and emotional functioning. As maturation and growth occur the aim is to return the student to the mainstream or to a less restrictive environment. Landreth (1983) writes "The basic rationale for utilizing a play therapy program in schools is to maximize children's learning opportunities by helping them work out problems which interfere with learning" (p. 201).

RATIONALE

It has been my experience that Milton Bradley's Jenga game is beneficial for students, aged 5 to 17, in various ways. Used in structure display, Jenga helps develop fine motor skills, increases impulse control and task oriented behavior, builds self-esteem and competence, encourages acceptance of rules, and allows the therapist to model losing as well as winning.

Landreth (1993) also states that, "Children's free play is an expression of what they want to do, and when they play freely and without direction, they are expressing and releasing the feelings and attitudes that have been pushing to get out into the open" (p. 51). I prefer to work using a client-centered, unstructured approach that focuses on free play. Landreth (1991) states, "Children may have considerable difficulty in trying to tell what they feel or how they have been affected by what they have experienced, but if permitted, in the presence of a caring, sensitive, and empathic adult, will show what they feel through the toys and material they choose, what they do with and to the materials, and the story acted out" (p. 51).

APPLICATIONS

The following cases illustrate how children use Jenga in their own unique ways. A latency-aged male from a chaotic household used the Jenga blocks to build escape stairs from a second floor dollhouse window (which represented his bedroom window) to the safety of a nearby castle.

A depressed, paranoid, ADHD adolescent in inpatient and outpatient treatment since 2½ years of age was unable to trust and needed to be in control. During the initial phase of his treatment, he engaged in solo play with Jenga over a period of weeks as he attempted to break his own record, only looking to me for admiration. While building, he was less resistant to discussing his life, past and present. Finally satisfied with his highest tower, he excitedly requested I take a picture of him with his tower. He wanted to hang his picture on my wall, next to that of a former student. After this session, his depression began to lift, and we entered the middle phase of treatment.

A 12-year-old utilized Jenga in a symbolic cathartic manner. The child had diagnoses of hypomania and encopresis with a history of severe neglect, homelessness, many losses, and various levels of placement over time. Since many social service agencies were actively involved in this case, my primary focus was on school related issues. A primary therapist had been engaged in individual and family treatment for over three years and a caseworker was making frequent home visits since the child's return to home from placement.

Child: ——— is leaving for another job and ——— can't see me anymore. [He explained what he had been told by the therapist and the caseworker].

Therapist: Oh! You're losing two special people at once!

The child responded with rationalizations of why each worker couldn't see him. Resistant to the feelings that were beginning to surface, and to defend against further comments from me, he took the Jenga blocks from the side of my desk and set up the tower between us. As we played, I began to help his pieces out of their former position and he did the same with mine. This was a form of cooperative play we had established in earlier sessions. Eventually the tower fell.

The student suddenly began to set up the blocks in an unstructured manner, forming a foundation with some small cracks in it. I began to put up corresponding blocks on my side of the new structure. The structure began to change—two big openings were clearly visible and, after a few more layers of block were added, he topped off the structure with a little plastic male figure.

He went to the other side of the room, picked up a foam ball and said:

Child: Watch out!

Therapist: What are you going to do?

Child: You'll see. [pause] Wait, can you take a picture of it?

Therapist: Sure. [I opened my desk, found the camera and took a picture.]

Let me take another picture from this side.

The student ran across the room to be in the second picture but became self-conscious and partially hid behind my desk. Returning to the other side of the room, he toppled the structure with the foam ball.

Over the years, it has become evident that photographs have symbolic meaning for some children. Given the option of taking a picture home, all have requested I add it to my office display. Recently, before going to college, a young man returned to visit after four successful years in his local high school. Although I am now in a different office, his picture is still displayed—he knows he is remembered.

References

Axline, V. (1969). *Play Therapy.* New York: Ballantine.

Ginsburg, B. G. (1993). *Catharsis.* In *The Therapeutic Powers of Play*. ed. C. E. Schaefer. Northvale, NJ: Jason Aronson

Landreth, G. L. (1983). Play therapy in elementary school settings. In *Handbook of Play Therapy*, ed. C. E. Schaefer and K. O'Connor. New York: Wiley.

——— (1991). *Play Therapy: The Art of the Relationship*. Muncie, IN: Accelerated Development.

——— (1993). Self-expressive communication. In *The Therapeutic Powers of Play*, ed. C. E. Schaefer. Northvale, NJ: Jason Aronson.

72

The Anger Shield

Teresa A. Glatthorn

INTRODUCTION

The Anger Shield is designed to help clients visualize and experience in an emotional and tactile mode the protective role of anger. It also allows clients to explore the myriad of ways that anger is expressed and the variety of situations in which they might get angry. Finally, it begins an exploration of what the anger protects them from and prepares clients for discussion of alternatives to an anger response, including ways to manage situations to prevent similar difficulties.

RATIONALE

Many clients present with difficulties relating to anger. Some act out or express anger inappropriately. Others turn it in on themselves and become depressed.

Listeners are not generally accepting of open expressions of anger. Furthermore, people are less able to listen to what is said in anger (Faber and Mazlish 1980, Lerner 1985). In addition, research is showing that venting of anger often increases the anger, hostility, and aggression, and solidifies the angry attitude rather than diffusing it (McKay et al. 1989).

Children (and adults) need to learn that anger is not a primary feeling. It is a learned protective response to shield a person from other emotions and difficulties. It can therefore be used as a warning signal. Clients benefit from learning the functions of their own anger and the emotions and stresses from which it protects them (Lerner 1985, McKay et al. 1989).

Once clients have learned the functions and sources of their anger, they need to be encouraged to express their primary feelings appropriately, rather than the anger itself. Clients can then be empowered to take responsibility for their anger. They can learn to problem-solve and/or work with others or change something themselves to make the situation better (Lerner 1985; McKay et al. 1989).

Metaphor is a powerful way to approach this teaching for several reasons. Hands-on metaphorical anger work is more interesting and less threatening than traditional approaches . It accesses the unconscious and speaks to clients of all ages in an understandable language. The lessons also last longer because they are stored in the unconscious and the learning involves more than one sensory modality (Barker 1985, Gil 1991, Mills and Crowley 1986).

DESCRIPTION

An age-appropriate introduction and summary of the main points indicated above in the rationale are provided. The client is then invited to make representations of anger on the outside of his or her shield (a large, pre-cut piece of cardboard) using markers, paints, crayons, magazines, comics, and glue. This can include what "causes" anger, what angry faces look like, what happens when someone is angry, what is said when someone is angry, and so on. Discussion of these aspects ensues during their creation.

On the inside of the shield, clients are encouraged to make representations of the feelings that come just before someone gets angry (i. e., hurt, sad, left-out, abandoned, disappointed) in the same manner as they did for the angry feelings. This discussion, which often begins with a brief self-disclosure or example, leads to a better understanding of the precursors to the client's anger.

APPLICATIONS

The Anger Shield is an appropriate activity for clients approximately 7 years of age and older, including groups and families as well as individuals. It is appropriate at the stage of therapy when the client is ready to develop this understanding in order to find a more empowering manner of managing his or her anger. It may not be appropriate for clients who are just beginning to experience anger for the first time, such as with incest survivors who are just beginning to get in touch with feelings about a non-protective parent; or depressed clients who are beginning to turn their anger outward (although it may be helpful later), or clients who, for any reason, are not ready to let go of anger as their defense.

Shawn was a very timid and anxious 8-year-old boy living in foster care. In the foster home, Shawn would act out in anger whenever he felt disappointed, hurt, frustrated, anxious, misunderstood, embarrassed, or jealous. A behavior program was initiated regarding his acting out. However, Shawn also needed to develop an understanding of his anger and learn alternative ways of managing it.

On the outside of Shawn's Anger Shield, he drew pictures of angry faces, fire, and smoke. He glued on magazine and comic pictures of situations depicting angry adults, children squabbling, words often said in anger, and people hitting and kicking one another. He also drew a monster character. During this activity, he talked of some of the times when he had gotten angry or others had gotten angry with him and how the anger was expressed. He talked about feeling strong when he felt like an "angry monster."

Shawn and the therapist reviewed some of the situations which "caused" his anger. They discussed what else he might have been feeling at those times and validated those feelings. On the inside of his shield, Shawn copied feeling faces from a poster representing some of his emotions. He glued on pictures of situations involving anxiety, frustration, jealousy, embarrassment, sadness, and other emotions. He added words associated with those feelings and words that can precipitate those feelings.

Shawn was very animated during this project. Upon completion, he immediately made a handle for it and a sword. He then literally strutted around the outside of the building six or seven times whacking at weeds and talking of times when he felt strong and protected. This is in contrast to his usual fearful approach to the outdoors in which he worried constantly about any dangers lurking. Shawn was very much in touch with the strength associated with the protective aspects of his anger and enjoyed honoring that.

In sessions following this activity, Shawn discussed recent episodes of anger and the more vulnerable feelings associated with the incident, referring to the metaphor of the shield. He became increasingly more able to recognize and label these feelings and to express them to his foster parents at the time of the incident or soon thereafter. He experienced a positive response from his foster parents about his type of expression, which further reinforced his style of communicating. Shawn was also taught other skills including relaxation, physical outlets for frustration, artistic self-expression, positive ways to gain attention, and assertiveness. He learned that these also could be used as armor to protect from hurtful feelings. He began to prefer the results using this new "armor" to using anger in many circumstances. He also gained a healthier form of strength and became less anxious.

References

Barker, P. (1985). *Using Metaphors in Psychotherapy*. New York: Brunner/Mazel.

Faber, A., and Mazlish, E. (1980). *How to Talk So Kids Will Listen and Listen So Kids Will Talk*. New York: Avon.

Gil, E. (1991). *The Healing Power of Play*. New York: Guilford.

Lerner, H. G. (1985). *The Dance of Anger*. New York: Harper & Row.

McKay, M., Rogers, P. D., and McKay, J. (1989). *When Anger Hurts*. Oakland, CA: New Harbinger.

Mills, J. C., and Crowley, R. J. (1986). *Therapeutic Metaphors for Children*. New York: Brunner/Mazel.

73

Using Self-Made Books to Prepare Children for Predictable Trauma or Crisis

Kevin O'Connor

INTRODUCTION

Within Ecosystemic Play Therapy, the modality practiced by the author, the primary goal of treatment is to help a child learn new and effective strategies for getting his or her needs met in ways that do not interfere with others getting their needs met. Children who exhibit problem behavior or emotional distress are seen as unable to get their needs met in ways that are both effective and socially acceptable. To resolve this problem the child and the play therapist must identify the child's needs, identify current factors that prevent those needs from being met, and then identify and master effective new strategies that the child can use to get those needs met. Alternatively, the therapist may need to find ways that the environment or those in it can be more effective in recognizing and addressing the child's needs.

RATIONALE

The majority of the time play therapy is an intervention that does not occur until after children are having difficulty getting their needs met and have developed symptoms or behavior that they or others find problematic. One of the most positive experiences a play therapist and a child client can have is that of undertaking a course of play therapy to *prevent* the development of symptoms. The opportunity for this type of intervention arises when the trauma a child will face can be predicted. In these cases the children can be inoculated against the stresses about to be faced and provided with an array of coping strategies that will allow them to continue to get their needs met in spite of the crises. Predictable crises include such things as the birth of a sibling, a family move, a change of schools, or, as will be discussed here, elective surgery.

DESCRIPTION

Creating a crisis/trauma-related book with the child in the play therapy sessions can be an excellent way to make both the traumatic event and the strategies for coping with it concrete. The ways in which this can be accomplished are as varied as the situations, children, and therapists who are involved. Rather than describe specific techniques or rules for creating the books it seems more expedient to describe a specific case in which the technique was used.

APPLICATIONS

Cory was a 3-year-old child facing surgery to replace his eardrums. While this surgery is relatively minor and typically not very painful it had the potential to be very traumatic for Cory because of the context in which it was occurring. Cory had lost his eardrums at about 20 months of age subsequent to violent, life-threatening abuse by his babysitter. As a complication of the abuse and the loss of his eardrums, Cory's language development was significantly delayed.

Cory was first brought to therapy by his parents when he was about 26 months old because he was frequently aggressive towards his sister (who was not abused by the sitter) and toward the family dog. A relatively brief course of treatment was effective in identifying Cory's underlying anger, his difficulty communicating it effectively, and his fear that his parents might let the abuse happen again. The parents were very effective in responding to Cory's needs, and his symptoms and behavior resolved quickly.

Consistent with their increased ability to read and respond to Cory's needs relative to his abuse experience, they recognized that there was a significant chance that he would misinterpret the surgery as further abuse. In response they arranged for two play therapy sessions to prepare him. Both Cory and his mother attended both of the preparatory sessions. During both sessions Cory, his mother, and the therapist engaged in three tasks. The therapist used Playmobil figures and the Playmobil surgical play set to demonstrate the process of Cory's surgery to him. Later, Cory was engaged in acting out the part of the surgeon in these pretend surgeries. All three engaged in various pretend and game activities related to the surgery, such as pretending to administer anesthesia to each other. Last, the therapist engaged Cory in creating a surgical coloring book.

Prior to the first session the therapist contacted the surgeon and got as complete a description of what Cory's experience of the surgery would be. Every aspect was covered, from the pre-surgical restrictions (not eating after midnight the night before, although the surgery wasn't scheduled until noon the next day), pre-surgical anesthesia, the post-surgical recovery process, and the long-term prognosis.

The book itself was 6 pages long, with drawings completed by the therapist and text created by Cory, his mother, and the therapist. It was set up as a coloring book so that Cory and his mother could take it with them and color in each page as the situation it depicted was encountered. The pages and their contents are described in Table 6-1.

PAGE	PICTURE	TEXT
1	Boy with hearing aids looking sad; a glass and a bowl each with a red "X" over them.	No food, no drinks = no throwing up!
2	Boy and mother in hospital playroom.	I'm still hungry but now there are toys to play with.
3	Boy's face with hearing aids and bottle of nasal spray in nose.	Nose medicine . . . WEIRD!
4	Boy on operating table with doctor in background.	While the medicine makes me stay asleep the doctor puts in a new eardrum.
5	Boy's face with big bandages over each ear but no hearing aids.	Wow, what a big bandage. I have an earache but at least now I get to EAT!
6	Boy's face smiling. No hearing aids.	No more bandage. No more hearing aids. YEAH!

Table 6–1.

During the first session, Cory made it clear that the part of this experience he feared the most was the administration of the pre-surgical anesthesia via injection. He was so anxious about this idea that he refused to entertain even the possibility of having the surgery. The therapist contacted the anesthesiologist between the first and second sessions and relayed both a portion of Cory's history and his extreme fear of injections. With some encouragement from the therapist the anesthesiologist agreed to use a pre-surgical anesthesia that was administered via a nasal spray rather than via injection.

At the second play session, the first part of the coloring book was amended to show the change in anesthesia. While Cory was greatly relieved he decided he did not want anybody spraying anything up his nose, either. At this point the therapist introduced a "nose spray" game. Two flexible, plastic baby bottles half-filled with water became the nose spray bottles. Cory and the therapist chased each other around the playroom trying to hit each other in the nose with the stream of water from their bottles. At the same time the therapist made it clear that Cory could choose between a shot and the nose spray, but that if he did not choose his parents would make the choice for him. After a little while Cory readily agreed to the nose spray as he seemed to have transformed it through the game from something dangerous to something very silly.

During the second session the coloring book was completed and given to Cory's mother to take with her and Cory through the surgery process. Additionally, further role playing and pretend demonstrations of the surgery were completed. At the end of the session the therapist gave Cory a get-well card to be opened only after the surgery and a follow-up session was scheduled for about one week after the operation.

On follow-up, Cory's mother reported that he had managed all aspects of the process very well except for one problem. We had neglected to include the fact that he would have to put on pajamas at the hospital in the coloring book. Cory had been furious at being asked to put on pajamas so shortly after having gotten up and seemed to equate it with being punished by being sent to bed early. Although the mother was able to manage this outburst it could have been avoided if it had been included in the preparatory sessions.

Play therapy and the creation of highly personal and specific books can be an excellent way to prepare children for predictable crises and trauma in their lives. Therapists who wish to use this technique must educate themselves as to the nature of the crisis or trauma, and its potential interaction with the child's developmental level and with the other persons or systems who will be involved. Good consultation skills will greatly enhance the process. The overall goal is to educate the child to the nature of the coming event, and to provide him or her with some strategies for maintaining a sense of control during the event and for coping with the stresses and anxieties that will arise as the event unfolds.

Reference

Ziegler, R. (1992). *Homemade Books to Help Kids Cope.* New York: Magination Press.

74

The Angry Feeling Scale Game

Joyce Meagher

INTRODUCTION

In fifteen years of doing play therapy, I have consistently seen that children have difficulty distinguishing ranges of emotion, especially anger. Thus, intensity of reaction to various levels of situations is often similar, or impulsive, because of previously learned styles of coping. I wanted to create a way for children to scale irritations, frustrations, and really angry feelings, and learn to intervene earlier in the cycle before out-of-control reactions occur.

I used beanbags thrown at a target with different intensity as a way to make levels of anger visual for the child.

RATIONALE

Children learn best from experience. Different learning styles can be accommodated by discussing, showing, and doing in this game. It is an easy game to play in any setting. It is nonthreatening because the therapist plays along and can role model healthy expression of levels of anger in a safe environment.

DESCRIPTION

A target is drawn on my whiteboard if the child has a particular issue that is upsetting him, or any hard surface can be used as a general target (a wall, a cupboard, a blackboard). The hard surface repels the beanbag with intensity equal to that with which the beanbag was thrown.

The child and I discuss how irritation is a small feeling of anger, and I throw the bag softly at the target in turn with the child, as we think of things that bother us each a little (i. e., "I get irritated when . . ."). Then we take turns throwing the beanbag moderately hard to practice, "I feel frustrated when . . ." Finally, we throw the beanbag hard and verbalize, "I feel angry when . . ." Ways to identify the earlier feeling of irritation are discussed (i. e., how does the child's body first tighten up when irritation starts?). Relaxation methods to combat irritation, frustration, and anger are all discussed. The goal is to create earlier identification and earlier resolution of upset feelings.

APPLICATIONS

This technique works especially well with aggressive, explosive, and impulsive children (such as children with ADHD). It helps them regain control of their actions and self-esteem.

One client recently drew a picture of his younger sister and then practiced identifying the different times when he felt irritated, frustrated, or angry in dealing with her. He was able to identify that his chest felt tight early on when irritated, and found ways to relax the tightness so as to deescalate his reactions to her.

75

Stomping Feet and Bubble Popping

Cathy Wunderlich

INTRODUCTION

This technique was introduced to younger elementary students who were having a difficult time expressing anger or frustration in ways that did not involve aggressive physical contact with other students. Their numbers seemed to grow on a daily basis in spite of the fact that teachers would explain that hurting someone else was against the rules, in spite of behavior charts, in spite of missed recesses. We began with Stomping Feet and soon introduced Bubble Popping to serve children in settings where the former technique proved too noisy.

RATIONALE

Using this technique allows children to hear that anger and frustration are OK, in fact very normal parts of life. It is how we let them "out of the pot" that often brings trouble. Stomping Feet and Bubble Popping allow the child to express those emotions in a way that releases the pressures in a socially acceptable manner. The child is given the concrete tools to express himself or herself and not just admonished to keep "in control." A harmful solution to problems is replaced with a life-coping skill.

DESCRIPTION

Stomping Feet are tagboard outlines of the child's own feet spread slightly apart. The child is allowed to color those feet in whatever manner he or she chooses. We then talk about how important it is to let anger come out so we can get on with our work or play. This is best done, I explain, by stomping fast and hard in a place right by our drawing. Usually we know when the anger is out because we not only feel better, but the bottoms of our feet get warm. That is a sure sign that you are almost finished stomping. Then we try it together (keep a pair of tennis shoes handy). When one of us pauses (I'm a lot older, so it's usually me), I turn my head sideways, as if trying to notice something. I ask the child if he can feel the bottoms of his feet feeling warmer. If the answer is no, then I say that we must not have stomped hard or fast enough and we go again. Hopefully, we arrive at the point (before I fall over in a dead heap) where the child agrees. This is the time to be very dramatic. I always ask if the angry feeling doesn't seem to be slipping out of our bodies, down through our feet, and out on the floor. Ask how his body feels (talk about taking deep breaths and feeling "softer" inside now than when he was angry, anything to help him visualize the anger being gone). Then the child draws a mad face at the top of the shoe and a happy face at the bottom. The instructions are to use Stomping Feet the next time anger sets in and stomp until his face looks happy. Some teachers have incorporated a "Stomping Corner" in their classrooms where children can stomp out their anger before it does damage.

Bubble Popping is an anger control tool that uses plastic bubble wrap from packages. It is helpful where Stomping Feet noises would not be appropriate. I ask the child to get rid of the anger by popping ten bubbles from the wrap. I then ask them if they can feel how that anger comes out of their "pointer and thumb." When it comes out correctly, a bubble pops. Usually after ten bubbles anger seems to be gone. Sometimes it takes more if we are really angry and sometimes it takes less. Then we talk about the anger going up in the air when the bubble pops, allowing us to feel calm again.

Usually after trying these techniques and getting the child calmed down, we are better able to talk about what the problem was that caused the anger. Then we can deal with making things right again.

This is a tool that I like to explain to parents for use at home as a model for all of their children. I have also had teachers use it in the classroom. Children need to see adults model "okay" ways of being mad.

APPLICATIONS

I have used these techniques with children who have a difficult time controlling anger and frustration. I have used the Stomping Feet with younger elementary students. I have used Bubble Popping with elementary through junior-high age.

One first grader was taught Bubble Popping. After we worked on that for a few weeks, he came in and wanted to write a story on my computer. It was about a little boy who "used to get really mad until a little bird came and sat on his shoulder. The little bird told him to pop bubbles when he got mad. The little boy was happy then. The end."

76

Knocking Down the Walls of Anger

Jennifer Leonetti

INTRODUCTION

One of the primary foci when working with children in play-focused therapy is to help them identify and express their feelings about a variety of issues. Frequently, this is an overwhelming and threatening process due to the powerful content. Many children become accustomed to reacting and expressing themselves in particular ways in order to adapt to abuse, neglect, and/or abandonment (e. g., suppression of emotional content, projection). Eventually, however, this mode of adaptation may interfere with other aspects of their lives as they develop and grow, requiring the need for intervention. Although the goal in therapy is to help the child learn new, more adaptive ways of relating and expressing her or himself, previous ways of adapting are often difficult for the child to relinquish, as these are all the child knows.

RATIONALE

Play therapy techniques that allow the child to express threatening feelings (e. g., anger) in a safe, nonthreatening context expose the child to alternative ways of expression without overwhelming her or him. The technique presented is designed to accomplish this task by incorporating verbal expression of feelings into a physical game that can involve the child alone or the child and the therapist. There is a lot of potential for using this technique in different ways and with different populations. It can be used to help the child express numerous feelings about one particular event, or to elicit feelings in a temporal manner, helping the child transition from discussing feelings related to recent or past events. In addition, depending on the child's ability to abstract, the therapist can identify "the wall" as a particular feeling, for example, anger related to abuse, and it is the child's task to destroy that wall of anger. By conceptualizing this technique as a metaphor, interpretive material and the therapeutic process can be enhanced, and most importantly the therapist becomes aware that the child's wall of anger, loneliness, grief, whatever the predominant feeling may be, can be knocked down slowly by expressing those feelings in physical and emotional ways through safe play. Finally, this activity becomes a catalyst for increased verbalizations. Because the game requires a verbal component, the child becomes accustomed to associating verbal expression with physical and emotional experiences.

DESCRIPTION

A medium-sized rubber ball and cardboard bricks or other type of lightweight building materials (e. g., cardboard boxes, blocks) are the only items needed. (The cardboard bricks can be ordered from Lillian Vernon.)

Prior to introducing the technique, a discussion about feeling states and helping the child identify the basics is important as you will be laying the foundation for further exploration of specific feelings. You may be in the stage of therapy where you have identified those feelings that are most intense for the child, and this provides an opportunity to suggest a fun way to express those feelings. The first step is to introduce the experience of kicking the ball against the wall as hard as the child can. This is relatively nonthreatening as it does not entail verbal interaction. Safety rules should be introduced at this time, though kept to a minimum so the child does not feel constricted. The child may need reassurance that it is okay for her or him to kick the ball against the wall. This can be accomplished by the therapist demonstrating this process while supporting the child's attempts to kick the ball. Eventually, structures and walls can be built with cardboard bricks, blocks, or boxes with the goal of knocking down these structures. This can be introduced with an enthusiastic, "Hey, we're getting pretty good at kicking this ball against the wall, now let's see if we can knock down a wall!"

Once the child is comfortable with the physical component, the verbal component is integrated slowly. Before the child is asked to interact verbally, this can be initiated by making basic, nonthreatening interpretations of observations regarding the child's feelings, behavior, and motives as she or he is kicking the ball. These interpretations may be centered around the intensity of the child's physical exertion and facial expressions, if verbalizations are limited, or comments she or he makes. The goal is to facilitate the child's acknowledgement and acceptance of her or his feelings, so she or he can then identify from where her or his feelings are stemming and therefore effectively address them. The therapist explains that the last part of the game is to state one thing that makes the child angry (eventually introducing sad, frustrating, lonely feelings, etc.) before kicking the ball as hard as she or he can. This aspect of the game should be explained as a rule: the child has to state one thing that makes her or him angry, with the words "I feel angry . . ." before she or he can kick the ball (e. g., "I feel angry when someone lies to me"). This can be encouraged by helping the child to visualize those angry feelings shooting out of her or his body through her or his toes into the ball (e. g., "Let's use those feelings to kick the ball the hardest ever. Send those feelings out your toes so the ball will hit that wall hard!"). As the child is stating those things that makes her or him angry, she or he is attempting to kick down the structure built by her or him and the therapist. After each attempt to knock down the structure, the ball is retrieved so the child has another opportunity to destroy the wall. As the child expresses those things that make her or him angry, sad, frustrated, and so on, there may be the opportunity for further interpretation. Initially, this should be kept to a minimum, as the game is devised to provide a nonthreatening medium of expression. As the child becomes more comfortable, increased interpretation may be appropriate. The level of interpretation utilized with this technique will depend on the therapist's training, the stage of the therapeutic relationship, and the client: where she or he is developmentally and therapeutically (where she or he is in the working through of threatening feelings).

APPLICATIONS

This technique can be used with most children who have difficulty expressing their emotions, and has been found effective with emotionally or physically restricted children. Due to the physical nature of the activity, children who may exhibit a limited range of motion, or who are withdrawn, may benefit from this technique as well. Nevertheless, this activity requires some coordination, so it may be frustrating for those children who have increased difficulties in this area. This technique may not be appropriate for aggressive children or for those who require increased external control and structure to behave acceptably, though modifications can certainly be made so that the technique is tailored to the child.

This technique was created and implemented while I was working with a bright, 9-year-old girl to help her appropriately express intense feelings of anger related to the abandonment and neglect by her mother, as well as physical and emotional abuse perpetrated by her mother's boyfriends. She demonstrated strong cognitive control when discussing her feelings related to past abusive experiences, and had a tendency to avoid these discussions altogether. She enjoyed being active in session, so this technique was particularly appealing to her and was effective in eliciting her anger.

The technique was presented to her as a game: a way to physically release her anger, and a way to eventually verbalize her angry feelings (the verbal component was introduced so she knew what to expect, though she was told it would come later after she was comfortable with the game). She was quick to kick the ball against the wall, and enthusiastic when I introduced the cardboard bricks. The verbal component was not met with too much resistance as it was slowly incorporated into the already established game. We began by taking turns and making general statements about what made us angry. When it was my turn, I addressed content that was applicable to her situation, which was often met with, "Yeah, that's a good one," or "Can I use that one, too?" As she had a tendency to suppress her feelings, this seemed to help her identify those situations that had made her angry and help her begin to release the anger associated with these experiences. Within the game, we transitioned to using situations that made us angry during the week, and then to addressing past experiences. She recounted situations and experiences from the past that she had not discussed previously. Many of these focused on her anger toward her mother for leaving her and not protecting her. I eventually had her view the wall as the feeling itself. Prior to this, we discussed how feelings get so bottled up they become a barrier or a wall to such things as feeling good and being close to friends and family members. I then acknowledged how hard it was to express painful feelings, but by doing that, as in her play, she was slowing knocking down her wall of anger, so she could begin to interact more positively. Eventually it got to the point where she would pick up the ball voluntarily and kick it against the wall when she needed to express anger. I always encouraged her to verbalize what she was feeling while she was playing the game, which subsequently increased her verbalizations during therapy. The process evolved from my instigating the game each session, to her picking up the ball when she was experiencing overwhelming feeling states, to her telling me about her feeling states. The need for the game diminished as she became more accustomed to verbalizing her feeling her present and past experiences.

77

Figures

Sylvia Fisher

INTRODUCTION

My experience as a former preschool teacher led me to specialize my clinical practice in working with children. I also received extensive training in sandplay therapy with Dora Kalff. Figures and small objects were a natural part of my office playroom.

In addition to the many shelves of figures, I also have some objects in baskets lined up on the floor under the shelves. The figures include cartoon characters, spiritual figures, "ordinary" people, mythical images, and real and imaginary animals. The figures are made of various materials: molded rubber, plastic, porcelain, glass, brass, ceramics, and wood.

RATIONALE

Most children are automatically drawn to the shelves and begin playing with the objects and figures on the floor or in the sand tray. These children create their fantasies or reenact their experiences with or without talking about it.

Some children may be overwhelmed by the number of toys, the orderliness of the shelves, and the unfamiliar experience of an adult having toys to play with. Some children find it difficult to initiate the play and may sit on the floor with their back turned to the shelves. Others simply do not know where to begin and have trouble focusing.

Some children are unclear about the expectations of play therapy and their role and therefore ask me to make choices about how we spend the session.

When certain emotional issues are difficult to express due to language limitations, conceptualization, or developmental considerations, the following technique may be helpful.

Figures are used as the vehicle of expression for the child. Each figure chosen represents a specific person who then interacts with other figures. The child provides all the dialogue and movement, unless the therapist is directed to move or speak for a figure. In this way, the child is the master of the universe, orchestrating the drama in a safe and protected environment. The inner voice is now externalized with no real-life consequences, and emotional expression is actualized through the figures.

DESCRIPTION

The most important step in therapy is establishing trust. The client must feel safe with the therapist and be able to develop a positive rapport. Once the therapeutic relationship begins, it is easier for the child to communicate freely.

Sometimes I have asked a child or adult to select a figure, approximately 2½" to 3" high, that represents how he or she is feeling right now. I might also use this technique in the following situations: when a client is reporting, intellectualizing, struggling with where to begin that session, anxious, shy, or too defensive. The client holds the figure while we begin a dialogue. We may discuss what that figure means to the client; what the client thinks the figure is feeling and why; what is going to happen next; times the client felt that way. The figure is allowed to absorb all the projections of the client's feelings and becomes the metaphor for the client's roles and relationships.

In other situations, when clients are more interactive and are trying to describe a feeling or experience that involves significant people in their lives, I'll invite the client to select a figure or object to represent each person. The figures are placed on the floor or on the table and the role playing begins. I use a variety of questions, which might include, "Can you show me what you mean with the figures?" The client is encouraged to move these figures around. The scenes may reflect the child's perception of his or her experiences or wishes. The unfolding of the drama becomes the focal point of expression. I ask the client to demonstrate what happens and who says what in the scene. The client often feels more free to express and even act on negative feelings with the figures.

I have also used this technique with adults, couples, and families.

APPLICATIONS

This technique has been especially helpful when a client is unable to articulate feelings. Children who have low self-esteem, shyness, or anxiety have responded well to selecting figures because the content is not focused on them. Difficult clients who are resistant or defensive use figures instead of talking. Those with a short attention span like using figures because they can express themselves kinesthically. Children with anger issues can often find the perfect "aggressor" and "victim." Trauma survivors find this a healing process in reenacting and resolving their complex issues. Separation, loss, and abandonment issues have been successfully worked through using figures and objects.

Although it is not necessary for this technique to be interactive, it is possible to deepen the experience for the client when there is validation and acceptance of the process. The figures are simple tools of expression.

An 8½-year-old girl with severe separation issues from her mother had a great deal of difficulty expressing herself. Rosie clung onto Mother, hugged, and kissed her many times before she could separate to leave the house, room, car, or waiting room. She didn't want to got to school, and didn't want to stay there if she went. At our thirteenth session, we had agreed to talk about her family. Since she didn't know what to say, I suggested she select a figure for each member. Mother was a figure in the pink prom dress; Rosie was a Barbie dressed in pink with white boots "doing nothing"; her 10-year-old brother was a baseball player with a glove; and Father was a bicyclist. After she sat them up on the floor, she remarked how much each figure reminded her of that person. As she began to play, her fears of separating from Mother emerged. She positioned Mother and herself very close to each other. I asked, "What if . . .

mother had to go out; was late in picking her up; had an appointment?" while I repositioned Mother slightly away from Rosie. As we worked with the figures, she was able to respond with an appropriate way of dealing with the situation in a safe, nonthreatening environment. In this way, she was able to address her fears, anticipate responses, and act out resolutions through the use of figures. Rosie's verbal expression increased with the use of figures as well.

While I was working at a preschool, a 4-year-old boy had a great deal of difficulty separating from either parent who brought him to school. He had excellent verbal skills and expressed himself clearly that he missed his mother or father. After sitting in my lap crying for a while, he went over to the sand table and used a red rubber volkswagen car that he named "Mother" and a blue one named "Father" and he "drove" them through the sand. The cars dropped him off at school and returned to pick him up. He repeated this ritual every day for about 10–15 minutes, with decreasing time over a two-week period. Finally, he announced he didn't need the cars anymore. I was supportive of his play, sat next to him, and mainly reflected his work. Several months later, a new girl came to school and cried when her mother left. While she was on my lap, the boy came over to ask what was wrong. When she replied, "I miss my mommy," he said, "why don't you play with the cars?"

I was working with a very bright 13-year-old boy, who was a middle child and his mother's antagonist. He was seeing me because of his bad temper and volatile relationship with his mother. Nick was uncomfortable talking about feelings and consistently blamed others for his misfortunes. He felt it was hopeless to talk to her and that she'd never change. During the twelfth session, I suggested that I could mediate a discussion between Nick and his mother. He seemed confused about how this could work. I demonstrated with the use of figures. I asked him to select one for him, his mother, and me. Mother was the Wicked Witch of the East (Wizard of Oz), he was Mickey Mouse as the Sorcerer, and I was Snow White. In the role play, I moved my figure around to show what it might be like to talk to each of them and feedback their responses. At the end of this play, Mickey knocked down and jumped on the Witch several times. Through his play with the figures, he felt empowered to express his anger in a safe way. Later, he was able to engage in appropriate dialogue with his mother.

Section Seven

Group Play Techniques

78

ElastaBlast

Kimberly Dye

INTRODUCTION

ElastaBlast (formerly Buddy Band), winner of the 1994 Parents' Choice Gold Award, was designed and created by dance and movement therapist, Kimberly Dye. It has been highly acclaimed in therapeutic, educational, and fitness settings with adults, seniors, families, and children. Designed originally as a movement tool for a psychiatric population, ElastaBlast's circular, visual, and textural appeal serves as an outside focal point to break the ice with groups of adults and children. ElastaBlast's dynamic, tensile properties facilitate movements that improve coordination, balance, and muscular strength. Its rebound effect alters one's relationship to gravity and brings out the risk taker in all of us!

RATIONALE

One of the magical moments ElastaBlast facilitates is when everyone moves as a single unit while still maintaining individual movements. Selfhood is maintained while becoming part of something greater than the sum of its parts. For those fearful of intimacy or of not belonging, or for whatever reason unable to participate in groups, ElastaBlast makes the bridge from self to community.

DESCRIPTION

Participants sit or stand holding the band so there is enough tensional pull to create a group synergy. Within a few minutes of play a group's interpersonal dynamics can be discerned around issues of power and control. One game, entitled Who's in Control, is a favorite with families. The leaders or controllers stand holding the band on the outside, while the followers stand inside with backs against the band. The controllers stretch, pull, and move with the band while the inside followers let themselves be led. Insiders reckon with the task of how to let go without getting out of control. This is therapeutic not only for child–parent relationships, but also for those with phobias or addictions.

ElastaBlast's tensile properties are helpful in facilitating tension or aggression release for therapy groups, faculty, or staff. In Tree Rooting, participants pull out into an expanded circle, widen their stance, plant their feet, and try to maintain their feet solidly on the ground while using their arms and full body weight to shift either neighbor off their balance. This exercise promotes a physical grounding, and confronts in a spirit of play, issues of competition and personal effectiveness.

Another method of releasing tension is to have participants expand the circle as far as they can. On the cue of the leader everyone runs towards the center of the circle making a sound, starting softly and gradually getting louder as they approach the center.

Push–pull dynamics can also simulate interpersonal tension. Working with couples to physicalize push/pull dynamics by using the band can release tension that prohibits moving together harmoniously.

For more information write:

BUDDYBANZ
117 19th Ave. E.
Seattle, WA 98112
206-324-0671

79

Group Building Activity

Glenda F. Short

INTRODUCTION

In working with children in groups, I found a need for an activity that would help the group to form. Children in particular often need a task to build cohesiveness and establish leadership. I had a group of boys with ADHD who were having difficulty concentrating and seemed to need excessive attention. This activity helped tremendously to establish group rapport and leadership.

DESCRIPTION

Children in the group are given a big basket of blocks (all sizes and all colors) and asked to build something together. There are two rules: first, that they must use all the blocks and second, that everyone must be allowed to help. A time limit is sometimes put on the project depending on how big the group is or how much time is left in the session.

Pictures of the finished product are made and given to the children, who are asked to take them home and put them somewhere that they can see their work and share the experience with a parent. During the group session, they are asked to discuss what the process was like for them and each group member comments about his or her part and how he or she feels about each group member before and after the task.

APPLICATIONS

I have had great results from this activity with groups of children, which was resulted in the children establishing firm cohesiveness early in group, which facilitates group process. This activity helps the group begin to understand about teamwork and building relationships.

80

The Captains of Avatar: A Space Adventure for Children in Transition

Tara M. Sinclair

INTRODUCTION

The Captains of Avatar was created within the theoretical framework of Psychosynthesis. Psychosynthesis is both a philosophy of psychology as well as a therapeutic modality that was developed by an Italian psychiatrist, Roberto Assagioli. A contemporary of Freud, Assagioli felt that the psychoanalytic framework excluded vital aspects of psychic life and needed to be expanded to include the full spectrum of consciousness. Thus, in addition to the lower unconscious and conscious mind, Assagioli posited the existence of the higher unconscious mind: the source of altruistic impulses, creative strivings, and the yearning for purpose and meaning in our lives.

Assagioli noted that, just as we repress lower unconscious sexual and aggressive impulses, we also repress higher unconscious wisdom and the drive toward life goals that transcend adaptation and survival. The theory and practice of Psychosynthesis strive to facilitate the integration of the personality and to promote the expansion of consciousness in ways that infuse life with a sense of joy and meaningful direction.

RATIONALE

The Captains of Avatar (C of A) is an interactive teaching story in the form of a space adventure. It unfolds over six weeks or sessions and was originally created for work with children of divorce. The children who participate take on the role of space captains. It is the year 2020 A.D. and the Captains, who come from various planets in the galaxy, are gathering at an intergalactic space station called Avatar to discuss the plight of Earth children in the late twentieth century.

The storytelling format is effective because it creates sufficient psychic distance from the actual events in the children's lives to liberate their creativity, and it promotes safe exploration of both intrapsychic and interpersonal dynamics. The activities in the story are designed to elicit both unconscious material and the children's own wisdom about what needs to happen next as they negotiate the challenge of family change.

DESCRIPTION

What follows is as specific a guide for re-creating the story as space allows.

Group size:

2-6 children

Ages:

7-10 years old

Materials:

Tape recorder with pause button, two cassette tapes, drawing paper, file folders, crayons, snack foods.

Preparation:

1. Prerecord the Message from Captain Will (Week II below). **Note: do not use your own voice. It breaks the spell.**

2. Make four separate signs that read: **AVATAR SPACE STATION, MISSION CONTROL, IMAGINATION STATION, VIRTUAL REALITY ROOM.**
3. Wrap six boxes of snack food in plain paper and label each **RATIONS.**

Intake:

Meet individually with each child who's been referred and say "Because your parents are divorced, you've been selected, if you choose, to go on an imaginary space adventure. I'm looking for kids who are experts on the subject of family change to come along. Would you like to go?"

Structure of each session:

45 minutes to 1 hour, depending on size of group and activity.

1. Briefing—introduction to the "mission" of the day.
2. Activity
3. Process exercise
4. Rations snack

APPLICATIONS

Week I:

The children are gathered together and, prior to entering the class or consultation room, are told, "When we get to the room, we're going to pretend that we're going into the future." The door to the room is labeled with the sign **AVATAR SPACE STATION.** The group enters the room and is instructed to sit on the floor. The facilitator says, "It's now the year 2020 and we're in outer space at the Avatar Space Station. Each of you is the captain of your own space ship and, because you are all experts on the subject of family change, you've been selected to participate in an imaginary space adventure. The best way for me to explain our unique missions is to tell you a story."

Briefing:

The Story:

"Once upon a time, long ago and many light-years away, the parents and children of planet Earth lived together until the children were grown. As time passed, things changed and parents started to separate from each other before the kids were grown.

"Well, this gave kids lots of problems they wished they didn't have. For instance, some of the kids thought that the parents' divorce was their fault, that they had actually caused the parents to break up. Of course, we know that's not true, but nonetheless, many Earth kids believed it was. Can you think of any other problems the Earth kids might have had?"

Open the floor for brief discussion. Possible answers might include: not getting along with parents or siblings, stepparents, having to relocate, visitation issues, parents fighting, less money, and so on.

Continue the story. "As the Captains of Avatar, our mission is to explore what happened to Earth kids during family changes and to see what we can do to help them. You have each been offered this mission because you're known to be experts on the subject. Does every one want to carry out our mission?"

If so, proceed to the area of the room (or a table) labeled with the sign MISSION CONTROL. Note: from now on throughout the story, the children are referred to as "Captain _____"(child's last name). The facilitator is referred to as the Navigator.

Activity:

Captain's Pledge: to be filled out as indicated and read in unison. This establishes the rules of the group. The Navigator has prewritten copies available which read as follows:

> I, Captain ____ [child fills in name] agree to be in command of my ship. I also agree to work with my fellow Captains and to steer clear of their air space. This means that when they are reporting about their mission, I will listen and wait my turn. Finally, I agree to follow the instructions of our Navigator [facilitator's name] so we can stay on course and find our way. Signed, ____________________ [Captain's signature]

Icebreaker Activity: Each Captain is given a blank file folder and is asked to draw a picture of the spaceship that transported them to the Avatar Space Station. To do this, they are sent to the IMAGINATION STATION. This can be a separate area of the room or the Mission Control sign can just be replaced.

Process Exercise:

Once the drawings are complete, the Captains are asked to describe their spaceships and to tell what special features it has. The Captains can be instructed that their ship's special features may not be visible in the drawing.

Once each Captain has shared, they are instructed that the file folders are their Captain's Journal and that they'll be keeping important papers from the adventure in them. The Captains are told to put their Captain's Pledge in the Journal, to hand them into the Navigator, and to reconvene at the Avatar Space Station at the appointed hour next week.

Rations:

Unwrap box of rations for snack. This completes each week of the adventure.

Week II: A Message from Captain Will.

Briefing:

"Today's mission is to find out more about what was going on in Earth families during their period of change. In order to do that, we need more information, so I've invited Captain Will from the spaceship Mandala to speak with us from his ship. It seems that his crew are young people from Earth whose families have gone through changes. Let's see if we can get him to come in on the intergalactic radio."

Activity and Process Exercise:

The Navigator now starts to play the prerecorded message from Captain Will. The tape starts with seven seconds of prerecorded silence, during which the Navigator says out loud, Space Station Avatar calling

Captain Will. Captain Will, do you read us?" After a few more seconds of silence, the tape signals that Captain Will is coming in via some sort of computer-generated space beep (a remote car door opener signal is the type of sound that's effective). Then the Captains hear the following pre-recorded message with pauses inserted as indicated.

This is Captain Will of Spaceship Mandala. I read you loud and clear. Navigator ______________, have you assembled the Captains of Avatar? [hit pause button as Navigator indicates that the Captains are present, then release]

Good, because the situation on my ship is critical and we desperately need their help.

As you know, several of my crew members (CMs) are experiencing changes in their families. Some of their parents have separated, some have divorced, and some have remarried. The CMs are trying their best to adjust, but it's not easy and, understandably, many need help to handle their feelings. I'm hoping that the Captains of Avatar and yourself can help me to better understand my crew and to give them what they need so that we can continue our journey in peace.

Let me tell you about a few of my CMs so you will have a clearer picture of our situation. The person I'm most worried about is my First Officer, Mr. Shock. His parents are going through a particularly rough divorce and he's acting as if nothing's wrong. I ask him how it's going and he says, "Fine." He doesn't want to talk about it, I guess.

Can you figure out what might be going on with him? Why don't you take a minute to discuss him and then I'll tell you about the next person. I'll hold while you talk. [Navigator hits pause button and asks the Captains, "What do you think is going on with Mr. Shock? Why is he pretending that everything's fine? How might he really be feeling?" After discussion, release the pause button.]

O.K. The second CM who's having a real hard time is Ensign Growl. He's very angry that his parents got divorced and is taking it out on anyone who gets in his way. Oh No! Here he is now. Can you hear him? [sound of someone—not the Navigator's voice—yelling in the background]. I'd better go see what the trouble is. Be right back. [Push pause and ask the Captains what they think in making Growl act so angry. "Who's he mad at? Why is he taking out on everyone? Do you imagine he's being especially mean to anyone in particular?" Release pause button.]

Well, I just had to settle another argument between Growl and a fellow CM. The other guy didn't know what he did that got Growl so angry. I don't even think Growl was sure how it got started. Poor Growl. He's such a valuable CM. Lots of energy and good ideas. I hope you can help him find a way to deal with his angry feelings without hurting others. That just gets him into more trouble. [brief prerecorded pause]

Anyhow, the next person in need of help is Dr. Fixx. Dr. Fixx keeps trying to fix things in the family so that her parents will get back together. She thinks that if she can just get herself and her brothers and sisters to act a certain way, her parents will change their minds about separating. Where do you think she got such an idea? I'll give you a moment to think about it. [pause button on]. Navigator asks Captains "What's going on with Dr. Fixx? What kinds of things might she be doing to get the parents together again?" [pause button off].

I only have time to tell you about one other person and that's Lieutenant Clinger. She's the one I'm least worried about because, although she's feeling quite sad and cries sometimes, she has at last begun to face the truth about her parents' divorce. She has finally accepted that her parents' divorce wasn't her fault. She didn't cause it and she couldn't stop it. That makes her feel sad and I guess that's normal, right? [pause button on]. Navigator asks what Clinger is feeling sad about since her parents' divorce. [pause button off]

So, Captains, that's a brief overview of the situation on board my spaceship. I'm confident that you will do your best to help us. After all, for a ship to accomplish it's mission, the Captain needs the cooperation of the whole crew. You each have your own ship, so of course, you understand this.

I look forward to hearing from you, Captains, Navigator ______ says you will send me a message after you have explored ways to help us. Until then, this is Captain Will, signing off. [space beeps, tape recorder off]

The Navigator asks the Captains if they can imagine the names of any other CMs who might be on board Captain Will's ship. (Examples from past groups include: A. Fraid, who's terrified about what's going to happen; I. M. Glad, who's happy because things at home are quieter now; and Nutty Butty, who's world is turned upside down). Navigator lists the names for future reference.

Rations.

Week III: Picking a Crew Member to Help.

Briefing:

The Captains are once again assembled at Mission Control. The Navigator tells the Captains that today's mission is for each of the Captains to pick a CM from the spaceship Mandala that they think they understand the best and can therefore help.

Before they do that, the Navigator reviews with the Captains the CMs described by Captain Will, as well as any others that the Captains thought might be on board.

This review is entered into the Avatar Space Station Computer. (A blank cassette is used for this recording.) The Captains are told that the Computer will be used periodically to keep a record of the mission and that, when the adventure is over, each of the Captains will get a copy of the recording.

Activity:

When the review is complete, the Captains are instructed to go to the Imagination Station to draw the CM of their choice. When they are done, the group meets back in Mission Control.

Process Exercise:

The group logs back onto the Avatar Space Station Computer and each Captain briefly tells which CM she or he chose, why that particular CM, and tells about the picture drawn of the CM. The Navigator can ask any questions appropriate to clarify the Captain's perception of the CM of choice.

Rations:

While the Captains eat rations, the Navigator tells them that, for next week's mission, each of them will visit the Virtual Reality Room aboard the Avatar Space Station, and that they'll be called to the Avatar Space Station one at a time. (Depending on the setting, the others will wait in their classrooms or the waiting room until they're called.)

Week IV: Time Travel Talk Show.

Preparation:

The Navigator has labeled an area of the Avatar Space Station with the sign VIRTUAL REALITY ROOM.

Briefing:

Each Captain is told that today's mission is to find out more about one CM, the CM of their choice. The way this will be done is to go to the Virtual Reality Room (where people on the Avatar Space Station go to play out their fantasies). Once there, the Captain will be a guest on a virtual reality talk show and the Navigator will be the Host. As a guest, the Captain will act as if she or he is the CM that she or he understands best and, from that CM's point of view, will answer questions which will help us figure out what the CM needs.

Activity:

The Virtual Interview.

Suggested Script:

Navigator: Good morning, and welcome to Time Travel Talk Show, the show that asks the question, "What did happen back then?" Today, we're happy to welcome our special guest, [CM's name, i.e., Crazy Dazey]. Crazy Dazey's parents went through a divorce some time ago and, this morning, Crazy Dazey is going to tell us what happened back then?

O.K., Crazy Dazey, I want you to go back in your imagination to the day you found out your parents were going to split up. Do you remember exactly how you felt?

[Crazy Dazey answers and, depending on the answer, Navigator/Host gears questions to uncover what was happening and how Crazy Dazey perceived and responded to events. "What did Crazy Dazey want to do when she found out? Since the separation, what has Crazy Dazey needed the most? What would help the most; help Crazy Dazey to feel better?"]

Navigator: And now for the final and most important question. Crazy Dazey, what are you hoping the Captains of Avatar can do for you? [Here the Navigator is trying to find what the CM needs to move on to the next stage of letting go.]

Navigator: O.K. It's time to go back to the future. Crazy Dazey, thank you for being a guest on our show.

This process is repeated for each of the Captains and the interviews are recorded on the Avatar Space Station Computer, to be shared (at the option of each Captain) as Rations are being eaten.

Rations.

Week V: The Helping Crew.

Briefing:

Today, the Captains of Avatar are going to work in the Imagination Station. Their mission is to create characters who can help the CMs on Captain Will's spaceship.

Activity:

The Captains of Avatar draw pictures of one or as many characters as they can imagine to be the Helping Crew.

Process:

The Captains of Avatar share their pictures with each other and describe their Helping Crew. The Navigator facilitates the discussion by drawing out the positive qualities embodied in the Helping Crew and relating these to the needs of the Crew aboard the Spaceship Mandala (including the CMs created by the Captains of Avatar).

If time allows, the group can brainstorm about what might happen if the Helping Crew were to materialize aboard the Spaceship Mandala. This discussion is recorded on the Avatar Space Station Computer.

Rations.

Week VI: A Message for Captain Will.

Briefing:

The final mission for the Captains of Avatar is to communicate with Captain Will about the groups findings.

Activity:

The Captains of Avatar go to the Imagination Station and answer questions about their adventure that they will record on the Avatar Station Computer to be sent to Captain Will. The questions are:

1. Why I chose to accept this mission.
2. What I found out that I already knew about Earth kids going through divorce.
3. What I found out that I didn't know.
4. What I think Captain Will's most difficult problem is in dealing with his crew.
5. My best advice for Captain Will at this time.

Each Captain of Avatar has a chance to respond to these questions over the Avatar Space Station Computer.

Rations.

References

Assagioli, R. (1980). *Psychosynthesis.* New York: Viking.

——— (1974). *The Act of Will.* New York: Viking.

Ferrucci, P. (1983). *What We May Be.* Los Angeles: Tarcher.

Fudgitt, E. (1983). *He Hit Me Back First!* Rolling Hills Estates, CA: Jalmar Press.

Hardy, J. (1987). *A Psychology with a Soul.* New York: Routeledge & Kegan Paul.

Weiser, J. & Yeomans, T. (eds) (1985). *Readings in Psychosynthesis.* Toronto: Ontario Institute for Studies in Education.

Whitmore, D. (1986). *Psychosynthesis in Education: The Joy of Learning.* Rochester, VT: Destiny Books.

Questions or comments are welcomed. They can be addressed to: Tara Sinclair, 1044 Abbott Blvd., Fort Lee, NJ 07024. E-mail address is: TSinclair@aol.com

81

Mr. Ugly

Mary May Schmidt

INTRODUCTION

Mr. Ugly is a stress reduction exercise similar to progressive muscle relaxation. This technique can be used with latency-aged children in group play therapy in a school setting. Mr. Ugly is the name I have given a rubber squeeze toy whose eyes, ears, and nose pop out when he is squeezed. There are many such toys available on the market that can easily be adapted for this exercise, but silliness enhances the overall effect.

RATIONALE

Children experience stress just as adults do, but children may not be able to identify the feeling as stress or identify the source of the stress. Because of their limited understanding, children may be even less able than adults to reduce that stress to more manageable levels. The Mr. Ugly technique borrows from another technique called progressive muscle relaxation, which is a technique of sequentially tensing and relaxing muscle groups to change the blood flow in the body, increase the available oxygen to the brain and body, and thereby change the body chemistry to healthier levels. With the release of bodily tension, the individual is better able to concentrate for problem solving, or do whatever is beneficial by changing the individual's relationship to the source of the stress. Progressive muscle relaxation is complicated for children to understand. Children need to feel better now, without a lengthy explanation, without a rule about "sequential" and "muscle groups." They need to have their own way to help them do that, something simple that gives them some personal control.

The Mr. Ugly technique is used in a group setting but can easily be used in many other settings. As the children become skilled, children can learn more discreet ways of relaxing and then apply the technique privately amidst large number of people and in formal settings.

DESCRIPTION

When a child discloses an "ugly" (ugly-stressful) thought or feeling, or an "ugly" situation that gives rise to those feelings, during the course of group play therapy, the therapist must give acknowledgment and facilitate an appropriate and brief discussion. It is important to value the child's experience before the Mr. Ugly technique, because if this is not done, the child may feel that his experience is being trivialized by squeezing a rubber toy. Then the therapist gives the Mr. Ugly squeeze toy to the child and instructs the child to squeeze the toy. While the child squeezes, the therapist explains that the ugly thoughts or feelings that are located in the child's mind need to be squeezed out of the mind, down the neck, across the shoulders, down the arms, and into the belly of Mr. Ugly. The other children in the group are asked to watch. If they see the child's face turning red, they will know that the child is giving good effort and should be cheered on. One child in the group can be given the job of counting to ten. The squeezing child must try to squeeze until the count of ten is over; then the child is asked to stop, relax, and breathe deeply. This routine is completed three times, with the others cheering for greater success at each trial.

If the child permits, the therapist can stand behind the squeezing child and gently poke the child across the shoulders. The therapist can explain that another way to tell if the child is giving good effort is to see how tense the shoulder muscles are. Tense muscles should feel tickled by the touch. The atmosphere created by the squeezing, cheering, and tickling is silly comraderie. Following the three trials, the child is asked to explain how he feels. Is the stressful feeling smaller and more manageable? Is it gone all together? How did the group cheering help? Does the child notice warmth in his muscles? How can counting to ten make a difference?

Depending on the age and ability of the children, the therapist can also discuss some more cognitive issues, such as changing thoughts in order to change feelings. For instance, a child can practice thinking "I can, I can" while involved in squeezing the toy. As children become more skilled at using this technique, they can be shown how to be more discreet and use the technique outside the play room. For instance, a child can quietly make a fist and relax the fist, repeatedly, while sitting at his or her classroom desk.

APPLICATIONS

This technique works well with latency-aged children. They are eager to learn how to gain mastery over their emotions. Withdrawn children become more expressive in an accepting environment. Acting-out children find an acceptable way to vent their strong emotions and therefore have less frustration and less acting out.

82

Therapeutic Puppet Group

Aileen Cunliffe

INTRODUCTION

I developed this technique while working as an elementary school counselor in an urban setting. I had an inordinately large case load due to the special issues of the setting, and pressure to deal with critical needs of the children in a limited amount of time. In order to help my client gain insight while reserving her need for privacy, I found this technique to be highly successful.

RATIONALE

My rationale for using this technique is to help enhance the child's view of the world. Many times when children are dealing with issues involving low self-esteem, poor connectedness with their surroundings, and limited awareness of their own feelings, it is extremely difficult to create insight for the feelings and needs of others. My therapeutic puppet group is a very concrete method for bringing thoughts and feelings into the counseling session.

DESCRIPTION

I ask the child to create the physical setting for a group. I provide the choices, which serve as the catalyst. The dialogue looks something like this—

You may choose chairs or bean bags.

You may put them in a circle or a semi-circle.

You need to choose at least 4, but no more than 6.

It looks like you have created a group. Now we need the group members.

Now the fun part. You choose the puppets.

It looks like the group members are ready. I think it would be a good idea to put their names on the board so the group leader can remember them.

At this point, it is important to stay very focused and to slow the tempo. The child is doing some very important work. She is choosing the aspects she needs to deal with in this group. Each puppet is something or someone very important to her. I let the child choose who will lead the group. Eventually, I want the child to take the lead, but sometimes it is too overwhelming, so I am glad to lead. I also let the child choose who will speak for each puppet, and we establish the same kind of rules characteristic of any other small group. In this manner, we are able to have some very therapeutic sessions together. Ideas are shared, awareness is created, and many feelings are accepted, and we can begin the process of learning to deal with the issues in this child's life.

APPLICATIONS

I have used this technique in a variety of cases that are common in an elementary school setting: aggression, isolation, withdrawal, children of alcoholics, children in homes where domestic violence is prevalent. This technique is useful in cases where there is blocking or denial of feelings.

83

Group Puppet Show

Glenda F. Short

INTRODUCTION

This activity was developed when I was a schoolteacher, and later used as a therapist with a girls' sexual abuse group, generally ages 8-10 years old. It was developed to help children find a creative way to express their trauma story, build their self-esteem about how they took care of themselves, and to learn how to get support from other group members.

DESCRIPTION

Each child chooses one animal that best shows how she feels and is most able to tell her story. They all get together with their animals and plan what they will say about their abuse. When it is time for the puppet show, all the girls and animals go behind the puppet stage. They pretend they are in the forest together and are sitting around a campfire talking. Each tells her story and gets support from the other animals. The therapist can encourage the animals to give details and tell how they protected themselves. Afterward, the girls tell how it felt for the animals to tell their stories. They are encouraged to tell the stories again by themselves without the animals. There are variations on this activity.

APPLICATIONS

This type of activity lends itself well to any age child, group, or even individual work with a therapist. Trauma is generally the issue, as the child can hide behind the animal to tell the story.

84

Mutual Storytelling through Puppet Play in Group Play Therapy

Mitch Jacobs

INTRODUCTION

The Mutual Storytelling Technique (MST) was developed by Richard Gardner (1970) as a way of administering therapeutic interventions using the self-generated stories of children. The therapist used the theme of the child's story to convey insights, values, and alternative behaviors to the child. MST has been used as a means to identify children's uncooperative or maladaptive behaviors, and teach more cooperative behaviors (Kottman and Stiles 1990). After a measure of trust had been established between the therapist and child, the child was asked to tell a story. The therapist identified the main characters and unresolved conflicts in the story, then retold that story, adding an ending that demonstrated more adaptive ways of coping.

Puppet play has been used as a therapeutic technique in individual and group play therapy as a means to facilitate the expression of impulses and conflicts (Woltmann 1971). Puppet play has been used in conjunction with MST (Oaklander 1978) in individual therapy with children guiding them toward a resolution of their conflicts. Use of MST in conjunction with puppet play can be used in group play therapy settings as well. I have adapted and applied what I shall term Mutual Storytelling

Through Puppet Play (MSTPP) techniques, working with children in a weekly play therapy group at a shelter for battered and abused women.

RATIONALE

The play therapy group consisted of up to six children, ranging in ages from 7 to 10 years. Over the course of the ten-week group, nondirective child-centered techniques and structured activities were used. Engaging the children in structured activities as a group was sometimes problematic because of differences in developmental stages and abilities. Sometimes MSTPP was used to involve all of them in one activity, rather than divide the children into groups by age and assign them different activities.

Children of different temperaments, levels of socialization and self-control, and emotional needs were all able to focus on and perform the puppet plays. Undercontrolled and agitated children were able to concentrate for longer periods of time watching or performing puppet plays. With some encouragement, such children were able to use this structure to organize and express themselves. Puppet play seemed to help over-controlled and shy children express their fantasies, conflicts, and concerns. Despite the wide age range of the children, they all seemed to be able to relate to and use the puppets and enact their stories.

MSTPP can be used in group assessment and intervention. In assessment, MSTPP can be useful as a means of identifying similarities in group members' issues, themes, and coping skills. By enacting his or her own story, the therapist can demonstrate more adaptive behaviors and encourage children to adopt new skills through vicarious learning. By watching other children's and the therapist's stories, children may discover that they share similar stories and identify with the feelings being acted out. As a result of sharing their stories, the children may feel reassured that their feelings are normal and experience increased self-acceptance.

DESCRIPTION

A store-bought red puppet theater with a black curtain was set up about three feet in front of a wall, and chairs were placed about six feet in front of the theater. A selection of puppets representing people and animals were placed behind the theater on the floor. Puppets representing people included a girl and boy and male and female adults. Puppets representing animals included a dog, elephant, snake, and alligator. I told the children that it was time for a puppet show, and that each child would have an opportunity to put on his or her own show, and that each show could be up to ten minutes in duration. I asked the children for a volunteer to perform the first show. After each show was over, I asked for another volunteer. The nature of the shows was usually left up to each child, although on one occasion I suggested the topic of the shows to be enacted.

During each show, I silently assessed each child's enactment of his or her puppet show. The puppets used and the roles that seem to have been assigned to each puppet were noted. The feelings expressed and the conflicts that developed between characters were identified. Actions taken by the child, if any, to resolve conflicts among puppet characters were also noted. I internally summarized the behavioral and emotional themes of the enactment at the conclusion of each child's puppet show. Some of the feelings expressed and actions taken were tracked and verbalized to the child performing the show. The summaries of all of the puppet shows were then used to identify the feelings, behaviors, and general themes shared by the children. This information was then used as a basis for my story.

When all of the children who wished to conduct a puppet show had done so, I told the children that it was my turn to conduct a show. This show incorporated most of the puppets used and common themes acted out in the children's stories. Some of the roles portrayed by conflicted puppets, as seen in the previous stories, were reenacted. The emotional themes that were shared by most of the stories were maintained. However, the ending of the story was changed to reflect positive emotional and behavioral changes in individual puppet characters.

Puppets that were portrayed by the children as conflicted and/or attempting to resolve conflicts were used to demonstrate improved adaptations. Those puppets that were thought to primarily represent a child were used to display problem solving, conflict resolution, and coping skills. Those puppets that might have represented other people in the children's lives sometimes remained unchanged, leaving the responsibility for behavioral change on the "child puppet," as can often be the case in a child's real life with his or her significant caretakers. By the end of this story, at least one conflict had been resolved by one or more characters, and the feelings expressed had changed from fear, shame, sadness, and anger to confidence, pride, happiness, and resolve.

There is an important consideration in applying MSTPP in the way described. When each child performed a puppet show, one after another, in a group session, some of the children tended to copy what they had just seen the previous child do in his or her show. Such children were encouraged to continue their shows beyond their own stopping point if they had not exceeded the ten-minute limit. This seemed to help them find their own stories and express their unique inner worlds more spontaneously. A second possible solution might involve limiting puppet shows to two or three children per group session, allowing several minutes to pass between shows. This may reduce the likelihood of imitation of one child by another. Alternatively, the therapist could arrange for each child to take turns, one child per session, telling his or her story through puppet play. In each case, the therapist would retell that child's story or a composite of the children's stories with a more adaptive ending for the benefit of all of the children.

APPLICATIONS

The use of MSTPP in group play therapy may be indicated when involvement of all of the children in an activity is desired, and the age range between the youngest and oldest child exceeds two years. Puppet play and storytelling can be utilized by most children. This technique may be useful in short-term, time-limited groups. Child puppet show performers and audience members may benefit from the same therapist-guided learning experience through direct participation and vicarious learning. Many differences and similarities in issues expressed by the child performers can be represented by the therapist's retelling of one unified story. MSTPP may help undercontrolled children organize their inner world and offer them a framework for expressing themselves. With this technique and the support of an empathic therapist, overcontrolled and shy children can find a familiar vehicle for self-expression and behavior change. This technique may be contraindicated for severely abused children who might experience an enactment of such abuse through puppet play as revictimization.

References

Gardner, R. (1970). Mutual storytelling as a technique in child psychotherapy and psychoanalysis. In *Science and Psychoanalysis,* vol. 14, ed. J. Masserman pp. 123-125. New York: Grune and Stratton.

Kottman, T., and Stiles, K. (1990). The mutual storytelling technique: an Adlerian application in child therapy. *Journal of Individual Psychology* 46: 148-156.

Oaklander, V. (1978). *Windows to Our Children.* Moab, UT: Real People Press.

Woltmann, A. G. (1971). Spontaneous puppetry by children as a projective method. In *Projective Techniques with Children,* ed. A. I. Rabin and M. R. Haworth, pp. 305–312. New York: Grune and Stratton.

Section Eight

Other Techniques

85

Using Drawings of Early Recollections to Facilitate Life Style Analysis for Children in Play Therapy

Harold M. Heidt

INTRODUCTION

Dreikers (1958) believed that it is "relatively easy to change the child's latent and sometimes obscure plan of behavior up to about the sixth year" (p. 28). As people get older they become more rehearsed and solidified in their beliefs, and shifting thus becomes more difficult. In order for counselors to understand and effectively influence children's beliefs, attitudes, behaviors, and ways of approaching life, counselors need to gain insight and understanding of the children's developing life style and perception of self in relationship to others. The use of early recollections has proven to be a useful projective tool in assessing children's lifestyle and clarifying treatment goals (Clark 1994, Dinkmeyer and Dinkmeyer 1981, Kottman 1995). Because younger children are limited in their ability to formulate and express early memories verbally, the assessment value of early recollections with children younger than age 8 has been in question (Clark 1994).

Several therapists have introduced the idea of allowing adults (McAbee 1994) and children (Kottman 1995) to draw pictures of early recollections. In working with primary and school-age children, drawing on early recollections has proven to be of great assessment and therapeutic value, for several reasons. First, drawing an early recollection takes little time to administer, is generally fun for children, is of a skill level that most children can understand and complete, and requires little or no written or verbal skills. Second, through the use of drawing, counselors are exposed to additional interpsychic information, otherwise missed if presented verbally. Third, by obtaining additional drawings of early recollections over the course of counseling, counselors are able to assess children's progress. With this increased understanding of the younger child, counselors are in better position to clarify counseling goals, formulate treatment plans, and monitor progress over time.

RATIONALE

According to Alfred Alder (1992) one's life style is a person's basic personality pattern that is developed early in childhood. It is during these formative years that each child develops a concept of him- or herself and of life and behaves accordingly. These concepts and patterns of behaviors are maintained throughout life. Dinkmeyer, Dinkmeyer, and Sperry (1989) state "the life style denotes the basic premises and assumptions on which psychological movement through life is based. Life style can be expressed in terms of the syllogism 'I am ———; the world is ———; therefore ———. . . .' We believe, feel, intend, and act upon these premises, and we move psychologically to justify our point of view" (p. 104).

Early recollections are of extreme value, for they present a crucial type of information the counselor collects in the course of formulating a person's life style. According to Adler, such recollections are valuable because they are indicators of one's present attitudes, beliefs, motives, basic mistaken attitudes, self-defeating perceptions, and unique laws of psychological movement. People remember only those events from early childhood that are consistent with their present views of themselves and the world (Dinkmeyer, et al. 1989).

> "Among all psychic expressions, some of the most revealing are individual memories. Her memories are reminders she carries about with her of her own limitations and of the meaning of events. There are no "chance memories." Out of the incalculable number of impressions that an individual receives, she chooses to remember only those she considers, however dimly, to have a bearing on her problems. These memories represent her "Story of My Life," a story she repeats to her-

> self for warmth or comfort, to keep her concentrated on her goal, to prepare her, by means of past experiences, to meet the future with a tried and tested approach. [Adler 1992, p. 70]

Clark (1994) suggests that counselors can make inferences through early recollections about one's personality characteristics. Powers and Griffith (1987) indicate that, through early recollections, one is able to detect how a person may answer these questions: "What kind of a world is this? What kind of a person am I? What must a person such as I do in a world such as this to find a place of security (to fit in) and significance (to stand out)? What are my chances of success in all of this?" (p. 186).

Drawings of early recollections have proven to be an added valuable method of self-discovery. Drawings, within themselves, provide a method that individuals can use to show their experiences of their world. Through the use of drawings, therapists can gain additional unconscious information and deal directly with the images and themes presented, which may be eliminated, distorted, or censored if provided only through verbal translations (McAbee 1994). Furth (1988) states,

> To know ourselves, we need to bring into conscious what is submerged in our unconscious. Our unconscious thoughts come to us in the symbolic language of dreams, paintings, and drawings. . . . Fantasies and images from the waking state as expressed in drawings also reveal conditions of the various parts of one's total personality, mind, and body. . . . Through analytic interpretation of these expressions we learn to recognize our weaknesses, fears, and negative traits, as well as our strengths, accomplishments, and untapped potential, giving us further insight into who we are. [p. 15]

Klepsch and Logie (1982) describe art as "pictorial language" (p. 7). It captures symbolically on paper some of the person's thoughts and feelings and makes portions of his inner self visible. Early recollections have been used to determine the life style for children in individual and in group settings. The use of drawings of early recollections has been used, however, in a limited way. Terry Kottman (1995) in her work in Adlerian Play Therapy, has suggested that children can either draw or act out their early recollections with dolls or puppets.

DESCRIPTION

After the counselor has established a relationship with the child, the child is presented with paper and markers and instructed, "Draw a picture of something that you can remember happening one day when you were younger or one of the first things you can remember. It can be anything at all—good or bad, important or unimportant—something you remember happening one day." The memory and picture must be of a specific event, not a narrated report of events or experiences. In some cases prompting may be necessary. However, caution should be taken in not promoting a response in a particular direction. Three or more recollections are desired in order to get a merging theme or pattern of the child's attitudes towards events (Dinkmeyer and Dinkmeyer 1981).

Upon completion of the drawing, the child is instructed to share the story of the picture. What the child shares should be written down verbatim. Clark (1994) recommends that when the child stops talking the therapist ask three questions: (1) Is there anything else that you can recall in this memory? (2) What part do you remember most about the memory? (3) What feelings do you remember having then? Depending upon the skill level and degree of emotional discomfort elicited by the recollection, some younger children are unable to give detailed descriptions of the recollections. However, most children are able to describe the picture or identify different details of persons, characters, objects, or events of the drawing. Such comments should be noted. Additionally, some children may make up or provide fantasy recollections. The accuracy of the memory is unimportant for interpretative purposes. The significance is the child's interpretation of the event, for it represents the child's perception, attitude, and idea about him or herself and the world. Children with more developed communicative skills are encouraged to write five or six sentences describing the recollection.

APPLICATIONS

Interpretations from the drawings and recollections can be divided into three categories for the purpose of determining one's life style: themes, details, and syllogisms. Clark (1994) and Sweeney (1975) provide some guidelines for interpretation of thematic variables of early recollections. Some variables for counselors to identify include: What were the feelings at the time the event occurred? What are the themes or patterns of the recollections? Is the child included, alone or with others? Is the child active or passive; caregiver or receiver; taking or giving? Does the child go forth or withdraw? Is the child concerned with people, things, or ideas? Is the child competent or incompetent; superior or inferior; conforming or rebelling; secure or insecure; accepted or rejected; encouraged or discouraged? Does the child receive praise or blame?

Additional information may be obtained by analyzing the physical presentation and content of the drawings. Furth (1988) lists several focal points that are important in understanding and making interpretations of the drawings. Included are the following: examining the feelings generated by and conveyed in the picture, and observing placement of focal points, space arrangements, boundaries, oddities, barriers between or around persons, central points, size proportions of persons and objects, shape distortions, shades, and colors.

Through the interpretations of themes and details of children's drawings and early recollections, counselors can make inferences about the basic elements of their developing life style (beliefs and goals). Kottman (1995) suggests that counselors make guesses about how the child might complete the following sentence stems: "I am . . . or I must be . . . Others are . . . or Others treat me . . .; The world is . . . or Life is . . .; Therefore, it makes sense that they my behavior must be . . . or Therefore, I must act as if . . ." (p. 142). Ideally counselors are able to formulate a child's developing life style in terms of the following syllogism: "If ——— then ———", or "I am ———; the world is ———; therefore———."

Through the use of drawing an early recollection, counselors are better able to understand the developing life style, mistaken beliefs, and goals of children's behaviors. Not only is drawing an early recollection fun, and at a skill level that most children can participate, but it also provides valuable information regarding counseling goals and progress.

References

Adler, A. (1992). *What Life Could Mean to You,* new translation by Colin Brett. Oxford, England: Oneworld Publications.

Clark, A. J. (1994). Early recollections: a personality assessment tool for elementary school counselors. *Elementary School Guidance & Counseling* 29: 92–101.

Dinkmeyer, D., Jr., and Dinkmeyer, D., Sr. (1981). Concise counseling assessment: the children's life-style guide. In *Life Style: Theory Practice and Research* ed. L. Baruth and D. Eckstein pp. 68–71. Dubuque, IA.: Kendall/Hunt.

Dinkmeyer, D., Sr., Dinkmeyer, D., Jr., and Sperry L. (1989). *Adlerian Counseling and Psychotherapy.* Columbus, OH.: Merrill.

Dreikurs, R. (1958). *The Challenge of Parenthood.* New York: Penguin.

Furth, G. M. (1988). *The Secret World of Drawings.* Boston, MA: Sigo Press.

Klepsch, M., and Logie, L. (1982). *Children Draw and Tell.* New York: Brunner/Mazel.

Kottman, T. (1955). *Partners in Play: An Adlerian Approach to Play Therapy.* Alexandria, VA: American Counseling Association.

McAbee, N. L. (1994). *A New Technique To Assess Adlerian Life Style Using Client Drawings.* Myrtle Beach, SC: The S. C. Conference of Adlerian Psychology.

Powers, R. L., and Griffith, J. (1987). *Understanding Life-Style.* Chicago, IL: Americas Institute of Adlerian Studies, Ltd.

Sweeney, T. J. (1975). *Adlerian Counseling.* Boston, MA: Houghton Mifflin.

86

Self Figures for Sand Tray

L. Jean Ley and Jean Howze

INTRODUCTION

This technique for working with children and adults, couples and families, and groups is easy, inexpensive, and very effective. It was originally used by one of the authors in her kindergarten classroom so that the children could involve themselves and their peers in their sand play. It was then adapted for use in clinical sand tray work. The addition of a picture figure is very empowering, assists in improving self-esteem and self-image issues, and allows a person, group, or family to more clearly see how they fit in their worlds. It can also be used for floor play and in doll houses.

DESCRIPTION

The creation of the figures is quite simple. Materials needed are a 35mm camera (Polaroid will not work), either laminating material or a place to get laminating done, and 1" square wooden blocks. We will describe the process for a client's individual work, then expand to groups, families, and other issues.

Take a picture of the client. A standing position is often preferred, but sometimes a client will be more comfortable in a sitting position. Take a picture of two children at the same time to cut down on cost for groups. For individual work, take two pictures so the client can choose which one she or he feels most comfortable with. Sometimes, clients will want both a standing and a sitting pose, and once they get used to actually having themselves in the sandtray they may also want action poses. If you do not have access to a camera, clients may be able to bring photographs from home. Once the picture is developed, carefully cut out the shape of the client and laminate it. You can get laminating done at most copy centers, and many office supply stores sell individual sheets of self-adhesive laminating material. You can use clear Contact paper, but it clouds the image some and is not as durable for play. Once the figure is laminated, paste it to a wood block so it can stand on its own, and the figure is ready for play and/or work.

This picture self allows clients to put their own image in their worlds. For some clients, and with some issues, this is too overwhelming at first, and they will need to work with representational objects before they can see their picture selves in the worlds. Some clients will want to use their picture selves immediately, and then, as the work deepens, it will become harder for them to use the picture and it may sit unnoticed for a period of time. The picture process also allows for the addition of other people in the client's life. Many clients (especially children) like to bring in a picture of their pet to have laminated and added to the sand tray collection. Sometimes they will bring in a picture of a friend, a favorite relative, or family members. One child almost always used a picture of his favorite uncle, now deceased, as a "witness" to the work.

In group work, clients have one or two pictures of themselves, and the group can do sand trays together that allow them to see and experience the group dynamics that involve them, but in a way that has some distance from the real experience and can be seen and worked on in a contained space. This is also an excellent way to facilitate problem-solving dialogue between two or more people having relational difficulties. Once the group members begin to trust one another, they can ask permission of each other to include their pictures in their worlds as support, advisors, and protectors.

For family work, every member of the family needs to have at least one picture. The worlds built may be done together, done individually, or done in various family groupings. Again, this level of "reality" will be difficult for some families, and they may require work with representational objects prior to being able to use their picture selves. Family dynamics often become clearer when the family members can see where they actually are in the worlds, how they interact (or don't), and who has what positions of power. Work can also be done with the images themselves. For example: Who chose a picture standing or sitting, and why? Are they facing the camera (and, therefore, the other members of the family) or are they in a position to always be turned away? Were they able to just be in the picture, or did they have to be doing something? Who is frowning, laughing, clowning, avoiding? As the work progresses, different family members may need to change their picture as their style of being in the family changes.

Store the figures away from the rest of the sandtray collection to ensure confidentiality. For children, the senior author often supplies a small box of some sort that the child can decorate and create a "home" for the picture self between sessions. That way, the picture self is always safe and protected. This is especially important for children who have been abused and for children that come from families that have no personal boundaries. This option is also offered to adult clients, but they are less likely to use it.

APPLICATIONS

In clinical sandtray work, this technique can be used for most issues. Its limitation is in the ability of clients to be able to actually have a concrete visual representation of themselves in their worlds. Just being able to do that will often first require extensive work on self-image, self-esteem, and self-protection. The use of picture selves can be very nice in attachment and relationship work, as well as separation-individuation work. When a client is working on intensive trauma, the use of the picture self may be too much for quite some time, but eventually can assist the client in becoming empowered to take appropriate control of his or her own life situation. For clients whose trauma happened a long time ago, bringing in pictures of how they looked at the time of the trauma can often be useful. When a client is working on grief issues, the use of picture selves can add a concrete element to the dialogue between the client and the other person(s) involved. The picture self has the potential to be used by some self-mutilating clients, both in terms of self-image and self-empowerment and in terms of mutilating a representation of self rather than self. This, however, requires an extensive understanding of the process and ritual of self-injury, and can be more damaging than helpful if not fully accepted by the client.

Once a client has worked through trauma issues to the point of being ready to "confront" her offender, adding a picture of the offender can be helpful. If an actual picture is not available, many clients are able to find a suitable picture in a magazine. They can then act out fantasy retaliation and eventually get to a place of direct confrontation without endangering themselves or any one else. If a client is going to face an offender in court, the court experience can first be experienced in the containment of the sandtray world. This is also true if a client is getting ready for a clarification session with their offender.

This technique has been very successful with children and they are very creative in finding new ways to use it. It gives them a very real experience of their own creativity, power, and problem-solving ability. Adults seem to be less able to be "playful" with the idea, but it has opened up new possibilities for some clients. In a general way, it is even diagnostic, as the clinician pays attention to how each client reacts to the idea, the picture, and the play using a picture self.

87

The Worry List

Richard Sloves

INTRODUCTION

Here is a technique that allows children to quite literally seize and take control of strong, overpowering thoughts and emotions that might otherwise disrupt their ability to attend, concentrate, and reason through the problems of daily living. The goal is to provide children with a modest tool that is flexible enough to (1) effectively shield and arm them against attack, (2) defend and insulate them from being flooded by potentially disorganizing affects, and (3) provide them with a metaphor that turns passive into active. The clinician illustrates and demonstrates the effective use of psychological defense against a destabilizing state of affairs. Children are offered a means to demystify what at first glance was perceived as a frightening entanglement of disturbing, conflicting, or terrifying emotions.

The opportunity for its use occurs when children have exhausted their intuitive capacity to solve a problem and appear overwhelmed especially by a worry, fear, or anxiety. This approach works best for children who feel flooded by strong emotions. Children need not have a primary diagnosis of an anxiety disorder for this technique to work. It is sufficiently flexible that it can be easily tailored to fit almost any circumstance confronted by children in psychotherapy. The clinician works interactively with the child to determine exactly what it is that makes them feel most vulnerable. An explicit strategy to inoculate them against the unsettling effects of anxiety is formulated and then a plan of attack is devised. Children are helped to label, concretize, and manipulate a particular subset of worries. It offers children the means by which to grab hold of and discipline ephemeral, amorphous phenomena and recast them into something that has a clearly defined shape and texture. This allows children to apply a whole host of cognitive, affective, and social manipulations to render them safe and manageable.

RATIONALE

This eclectic approach works at several levels. It uses to good effect the magical imperatives and directives derived from the work of Milton Erickson (Haley 1973), incorporates the direct, educational approach of cognitive behaviorism (Meichenbaum 1974), and makes conscious the unconscious mechanisms of defense explicated by psychodynamic theory.

Anxiety management training is woven into fabric of this structured model of play therapy (Sloves and Peterlin 1994). When vague, ethereal, intangible, or abstract experiences are concretized they are more easily brought under conscious control. The more tangible the imagery, the more easily it can be manipulated. When diffuse emotions are named and concretized, children learn a method of intellectual detachment and master the appropriate use of isolation of affect. Once fears and worries are actually placed on the table, they are more easily examined, manipulated, reworked, and refashioned. At the very least, they are affectively neutralized. Something simultaneously logical and magical occurs when an indistinct fear is clothed in familiar garb. Random, intrusive, and alarming experiences that formerly burst uninvited into consciousness to flood an immature defensive system are now *ordered* by the child into awareness and offered an "assigned seat" in their daily routine. Children are not asked to ignore or forget their concerns. On the contrary, the clinician prescribes the symptom. But children pick the time and place to experience what they previously avoided. The clinician models age-appropriate problem-solving skills. In a calm and reasoned atmosphere of therapy, a form of desensitization occurs. Children experience finite, planned doses of anxiety without their anticipated negative consequences.

This problem-oriented approach strengthens children's mediational proficiency. They are not taught what to think but rather *how* to think. Basically, children are trained in the effective use of psychological defense and how to use language and imagery to shape the problem-solving process. When age-appropriate defense mechanisms fail to function properly, this technique methodically demonstrates the use of compartmentalization. The procedure fortifies the strength of signal anxiety, which is "a warning signal in your body, like a car alarm or a smoke alarm that gets your attention and tells you there is a problem so you can figure out what to do about it."

DESCRIPTION

1. Children are helped to help identify what it is that worries them. If they have difficulty expressing themselves linguistically, diagnostic play or art therapy materials are used to illustrate and dramatize their concerns.

2. The clinician keeps track of each explicit or implicit worry, fear, or concern mentioned during the session. This is accomplished in as natural, direct, and open a manner as possible. It is important to develop the list in front of the child and to write it down in a manner that is commensurate with his or her developmental level. With younger children try to mimic the way they draw and write by using bright colors, primitive yet clear pictures, and large block lettering. Very young children, preschoolers through the first grade, or the reading disabled need colorful drawings to symbolize the point under discussion. Most older children do not find this to be a particularly intrusive procedure, especially when told, "These things are private and at the end of the session you can decide to put them in a special folder for safekeeping or to throw them in the garbage."

3. The entire process should resemble a brainstorming session, so it makes little difference whether the concerns are based in reality or totally the produce of children's imagination. No judgments are made as the list is compiled; prioritizing comes later. Keep in mind that we want to disassemble an overbearing concern into more manageable component parts. Some children need the clinician to help jog an errant thought or memory, but this is always done using the vocabulary, imagery, and symbols of their language system. For example, "Didn't you tell me something about how you feel when your mom has to come home late from

work?" Ideas have to be phrased in a way children can recognize as familiar.

4. This technique works best when the list contains at least five but not more than ten concerns or worries.

5. Something concrete must be done with the worry that is psychologically correct.

APPLICATIONS

Kevin is a 9-year-old boy who for the past seven years has lived with his foster mother. Despite clinical testimony in Family Court to the contrary, Kevin was returned to his birth mother on a trial basis. As predicted, this reunion was an unmitigated disaster. Six months later, when Kevin returned to his foster mother, this once confident, poised, and cheerful child was transformed into someone who was inordinately fearful, distracted, preoccupied, and irritable. In school Kevin's teacher described him as "lost in space . . . you can tell he is in another world most of the time . . . he's just not with it." The same was true at home where "he daydreams . . . sometimes I catch him just staring into space or he follows me around like a baby."

During one particular session Kevin and I worked to reframe the presenting complaints into something less pejorative and more accessible to treatment. Kevin agreed that "thinking and worrying" was a more accurate description of what his teacher and foster mother called "daydreaming." As we talked I doodled and "wrote out loud" with a pencil and colored markers. I made several lists, drew lines and arrows to join interrelated or interdependent ideas, and made a genogram of his birth and foster family. When I knew that certain psychological concepts or processes were beyond his understanding, I sketched pictographs and cartoon figures to illustrate them. Finally we had a reasonable number of concerns, most of which revolved about the irrational belief that not only was Kevin responsible for the original banishment from the foster home but that he felt that he was constantly on the verge of precipitating yet another separation.

I showed Kevin my scribbling. "They're going to send me back to her. It was my fault I got sent away." He cited as evidence an unusually low grade on a math test, recalled once sneaking outside without permission, and then there was the time "I broke the TV by mistake." Kevin was concerned that "I'm going to mess up again." To guard against what he regarded as the inevitable, Kevin developed magical notions and ritual procedures, and thought up elaborate yet ultimately self-defeating ways to avoid "screwing up." He obsessed over minute infractions and berated himself for mistakes that only he noticed. At one point I asked, "What about me? Am I on your side or am I a spy for the Family Court?" After all, Kevin had mentioned, "You told mommy I had to get punished for taking that dollar." It was close to the end of the session that a list of Kevin's worries led to this focused intervention.

Therapist: That's quite a lot of worries. Why don't we make a list of them, a Worry List? You're an artist, so why don't you draw a little picture next to each one. Help me out and then I'll show you what we are going to do with them.

Kevin: Give me! [He draws small pictures next to each worry.]

Therapist: There are so many of them all bunched together. We need to get some control over them. Got to make them smaller.

Kevin: Throw them away! [Moves toward the garbage pail.]

Therapist: Hold on. If you do that they might creep back again.

Kevin: Cross them off.

Therapist: Good idea, but we don't want them to disappear yet. They're all so important. You can handle them one at a time, but look what a mess they make all bunched up together. They make is so hard for you to concentrate on school and stuff. I know! [I hand him a scissors.]

Kevin: Yeah, cut them up.

Therapist: Right. Why don't you separate them from one another?

Kevin: Cool. [He cuts them into strips.] Look like those fortune cookie things.

Therapist: They do. Now we have five separate worries. Instead of one big messy worry, we have five smaller ones.

Kevin: Now we can throw them away?

Therapist: Nope. You really want to get rid of them, don't you?

Kevin: Yeah.

Therapist: [Picking up one of the worries] Now the good part. When is the best time of the day to worry about this worry?

Kevin: Art class, cause they let you draw there.

Therapist: Perfect. Where do you want to put the rest of these worries while you work on this one?

Kevin: I'll leave them here.

Therapist: All of them? I don't know. Where would you put them that's safe?

Kevin: In your desk.

Therapist: Good idea. [Taking out an envelope.] Here, write your name on this. You can leave them here for now. When you come back next week we can take them out and figure out what to do with them.

One variation on the desk drawer as a safe storage area, referred to by one child as "the vault," is as follows. The child, with the clinician's help, constructs a fort out of wooden blocks, taking care to insure that the structure has one room for each worry contained on the list. Each worry, with the exception of the one being taken home by the child, is then placed in its own room. The child is told, "Each worry is locked inside its own strong room and it can only come out when you decide to unlock the door and let it out to play. So if you are having a math test or doing something important it won't come out and bother you."

References

Haley, J. (1973). *Uncommon Therapy: The Psychiatric Techniques of Milton Erickson, M.D.* New York: Norton.

Meichenbaum, D. (1974). *Cognitive-Behavior Modification.* New York: Plenum.

Sloves, R., and Peterlin, K. (1994). Time-limited play therapy with children. In *Handbook of Play Therapy: Volume II,* ed. C. Schaefer and K. O'Connor pp. 27–59. New York: Wiley.

88

My Baby Book

Karen Pitzen

INTRODUCTION

The activity called *My Baby Book* has been used with young children who have been removed from their birth parents and who have little or no history or pictures from their early lives. The birth parents are either physically or emotionally unavailable to give needed information about the child's early experiences and development. Foster children and adopted children ages 8 and above have used this activity to create an emotional record of their early lives. *My Baby Book* can uncover an explanation for the child's troubling behaviors or a connection to the source of persistent feelings for the child.

The activity was inspired by a 9-year-old boy who called his foster mother from the school office and asked her what he was like as a baby. He had been given the assignment to write an autobiography. Because he had moved into his foster home at age 5, his foster mother did not know him as a baby. Fortunately, his foster mother was able to respond to him in spirit, saying such things as, "I am sure you were a cuddly, lovable baby boy." His curiosity about his life as an infant led to the creation of *My Baby Book*.

RATIONALE

The activity is to make a simple book of baby pictures to help the child explore his or her early attachment to his or her mother and to help to explain to the child why he or she still has certain troubling behaviors and feelings. Many children have an innate understanding and curiosity about babies. These natural skills can be used to create understanding of and mastery over early childhood experiences, many of which may never have been put into words before doing this activity. Because children often have strong loyalties to their birth families, they are closed to having negative thoughts and feelings about them. It is as if saying anything negative would literally cause the loss of their birth family. The child would then have an even stronger reason to blame him or herself for their loss. However, the child may be struggling with behaviors and feelings that have their origins in early childhood experiences. To respect the child's loyalties, the activity starts with questions that are more general and continues with questions that more directly address the child's experience with his or her birth family. The therapist and child can stop at any level of question about the baby in the picture.

DESCRIPTION

Begin with a selection of ten to fifteen baby pictures copied from a book about babies or early child development. *Your Baby and Child* by Penelope Leach has excellent evocative pictures showing babies having their needs met in a variety of ways: nursing, being bathed, playing, having a tantrum, and others. Have 8½" × 11" paper, glue, pens, and scissors ready.

Explain to the child that you will be working together to learn more about what she or he was like as a baby, what kind of care the child received, and how the child may have felt as a baby. The therapist explains to the child that together using the book they will be better able to understand the problem the child is having currently. The child selects one of the baby pictures. It is cut out and glued to the page. The therapist asks the child some or all of the following questions. While the child dictates, the therapist writes the child's descriptions below the picture. The questions are:

1. What is happening in the picture? What is the baby doing? Who is taking care of the baby? How is the person taking care of the baby?
2. How does the baby feel in the picture? How does the parent feel?
3. What happens if the baby gets good care: was fed, was kept clean, was played with? What kind of person does the baby grow up to be?
4. What happens if the baby does not get good care? (Suggest some of the experiences that you think may have happened for this child: parents fighting, drug abuse, neglect, etc.) What kind of person does the baby grow up to be?
5. What do you think it was like for you?

Collect the pages to make into a book, completing one or two per session. The child can make a cover and give the book a title: My Baby Book or My Life Book have been used. The child may choose to share the book with his or her parents.

APPLICATIONS

Making a book about early experiences can be helpful with children who have experienced early or preverbal trauma. The book helps the child put words and pictures to his or her needs as an infant and connects those unmet needs to later childhood problems. This process can be helpful to children who have spent part or all of their first five years in families where there was drug abuse, mental illness of a parent, severe poverty, violence directed toward the child or spouse, maternal absence, or neglect. These are children who often have trouble trusting others to meet their needs and who feel extremely powerless in relationships. Foster or adoptive children who are working to form attachments to new caregivers can use this process to explore their earliest attachment experiences. Children who struggle with persistent behavior problems such as hoarding food, lying, stealing, or other "survival" behaviors can use this technique to discover the reasons behind their behavior and consider its current utility. Children who have a hard time being genuine with others can look more closely at their earliest relationships and the primitive emotions which connect people. My Baby Book can be used by a child beginning the process of grieving for a lost parent and grieving the loss of not getting his or her earliest needs met.

89

The Song Flute or Recorder

Robert W. Freeman

INTRODUCTION

Just as the playing of music has been used to charm (the savage beast), to hypnotize (snakes in India), to exterminate (the rats of Hamelin), to mollify (lullabies for babies), to improve egg production (symphonies in the henhouse), to relax shoppers (canned music in stores or elevators), so also can it be used as a therapeutic intervention with children.

Use of music as a therapeutic intervention has a long history (Boxill 1985). Historically, music has been used as a method of healing. Its restorative aspect has been extolled in examples such as Plato's description of promoting health and harmony through music, David soothing Saul by playing the harp, Apollo delighting the gods of Olympus with the harmony of the lyre (Larousse 1959).

With the rise of the notion of the "therapeutic milieu" (Bettelheim and Sylvester 1949, Jones 1953), treatment branched out to many nonverbal areas: art, dance, physical movement, music. These activities were viewed as enhancing the therapeutic or mental health environment. Music therapy became a part of work in hospitals, schools, and institutional settings. Music was first used to entertain and involve patients, but gained popularity as a therapeutic agent "in the integration and treatment of human personality" (Music Therapy Training Manual 1964). Music therapy in the mental health setting appeared in large group activities such as variety shows, plays, and talent shows, smaller group activities such as choirs, choruses, instrumental, and rhythm groups, and in individual activities such as lessons.

Music was used to affect moods. In hospitals, soothing and calming music was used with distraught and disturbed patients. Catatonic patients were roused by martial and stimulating music. Viewed overall, music therapy was described as "the controlled use of music in the treatment rehabilitation, education, and training of children and adults suffering from physical, mental, or emotional disorder" (Alvin 1966). While music therapy covers a broad area, the focus here is on the use of music in therapy as an intervention.

The idea of using the song-flute or recorder as a therapeutic adjunct first occurred when the author was working with a 10-year-old boy who was functioning in a random, undirected way. While initially there was value to letting this behavior play out, in order to gain some awareness of the background of the problem some method of measuring change and progress was needed to show him that change was possible. He was doing poorly in all school subjects. Reading was going nowhere, and at 10 he couldn't even ride a bike. He was stuck, and with so much discouragement and low self-esteem he needed some way to identify progress. The recorder was introduced into therapy as a tangible way to measure change, as we moved slowly from three notes and simple pieces to thirteen or fourteen notes and duets. Along with other therapeutic work the recorder progress was specific and tangible evidence of growth, change, and progress.

In Barnard's chapter (1953) on the philosophy of the theory of music therapy, the term "adjuvant" was used to identify music as an auxiliary action or something that facilitates and enhances a treatment. That is the effort here, to employ an adjuvant action that aids, facilitates, and enhances the treatment.

RATIONALE

Once-a-week therapeutic contact with children often moves slowly, and progress is hard to identify in a tangible way. A measurable way of demonstrating change is needed. The teaching of something new and different that incorporates visual, auditory, and kinesthetic action seems useful. The activity needs to start at a very basic level and build up. It needs to facilitate progress and change in addition to augmenting treatment. The song flute or recorder is ideal for this purpose. It is a simple instrument and can be taught to a variety of children. Change and development can be emphasized by expanding the repertoire of notes learned as well as visibly noting the progression of songbook pages accomplished.

Recorder playing also provides for interaction. In this variation, the therapist plays with the youngster, which serves as a support function, from warming up by playing a scale or notes learned to the actual playing of pieces. Recorder playing quickly becomes a cooperative activity. Therapist and client are doing something together that is a paradigm for the whole therapy process—working together for progress and change. The time spent together may serve as a predictable part of the session and a cementing aspect of the relationship.

Gaston (1968), writing of basic principles for music therapy, mentions two of these as: "The establishment of re-establishment of interpersonal relationships," and "the bringing about of self-esteem through self-actualization" (p. 7). Dickinson (1976) lists a number of benefits from the use of music with children with problems. These include improved concentration, extension of attention span, improved articulation, stimulation of interest and curiosity, and satisfaction of achievement. All of the above have been experienced in using the recorder.

Barnard (1953) makes a statement about the benefits of playing piano scales that could easily be applied to the use of the recorder by describing the benefits:

> This can be an experience in adapting oneself to authority and following prescribed rules for an impulsive anti-social person; it can be a creative experience for the person who has never done anything for the sheer pleasure to be derived; it can be a gratifying experience for the person burdened with "I can't learn anything" attitude; it can be a task to perfect for the compulsive person; it can be a medium for aggressive pounding and banging (blowing hard and taking the recorder apart) where needed; it can be a never-ending task for the guilt-ridden person; it can be a stepping stone to verbal communication for the withdrawn person; and so on with endless variation. [p. 47]

DESCRIPTION

The song flute or recorder is one of several flutes that have existed in a formal way at least from the eleventh century in France (Sachs 1940), although certainly use of willow branches, bamboo shoots, and bird bones as flutes goes back much farther in history.

There are two elements which support the use of the recorder:

1. It is easy. The soprano recorder was selected for use because of the straightforward blow and fingering to make sounds, and the simplicity of learning to play recognizable tunes. The simplicity of producing fairly accurate sounds virtually guarantees an identifiable tune such as "Hot Cross Buns" or "Frere Jacques" can be played within 10–15 minutes of instruction and practice.

Musical talent is not required. While the therapist should have some familiarity with music and be able to count, this is an example of a situation where the teacher can be a few pages ahead of the pupil and function adequately.

An instruction book that uses a spaced letter notation is recommended, since "it enables students to play more music and to use complicated rhythms sooner than is typically possible with staff notations" (Hoenack 1986). Experience with many youngsters suggests that once they master the letter notes, later transition to musical notes is accomplished with little difficulty.

2. It is learnable. The actual procedure is first to show the youngster how to hold the flute. Then teach the B fingering position (covering the top front hold with the index finger of the left hand and covering the dorsal hole with the thumb of the left hand), and show, play, play with the child. (The Hoenack book gives more complete instructions.) Then teach the A fingering position, and show, play, play with the child. Teach the G fingering position, and so on. After minimal practice of the three notes (B,A,G) proceed to the first song in the book. There are nine songs in the Hoenack book that can be learned before going on to the next note. Often youngsters wish to play a note or a piece by themselves. This is fine, yet in general having the teacher–therapist play along with the learner helps to correct and make clearer the correct note by having a standard. It also encourages the cooperative process.

APPLICATIONS

The simplicity of the task means it can be introduced at any time in the course of therapy, but it may be most effective when some trust has developed. Hopefully, this will be early in the treatment to maximize growth.

Consistency is important, with once-a-week practice. Practice time can be brief, usually three to five minutes a session. The short exposure still permits learning over time. No practicing outside the session is required, which diminishes complaints and does not put undue pressure on the child. The satisfaction and reinforcing effect of both easy learning and easy progress reduce the resistance to learning that is characteristic of many problem children.

Teaching recorder is possible with a variety of cases. Youngsters who are withdrawn can be helped to participate. The short weekly practice has advantages when used with youngsters who resist pressure. Developmentally delayed youngsters have shown a remarkable ability to learn and enjoy recorder playing. The slow but measurable steps to improvement are apparent and appreciated. Youngsters with attention problems are usually able to endure the brief practice and, as their repertoire grows, take pride in this progress. It has been used with success with a visually impaired child who learned the fingering (slowly) yet took great joy and pride in the accomplishment of playing simple tunes. The child who has poor motor control and poor coordination can be brought to cover the holes, with practice. As a metaphor for handling the child's disruptive behavior the lesson often included, "You need to tell your fingers what to do," as a way of saying, "You have control over your own actions."

Although used with a variety of behavior problems, the most moving changes came with developmentally delayed youngsters. The length of therapy may have been a factor here since these youngsters were long-term cases. A breakthrough was hearing Martin playing Beethoven's Ode to Joy (p. 24 in Hoenack's book, requiring the knowledge of only six notes), or Kevin, who had been diagnosed early as autistic and typically responded in a hollow or empty way. He progressed to the point where he could play simple duets, which meant he had to listen to himself and also to the therapist so we could play together.

Teaching and playing the recorder as an adjunct to therapy can have benefits and it is a cooperative, learnable, and easy activity in which the therapist and youngster can engage.

References

Alvin, J. (1966). *Music Therapy.* New York: Basic Books.

Barnard, R. (1953). The philosophy and theory of music therapy as a adjuvant therapy. In *Music Therapy,* 1952, ed. E. G. Gilliland, pp. 45–49. Lawrence, KS: Allen Press.

Bettelheim, B., and Sylvester, E. (1949). Milieu therapy: indications and illustrations. *Psychoanalytic Review* 36(1): 54–68.

Boxill, E. W. (1985). *Music Therapy for the Developmentally Disabled.* Rockville, MD: Aspen.

Dickinson, P. (1976). *Music with ESN Children.* Atlantic Highlands, NJ: Humanities Press.

Gaston, E. T., ed. (1968). *Music in Therapy.* New York: Macmillan.

Hoenack, P. (1986). *Let's Sing and Play, Book 1.* Bethesda, MD: Music for Young People.

Jones, M. (1953). *The Therapeutic Community.* New York: Basic Books.

Larousse Encyclopedia of Mythology (1959). New York: Prometheus Press.

Music Therapy Training Manual (1964). Westville, IN: Norman M. Beatty Memorial Hospital.

Sachs, C. (1940). *The History of Musical Instruments.* New York: Norton.

90

The Starting Over Wedding Gown Ceremony

Patricia B. Grigoryev

INTRODUCTION

Shame is a potent poison to self esteem (Shore 1994, Lewis 1991). Shame is also a common experience for children who have been sexually violated. Even after therapy has begun to help resolve problems with self-blame, loss of power, and anger, many sexually abused children continue to suffer a sense of having been made unclean or dirtied. There can be a belief that the body and self have been contaminated, defiled, or negatively altered in some way as to continue to hold the abuse. This may be expressed directly or be seen in a variety of play themes such as repetitious cleansing and washing play, avoidance of messy play, or overindulgence in messy play. These children may appear to lack playfulness and spontaneity, have somatic complaints or other signs of depression (Gil 1991).

RATIONALE

A technique that helps address this pain is to offer the experience of a cleansing ritual. Toward this end, a wedding dress in the playroom has been particularly useful and much enjoyed by girls of all ages. Children are generally well inculturated with the symbolism of whiteness, purity, and new beginnings associated with a white wedding gown.

A starting over wedding ceremony play experience can be powerfully helpful as the child can incorporate a positive sense of newness and restoration to the body. Repetition of this play is common, as the child may wish to solidify the memory of the cleansing experience. The child may be so moved by the play as to inquire as to whether or not it's real. A helpful response may be, "It's really fun to believe in, and yes, you are truly starting over, all brand new."

DESCRIPTION

This play can be accomplished in both individual and group settings. A clean, white bridal gown in good shape is needed. Second-hand clothing stores are a good source. A gown that is soiled or torn will not be effective. A bridal veil with a blush to go over the face is helpful to further allow anonymity and distance of self. A silk bridal flower bouquet can be held. In group play settings, the child may choose to have "attendants" and "witnesses" for the ceremony. The therapist can assist the child in custom designing the format of the ceremony, which can be playfully conducted with much pomp and circumstance. The climax of the ceremony occurs when the therapist ceremoniously officiates (I wave a magic wand) at the wedding with a solemn expression of purification. "Magic, magic pudding and pie, on the count of three all that is past is past, and you get to start over, all brand new, squeaky clean. All bad, yucky feelings from the bad touch have to go. One, two three! Now it's done, and the starting over has begun. You are now free to start over." The child can play out the celebration in many ways. Some have enjoyed promenading through the playroom, attendants in tow, and even through the lobby, to show off for the receptionist and parents. Following the ceremony, the child can play that she now has the magic to share with others. Given the wand, she can offer the same kind of purification to others in the group or to dolls and puppets. The therapist should be cautious in emphasizing that the ceremony is one of new beginnings and renewal. The child should not be led to believe that there will be a complete and automatic change.

APPLICATIONS

KC reluctantly joined a therapy group for latency-aged girls with a history of sexual abuse. She was pale, thin, and easily overwhelmed by common social demands. Despite friendly overtures from the therapist and peers, she hid herself under the playroom table, curled in a ball, nonresponsive. This continued for several sessions and she made little use of the playroom. Then the wedding gown was added to the dress-up area. The therapist suggested that the group have starting over wedding ceremonies.

"I have an idea that it might be fun to dress up and have official starting over wedding ceremonies. We have talked a lot about how kids feel stuck and feel like it's hard to get rid of the feelings from bad touch on your bodies. Some kids have told me that it's hard to feel really clean, even after a long shower. Did you ever have that feeling?" Group discussion can be encouraged to capture and validate feelings and thoughts about body damage. Generally the children are surprised and comforted to learn that others have harbored similar fantasies and fears. "Yeah, I have that, and I still sometimes can smell the way he smelled and it's so gross." "Me too, I hate it, sometimes I just feel smelly like him." "I used to think that the stuff he made in me was still there, but my Mom says it's not, but sometimes. . . ."

The therapist can use this time to educate the children about the reality of their cleanliness. This play can further help to form a solid memory of having been officially cleansed. The child may begin to internalize a renewed representation of self that includes a clean, fresh body.

In KC's group, the idea to have starting over ceremonies was received with much excitement and the children immediately elected to draw up a list of names ordering each person's time to be "bride." KC shyly watched with new animation and interest. When her time arrived, she dressed herself quietly, drew the bridal blush over her face, and solemnly walked through the ceremony. Her demeanor changed greatly after this session. She began to initiate play with others, quietly drawing one child at a time to join her in a favorite board game. Week after week she appeared to open like to flower within the safety and openness of the group. She eventually asked her mother to come in after group so that she could see her in her starting over wedding gown. She began to laugh, play, and become more childlike and happy as she moved through more avenues of therapy. The gown play allowed KC to begin to redefine her inner sense of self from broken and dirtied to new and cleansed. Her devastating abuse experience had occurred in secret. Therefore, the experience of having friends and family witness her cleansing ceremony was even more important. She was able to enact and form a powerful memory of her newness, both witnessed and validated.

Children who have suffered a damaged self-image may benefit from this play. It has been especially helpful in group play, family play (both mothers and daughters can be encouraged to state their own ceremonies), and individual play.

References

Gil, E. (1991). *The Healing Power of Play: Working with Abused Children.* New York: Guilford.

Lewis, M. (1992). *Shame: The Exposed Self.* New York: Free Press.

Shore, A. (1994). *Affect Regulation and the Origin of the Self: The Neurobiology of Emotional Development.* Hillsdale, NJ: Lawrence Erlbaum.

91

Play Therapy and Pets

Mary-Lynn Harrison

INTRODUCTION

Pets are increasingly being used therapeutically across the country. Animals are being taken into hospitals, nursing homes, jails, residential treatment centers, schools, and therapy offices to provide nonthreatening, unconditionally accepting, warm and fuzzy contact with patients, clients, inmates, and students.

The Delta Society of Renton, Washington, serves as an umbrella organization for more than 2,500 people active in animal-assisted programs nationwide, up from fewer than 50 in the 1970s. The Delta Society's list of animals approved for emotional therapy work includes dogs, potbellied pigs, donkeys, llamas, guinea pigs, cats, and rabbits (Wolcott 1993).

Research conducted at the Devereux Foundation, the country's largest collection of treatment facilities for children in need of special education and care, has produced evidence in favor of animal-assisted therapy and education. In a Philadelphia-based study of 50 boys ages 9–15, exposure to animals seemed not only to reduce symptoms of hyperactivity and oppositional behavior, but increased the children's learning capacities (Golin and Walsh 1994).

Because pets both give and receive affection, they can be emotional substitutes and contribute to maintaining morale when people are alone or going through difficult periods of transition (Sable 1995). In Brewster, New York, a residential treatment program called Green Chimney's Children's Services provides healing opportunities with farm animals and wildlife to children with severe backgrounds of abuse, neglect, school failure, loss, and separation. Farm animals provide tactile stimulation and safe opportunities to hug and hold living things. Through wildlife rehabilitation, the children can identify with the birds that have broken legs or wings, and gain encouragement and hope from seeing them heal (Golin and Walsh 1994).

In Tallahassee, Florida, pet therapy is being successfully used with children who were born addicted to crack. And at the Julia Dyckman Andrus residential home in Yonkers, New York, emotionally disturbed children who were visited weekly for eight weeks by college students with dogs and cats exhibited less acting-out behavior (Burke 1992).

According to Beck and Katcher (1983), well-known researchers on the health enhancing effects of pets and authors of *Between People and Pets,* animals can make a unique contribution to therapy because of their capacity to make people feel safe, loved, and worthwhile. Animals do not use words, and patients can safely approach them when they cannot approach people. Also, the pet has the capacity to call forth speech from those who have given up speaking. Dolphin-assisted therapy seems to accelerate the vocal and physical development of autistic and mentally retarded children (Blow 1995).

While pet-facilitated therapy (PFT) most often refers to a professional or volunteer bringing a pet to a patient, the technique described here involves the client bringing his or her own pet to a therapy session.

Having clients bring in their pets is therapeutic for many reasons. A child usually loves its pet, who is often regarded as another family member, even as a child's peer (Nebbe 1991). A child is usually eager to share a pet with the therapist and the sharing strengthens the therapeutic alliance. The presence of the pet offers serendipity: the child and therapist experience the spontaneity of the pet's personality together. The child's trust and respect for the therapist is enhanced because of the common interest in the animal (Nebbe 1991). Pets in therapy provide opportunities for child and therapist to laugh together, a critical component of bonding and good mental health. Using a child's pets in therapy also increases a child's self-esteem: the child, as the pet's "expert," can teach the therapist about the pet, and experience the humility of the therapist who is willing to be taught.

In her book *Children at Play, a Preparation for Life,* Heidi Britz-Crecelius speaks of doll play, which usually begins in the second year, as "the game that touches the depths of the personality . . . here, the child meets itself" (p. 82). She says, "The favorite doll—it can also be a teddy bear or some other small animal—is endowed with a bit of the child's own soul" (p. 83). I'd like to suggest that, like the favorite doll, a child's pet carries a part of the child's soul until the child is ready to reclaim it. The act of sharing the pet with the therapist helps the child reclaim lost pieces of him- or herself.

Pets in session are not only therapeutic for children but also diagnostic, and provide ample opportunities for the therapist to observe a child's ability to make contact, empathize, nurture and set boundaries.

DESCRIPTION

A pet can be brought into a session with little or no preparation. Usually I know one week in advance that a child will bring in his or her pet.

I ask at the time of the intake what pets are part of a family. Later on, when the child mentions a pet in the course of therapy, I ask if my client would like to bring in his or her pet. This suggestion is usually met enthusiastically and with gleeful anticipation.

When the pet is brought in, I encourage the child to introduce me to the pet. If I am invited to hold the pet, I do. I model connection with the animal, and talk to it myself. I let the child lead the way and provide supportive presence. Staying in the moment with the child and the pet is important, providing that "free and protected" space of therapy, with time to talk, listen, laugh, and watch.

I also observe how the child interacts with the pet. I gently encourage the child to share about the pet if he or she wants to. I might ask: Where did the pet come from? How long has it been in the family? How was this particular animal chosen and named? Where does it sleep? How does the child feed and care for it? Importantly, what does the child like best and least about the pet and in what ways is the child like his pet? How does the child feel about the pet? I may also ask, "If your pet could tell you something special, what would it say to you?" and then, "What would you like to say to your pet? If he could talk, what would he say back to you?"

There may also be specific relationship issues about a pet that call for the child to bring it to one or more sessions. Nebbe (1991) described a series of sessions with a fourth-grade girl and her "mean" parakeet who needed to learn to be nice.

APPLICATIONS

Animals have been known to be especially helpful in cases of withdrawn and alienated children, but I believe that regardless of diagnosis, using this technique, any child who is willing to share his or her pet can benefit from one or more sessions with the pet.

In one instance, a 10-year-old, female client of mine brought her guinea pig lovingly cradled in her arms and wrapped in swaddling towels. She set it on the table, and we petted it and talked about it. We took pictures of it, and she let it run on the floor and hide in the toys. Her enthusiasm in this session was significant. This was a child who hoped to be a veterinarian when she grew up. She was being treated for difficulties in completing tasks at home and at school, and for relationship problems with family members and peers.

In another situation, a 9-year-old girl who had been sexually molested brought her chameleon in a carry case. She allowed me to let it crawl up my arm, and delighted in my initial tentativeness, and then my acceptance and curiosity about it. She knew all about it, and could instruct me in how to handle it.

It is interesting to note whether a client's pets change over time. The client with the chameleon later got a rabbit. The addition of the rabbit took place as the client became more visible and self-identified. She then cared for both the animal that represented part of herself as she was and the new fluffy white animal that symbolized rebirth and spring.

Sessions with pets and children can be great successes and a common experience that enhances the therapeutic bond.

References

Beck, A., and Katcher, A. (1983). *Between Pets and People.* New York: Putnam.

Blow, R. (1995). Dr. Dolphin: Why does swimming with dolphins help humans heal? *Mother Jones* 20(1): 28-31.

Britz-Crecelius, H. (1972). *Children at Play. Preparation for Life.* Rochester, VT: Inner Traditions International.

Burke, S. (1992). In the presence of animals: health professionals no longer scoff at the therapeutic effect of pets. *U.S. News & World Report* 112(7): 64-66.

Golin, M., and Walsh, T. (1994). Heal emotions with fur, feathers, and love. Animal Assisted therapy and education for children. *Prevention* 46 (12): 80-84.

Nebbe, L. L., (1991). The human-animal bond and the elementary counselor. *School Counselor* 38(5): 362-371.

Sable, P. (1995). Pets, attachment, and well-being across the life cycle. *Social Work* 40(3): 334-341.

Wolcott, J. (1993). Pet therapy gains credibility in Northwest hospitals. *Business Journal-Portland* 10(8): 8A(2).

92

The Twelve-to-One Technique

Mary May Schmidt

INTRODUCTION

The Twelve-to-One Technique is a simple exercise that I have adapted for group play therapy with latency-aged children in a school setting. Essentially, twelve positive statements are made to counter the painful impact of a single hurtful remark or insult. The use of single visual aids and the encouraged participation of group members make this technique joyful and eloquent.

RATIONALE

Children are defenseless against adult criticism, sarcasm, derogatory punning, and such because they are not yet capable of understanding or using verbal gaming, but more importantly they are caught between needing and depending upon adult protection and nurturance on the one hand and fearing adult rejection on the other. The child experiences criticism as a separation from the adult, so a child dares not risk countering the adult with similar verbal responses because the child cannot bear to be responsible for adding to his own feelings of separation and loss. The child is very confused about the mixed messages of love and distancing that he or she receives from the critical adult and can, at best, conclude that the adult, being powerful, must be right. The child feels defective, lonely, and wounded.

Another powerful adult, the therapist, must champion the wounded child, heal the hurt, and teach the child some wisdom about recognizing his own worth. This adult may also be able to soften the perfect image that the child holds of the criticizing adult and thus make that adult more approachable for the child. Because criticism has such great impact, it is not enough to assume that one insult can be eradicated by one compliment. The Twelve-to-One Technique supplants the one criticism with twelve sincere compliments, compliments that the child will clearly recognize as true. This technique, used in a group therapy format, adds the participation of peers who identify with the hurt child's painful dilemma and who are also deeply and vicariously invested in this healing process.

DESCRIPTION

The therapist makes twelve cards of one color and one card of another contrasting color. The cards can be made from construction paper and laminated for strength. All cards should be the same size, a size that fits easily in the hand much like commercially made playing cards. I chose blue for the twelve cards that represent compliments because I use images such as "true blue" and "blue ribbon" to increase the kinds of positive associations that the children attach to the twelve positive statements. I chose orange as the color that represents the negative remark because I use images such as "glaring" or "slime mold from the back of the refrigerator" to help the children defuse the impact of the insult. The colors that the therapist chooses are a matter of personal style.

The therapist must generate a list of at least a dozen statements that can be personalized to fit most children. Some examples might include: "I know you are the kind of child who cares about being helpful to your (mom, dad, etc.) because you have told us about the times that you (set the table, turned down the volume on the TV without being asked, etc.)"; "I know you are the kind of a child who worries about doing the right thing because you have told us about the time when you remembered to ask your (mom, dad, etc.) before you borrowed (some personal item)"; "I have seen you pick up papers that another child dropped by accident in the cafeteria"; or "I have seen you practice good manners many times when. . . ." The therapist must be so familiar with this prepared list that the therapist can spontaneously use the list without referring to the list. I keep a list of about fifteen such statements on a small piece of paper located on my filing cabinet within easy sight for me but too disguised among many notes for others to readily see. Practicing the list makes the therapist appear spontaneous and fluid and increases the sincerity value of the whole exercise.

Use this technique when a child has disclosed to the group a painful experience with adult criticism, particularly when the criticism has no intrinsic teaching value, such as "Your room looks like an armpit!" Acknowledge the pain of the criticism and encourage the child and the peer group to think about what that feels like. Offer a brief reframing of the criticism, something that is appropriate to the child's situation and that also serves to protect the child's relationship with the criticizing adult. (Other therapeutic interventions may be appropriate outside the group setting if the therapist suspects the parents need parenting skills, or if the therapist suspects emotional or other abuse.) Then the therapist tells the child and the group, "We are going to bury that painful criticism right now." Place the orange card on the table for all to see and explain that this card represents the insult. Let the child pound on the card and make angry faces at it. Encourage the others to join in.

The therapist then fans the blue cards in her hand and waits for the children's expectant looks. Say, "These blue cards represent twelve true blue qualities that we all know that fit [child's name]." The therapist should be mildly theatrical but also sincere and matter-of-fact. With each blue card held for all to see, the therapist repeats a positive statement and begins to bury the orange card on the table. The therapist can invite the peers to offer a compliment or invite them to cheer after each one. The more active the group involvement, the more therapeutic the impact. Group cohesiveness and friendship carry the import of this activity out of the playroom and into the rest of the child's day. By the fifth or sixth blue card, the orange card should no longer be visible. The therapist can stop briefly to show the children how cleverly the insult has been buried, and to show the children how many more positive statements are yet to come.

When the twelve blue cards are all used, it is helpful to admire the work. This is a triumphant moment for the child and for the group. Slowly uncover the orange card and then cover it up again. Do not repeat the words attached to the orange card.

A few absolute rules:

1. If the therapist has a deck of twelve blue cards, the therapist must use all twelve. Do not end the exercise with unused cards in your hand.
2. Use a consistent pace from card to card. Children respond to rythmn. A consistent pace will convey the idea that each compliment is just as easily accessible to the therapist as the others.
3. Keep the positives concrete and personal. The insult certainly was!

APPLICATIONS

This technique is effective with most kinds of experiences in a child's life where adults have misused or misjudged their authority and have injured a child's self-esteem.

93

The Therapist on the Inside

Patricia B. Grigoryev

INTRODUCTION

The therapist is challenged to find ways to assist the child in the development of internal structures for self-regulation and the ability to tolerate negative affect. Learning to evoke the memory of the therapist to directly form a soothing internal object may assist the child who is underregulated.

RATIONALE

A primary task for the play therapist is to help the child to develop an ability to self-soothe, self-regulate, and tolerate negative feelings. Unregulated negative affect reactions can lead to a loss of the sense of inner self-cohesion (Shore 1995). Behavioral acting out may reflect the loss to esteem that occurs when painful affects are experienced without inner regulation.

The child can be benefitted if he or she can find a way to access the memory of the soothing, regulating experience afforded by the therapist during face-to-face sessions. Gradually, attempts to internalize the therapist will lead to positive changes in the self. Over time, the internalization of good objects allows the self to become more cohesive and more self-sufficient (Kahn 1991).

DESCRIPTION

A particular problem area, such as sexualized behaviors, stealing, nighttime fearfulness, or fighting with peers, is first identified with the child. The child is encouraged to directly evoke a memory of the therapist offering soothing and helpful support when next the problem is encountered. The following explanation to the child is instructive: "You know me so well now. You know so much about the way I am with you. And you know about the way you are with me. You know about the way I talk to you and how things go with us. You know how I think and feel about a lot of things now. You really have a lot of parts of me, and you and me together, on the inside of you now. I'm just wondering about something. How might it be if the next time you feel scared or mad or alone you try something very powerful? How about you just pretend I'm right there with you and able to talk to you? I wonder if you can imagine what I might say to you. How might I help if I could be with you right then and there?" At this point the child and therapist can imagine and visualize the conversation and calm feelings that might occur.

If imagining a situation is too abstract, as will be the case with younger children, the same result can be accomplished through more concrete means. For example, the child may be able to draw or describe a problem (or some metaphor for a problem). Next, have the child draw the problem again with the therapist (or some metaphor for the therapist) directly involved and helping, and then to draw the problem a final time with the problem resolved (all better). Another method is to use puppet play. The therapist can enact a play in which one puppet is comforted by another, then "teaches" the comforted puppet to "remember me" while the comforter hides out of sight. In this way the structure of internalizing and retrieving an image of the soothing therapist can be established.

The same technique can be used to foster internalization of other appropriate nurturing objects for the child, e.g., an appropriate new parent figure who is experienced as one who supplies soothing and regulating structure.

APPLICATIONS

Children who have difficulty with self-regulation of strong emotions due to insufficient internalization of parent objects and self-soothing structures may benefit from this technique.

Nancy was a 9-year-old with a history of sexual abuse, a mother with borderline personality features, and a continuously chaotic home environment. Her mother had little ability to regulate her own affect and was subject to severe rage. With a few opportunities to experience and internalize affect regulation from her primary caretaker, Nancy had limited ability to regulate fear and rage.

In group play therapy she began to show some increased ability to control sudden rage. However, she continued to have difficulty at home and school and was frequently in trouble for engaging in physical fighting with peers. In group she was taught a cognitive problem-solving strategy to avert rage and fighting cycles. However, she could not consistently or successfully use this to avoid fighting in settings outside of the group therapy playroom. She was then encouraged to consult the Therapist on the Inside whenever she felt scared or alone.

Nancy entered the playroom and announced that she had once again been placed on in-house school suspension for fighting with a peer. We discussed the situation, the events leading up to the fight, and her attempt to use the cognitive problem-solving techniques already available to her. "I did, but it didn't work," she stated with little emotion. "All right, let's try something very powerful then," I said, capturing her interest.

"You know me so well now. You know so much about the way I am with you, and the way you are with me. You know about the way I talk to you. And you know how things go with us. You know how I think and feel about a lot of things now. You really have a lot of parts of me, and you and me together, on the inside of you now. I'm just wondering about something. How might it be if the next time you feel scared or mad or alone you do something different? How about you just pretend I'm right there with you and able to talk to you? I wonder if you can imagine what I might say to you. How might I be able to help you if I could be with you right then and there? Lets say we try this at school, the next time you feel upset and have a problem that may lead to a fight. How would it be if you were to think about having me right there with you, and helping you? What would I probably say to you if I could be right with you next time a kid gets you so mad that you are about to get into a big fight?"

Nancy looked thoughtful and then smiled knowingly. "You'd say for me to stop, and breath deep, and think ways to get out of it."

"Right, great, so you really do know a lot about how I am! What would I say next?"

Nancy replied easily, "You'd say that I should go sit with my teacher, Miss Sims, I guess."

"Right, until you feel calm again. Would I be mad at you or anything like that?" I asked.

"No," she smiled.

"Right again. So I still like you?"

She looked thoughtful, and replied, "You're always the same, so you'd just be the same, you'd like me still."

"You do know me so well. You could remember how I put my arm on your shoulder like this, and say, "It's all right," and use my quiet voice, and say, "You're OK." I placed my hand on her shoulder and gently squeezed for emphasis. "Now this is the really powerful part. I would like it if you talk to me any time you want. You can talk to me on the inside, in your thinking and feeling part. Then we can talk about it in person when you come back. Could you try that?"

Nancy agreed to try this the next time she felt out of control. She later reported that she had been able to remember being together and to pretend I was there and supporting her. She said that she could think of the playroom, the therapist, and our conversations at will. In fact, she began to be better able to control the fear, rage, and fighting behavior much more often. She was able to access more directly an inner object for soothing and regulation. With practice, this object was to become more and more refined and available as a self-soothing structure. Nancy was able to become more controlled because she did not feel as utterly alone and without help when her feelings became intensely negative.

References

Kahn, M. (1991). *Between Therapist and Client: The New Relationship*. New York: Freeman.

Shore, A. (1995). *Affect Regulation and the Origin of the Self: The Neurobiology of Emotional Development*. Hillsdale, NJ: Lawrence Erlbaum.

94

Play-by-Play

David A. Snyder

INTRODUCTION

This technique is one that builds on or springs from my orientation toward child-centered play therapy. This technique is a "dressed up" form of reflection, giving back to the child what the therapist observes in his or her play.

RATIONALE

The rationale behind this technique is therefore parallel to why we use other types of reflection: to confirm or validate the child's expression as demonstrated in play. This technique has the potential to extend beyond mere reflection by offering the child new descriptors for feelings that may be displayed. The therapist may also "smuggle in" interpretive content or provide more adaptive response options in a lighthearted way to help the child move beyond a behavior or feeling that has been displayed in play. The therapeutic value of the technique may also reside in the fact that through the use of exaggeration and dramatic emphasis the difficulty that the child brings into the playroom may be externalized and thereby seen or felt to be more manageable.

DESCRIPTION

The technique calls on the therapist to employ a stage voice in offering a running, descriptive commentary on the play of the child, as if the therapist is the play-by-play announcer of a sporting event. Like a sportscaster the therapist should seek to include much dramatic flair, clichés that may be significant for the child, and feigned affect that may extend what is being displayed by the child. The technique may be used by a therapist who is strictly in an observer's role or while the therapist is actively engaged in play with the child.

APPLICATIONS

This technique can be used with a range of cases. I first used the technique with a very active boy as a way to validate his physical energy while gently adding commentary that pointed out the real or potential consequences of acting without thinking. I have also used the technique to reflect aggressive feelings and behavior. One boy's kicks and punches to a beanbag chair were turned into a mythic struggle between good and bad superheros that this boy often talked about. This technique may also be used with a depressed or withdrawn child as an indirect means to gently shift both activity and affect. As with any technique, this should be used sparingly and with careful attention given to the child's response.

95

The Time Line Tape Technique

Jo Ann L. Cook

INTRODUCTION

The Time Line Tape Technique described in this section was drawn from Neuro-Linguistic Programming (NLP) as described by Woodsmall and James (1988). The use of the present version allows a visible and less abstract conceptual basis that has been helpful with children in assisting them to grasp some temporal order and/or pattern of their history. They may then review and internalize successes and strengths from which to face and overcome difficult or traumatic events and move beyond them toward the future.

RATIONALE

Children experience difficulty grasping and organizing temporal concepts and projecting future coping methods or alternative perspectives due to their cognitive developmental levels. Use of specific points in time from which children can recall and describe recollections, their impacts, derived meanings, and related emotions allows them to relate their own life event histories, construct meanings as well as new understandings, and to step forward in time past previous fixation points.

DESCRIPTION

The application of the technique in the initial phase involves provision of a large piece of drawing paper and having available a straightedge or ruler, colored markers, pencils, or crayons. The therapist explores the method in which the child stores time, whether in left-to-right or right-to-left sequence, in a vertical process, or other variations, such as the past being behind oneself, present at the position where the person is seated or standing, and future moving forward. This can be discussed with reference to general or specific events that the person can describe. Children often willingly point to the position from which they mentally perceive their visual images or memories evolving. The paper is used to draw a Time Line of their lives, with the line running parallel to the discussed trajectory of their temporal perspective. The Time Line begins by requesting earliest recollections or associations and can be annotated with drawings, symbols, or words located on the Time Line at the position the child chooses with reference to a fixed point of their current age. Many seem to grasp the idea of describing events by ages or birthdays, others seem to describe memories more easily with reference to their grade in school at the time. The issues of concern can drive the methods of explorations; for example, grade, teacher, and class if the historical issues relate to school, or birthdays, holidays, or family vacations if the issues related to family situations.

With initial fixed points above, children often become quite interested and invested in compiling details and information, with additional drawings or words. Development of chronic patterns, changed patterns following difficult events, and other informative material can be explored. Using the drawing as a map, the children can then use wide masking tape to construct a time line of their lives on the floor using markers or color-contrasting tape to identify ages and events, often indicating them with symbols or drawings.

The process of movement can be evoked by actually physically walking through the times in their lives, while gathering strength through memories of successes. This prepares for return to previous negative or traumatic events from the current age, having developed increased awareness of strengths, resources, and insights regarding how to address the past. This allows movement forward, stepping though and beyond the events in the past and present and generalizing toward the future. For some children it has been helpful to pause and change drawings and illustrations at certain points of issue, or to leave some representational object behind and take chosen or meaningful objects forward in life with them. Processing the experience may include the ability to look back at the past without repeating it, carrying new learnings forward as well as grasping the chosen/meaningful memories in order to have them when facing future events. Having observed this experience with many children who were initially fearful of facing, discussing or even physically moving past a difficult period or current age marker, the ability to physically walk forward through the designations has been accompanied by a release and strength that have been notable. For example, many children have extended their time lines past their current year in school through middle and high school to college, projecting the forward movement of their success and self-esteem. Other children have extended their tape lines through the length of this office down a long hall and out the door "into the world." The joy and freedom that is exhibited by children previously emotionally held in time is often a vigorous powerful forward movement, signifying a release and a new perception and potential for facing life without their previous limitations.

Reference

Woodsmall, W. and James, T. (1988). *Time Line Therapy: And the Basis of Personality.* Los Angeles: Meta Publications.

96

Terminations Utilizing Metaphor

Teresa A. Glatthorn

INTRODUCTION

Termination is an opportunity to review and celebrate progress made in therapy, as well as to accomplish goals very specific to this phase of treatment (Kramer 1990). It is a window of opportunity in which clients are highly receptive to certain kinds of messages.

During the termination process, achievement of therapeutic goals is enhanced by the use of metaphor. Metaphorical terminations have several advantages. They use the natural language of the child and are therefore understood by clients of all ages (Gil 1991, Mills and Crowley 1986). Other advantages of metaphor are that this method is less threatening, more interesting, and more individualized than traditional techniques. Also, metaphorical messages access the unconscious directly and are therefore remembered longer (Barker 1985, Mills and Crowley 1986). Thus a metaphorical termination allows clients to carry forward for long periods of time the gains made and summarized during the termination process.

Termination is seen as a process during which a number of therapeutic approaches and/or techniques may be combined to achieve the goals noted below. The ideas and examples described herein are presented as a selection to stimulate the creativity of individual therapists to design the most meaningful and empowering metaphorical terminations for and with their clients.

Use of metaphor in termination with clients of all ages strengthens the endurance of the gains made in therapy. It summarizes the progress made and the termination messages in a way that is understandable and enjoyable, as well as deeply meaningful, moving, and lasting (Barker 1985, Mills and Crowley 1986). Envisioning termination as a graduation positively reframes this transition period and facilitates processing of the variety of emotions experienced. Joint planning of the termination process empowers the client and enables the therapist to capture the client's perception of the essence of their progress while planning for the future during terminating (Kramer 1990). Metaphorical terminations are highly individualized. They capture and hold termination messages and easily fit into a celebration of this important milestone in the client's life.

RATIONALE

Goals of metaphorical terminations are much the same as those of all terminations (Kramer 1990):

Review and celebrate progress made in therapy

Empower clients to use their strengths and tools

Identify areas for possible continued growth

Identify resources for future support and growth

Address issues related to endings in relationships

Express and accept the variety of emotions related to endings

Enable the client to experience a positive ending to a relationship

Maintain the client's trust and confidence in the therapeutic process

Identify and prepare for possible future pitfalls

Strengthen the client's sense of optimism and accomplishment

Solidify gains made during treatment to maintain them

Celebrate the new beginning and sense of autonomy

DESCRIPTION

Depending on the interests of the therapist and client and the nature of their work together, materials may be selected to create one or more of the projects below. Other projects and/or metaphors that the therapist and/or client feel can better capture the essence of the work can, and should, be substituted.

Seeds (ideally a selection of seeds with metaphorically significant names and/or natures), soil, container(s), water, and tools

Construction paper, lined paper, pens, markers, crayons, magazines, scissors, hole-punch, yarn, or other binding and laminating supplies (optional), to create a story or journal together, or as a gift to the client

Blank puzzles (and boxes in which to store them), key chains, refrigerator magnets, bookmarks, or button-making supplies, markers, crayons, paints, colored pencils

Oh, The Places You'll Go, by Dr. Seuss

Other children's books with appropriate messages

A metaphorical gift

In addition to the above materials, it is often appropriate as part of the celebration metaphor to have a celebratory snack, music, and/or graduation symbols. For example, depending on the age of the client, one might have cupcakes decorated with a graduation hat, a graduation card, empowering music, and/or a congratulatory balloon.

Ideally, termination is a process. During the early phases of the process, a discussion of termination and the accompanying feelings is part of the therapy. To assist in reframing the ending in a positive light and to provide empowerment during the termination process, clients often enjoy helping choose and plan the termination day and/or projects (Kramer 1990). Choices regarding activity, time lines, snacks, and symbols are appropriate and allow the therapist to individualize the process for each client or group of clients.

The therapist needs to review, either alone or with the client, what was gained during the therapeutic process, taking special note of turning points or key learning experiences and preferred natural metaphors. Therapists should note current strengths and resources as well as areas in which more growth is encouraged. Possible pitfalls need to be identified, along with skills and resources to deal with those pitfalls. The therapist needs to be aware of the positive aspects of the future for the client.

Once this review is complete, the therapist decides, again, either alone or with the client or in some combination, on an appropriate metaphorical language into which the above information will be translated for the client. This can include one or more of the following: an original story, a journal of growth, creation of a symbol of what was learned, planting seeds, reading stories with important messages and/or directives, listening to music with pertinent messages, presentation of a metaphorical gift, or some type of celebration. Ideally, the termination process is designed to include sufficient time for the creation of the metaphor(s) and the celebration.

The therapist and client discuss feelings during the process and work with the metaphor to achieve the termination goals. Then therapist and client celebrate the progress and future, while they express any sadness, similar to the process involved at a graduation (Kramer 1990).

APPLICATIONS

Metaphorical terminations are appropriate for and beneficial to clients 3 years of age and older, for whom metaphor and/or play are appropriate languages. The type of metaphor, and whether the metaphor is concrete and/or verbal, depends on the client's preferred mode of communication, developmental level, and level of intelligence, and the therapist's particular style and preference.

Metaphorical terminations are equally appropriate for groups, couples, families, and individuals.

Termination utilizing metaphor can be employed by anyone who is comfortable working in metaphor and/or play. As with all terminations, the therapist must be able to view terminations in a positive light and be aware of his or her own issues regarding termination. Therapists must be willing to deal with their own issues outside of the therapy room with a supervisor, therapist, or colleague (Kramer 1990). The process involves some preparation in terms of reviewing the progress made during the therapeutic process and delineating the specific termination goals. The therapist picks out key gains made, as well as the client's preferred metaphors.

Jeffrey is a 10-year-old boy who was referred to work on peer relationships and speaking up appropriately at home rather than acting out. During therapy, he learned to manage his anger and to ask for what he needed. Jeffrey's mother was a hypochondriac who found it necessary to constantly find illness and dysfunction in her children as well as herself. It was important for Jeffrey to feel he was no longer "ill." He also needed to understand that his mother was the one who now needed help. Mother accepted a referral for treatment.

When asked to design his termination celebration, Jeffrey successfully shared his wishes: sparklers to be lit in the field behind the office, and a snack of Lebanon bologna, cheddar cheese, crackers, and yellow mustard (items not commonly suggested by the therapist as celebratory treats, but very individualized to this child).

Termination day included a metaphorical story about a young injured hawk, his healing process, and his renewed ability to seek out what he needed in his life, knowing how to obtain the various foods he craved. The hawk had also learned how to avoid the injury he originally sustained while caring for an ornery, injured bear he loved, whose wounds he was unable to heal himself. The bear received assistance from other grown bears. And although the bear was still not healed, because its injuries were quite severe, it was gaining strength each day and would be continually cared for by the grown bears until it was well.

Jeffrey and the therapist enjoyed lighting sparklers in the field and then shared the specified snack. Jeffrey asked the therapist to keep the burnt remainders of the sparklers in her drawer "forever." The sparklers are still there, as is the memory of this young boy.

Melanie was a 15-year-old girl living in a group home. She had been sexually abused by both parents and was labeled as having oppositional defiant disorder. She was very defensive and refused to let adults get close to her. She also had a fatalistic outlook. Though her treatment ended prematurely due to financial issues, she had made very good progress. A breakthrough for Melanie had been made following an "oppositional" session in which she refused to talk, but allowed the therapist to talk about whatever came to her mind.

Melanie was told during this "oppositional" session about lobsters (which are referred to as crayfish after Melanie shared that she played with crayfish in a creek when she was little). Melanie learned that the shell of a crayfish does not grow. She learned that at many crucial points in the crayfish's life, it feels very constrained inside its shell and knows that if it is to survive and grow, it needs to shed its protective shell. The therapist discussed how vulnerable the crayfish was during this phase, and its other means of protection until it could grow a new shell that leaves room to grow.

Termination with Melanie included making a dream catcher with the therapist and discussing the power of believing in dreams and working toward realizing our own dreams. The time line for termination was also altered slightly when an appropriate request to do so was made by Melanie. She requested this in order to receive enough assistance from the therapist to finish the difficult aspects of the dream catcher, so she could complete it on her own when she left therapy. She was also presented with a necklace with a pewter crayfish pendant, a card with a symbol of another important metaphor for her on it, and, of course, a graduation cupcake.

It is important to note that part of the metaphor in this termination, as well as the one above, is in the process, not just the content. In each case, the clients were empowered to ask for and receive what they needed. In the second example, the metaphor also included Melanie's increased ability to accept the amount of help from adults that she required and then continue the work on her own.

Danielle, a 7-year-old foster child with severe acting out and a history of abuse, was working, among other goals, on issues around her placement versus eventual return to her mother. She had been returned once, only to be removed again. In the course of treatment, Danielle found acorns and began to plant them haphazardly in places where they had no chance of surviving. Discussion of the needs of the acorns led her to unearth them and plant three into pots. Danielle independently decided to leave one in the therapist's office and take two to her foster home, asking her foster mother to help nurture them for her. She planned to leave one with the foster parents and plant the other one that the foster parents helped nurture at her mother's home when it was ready to be transplanted there.

Termination for Danielle was an ongoing issue that was often discussed in terms of the needs of those plants. Discussions focused on how one knows if the plants are ready to be transplanted, what helps the plants get strong and healthy, what risks there are for the plants, how and how well the foster parents are nurturing the plants, what happens if they are transplanted too early, how to care for them once they are transplanted, what to do if the mother is too busy with the three children to tend the plant, and other related issues. When Danielle was transferred to another foster home closer to her mother, part of her termination was taking the plant left in the therapist's office to her next therapist to care for, and taking the foster parents' plants and giving them to the new foster parents to care for until they were ready to be transplanted.

Additional brief examples:

A couple made each other termination mementos: he made her a key chain depicting a bottle of glue in a red circle with a red line through it and announced that she "need not be the glue that binds the family together."

A 48-year-old woman, who had always neglected self-care and engaged heavily in care of others, made herself a "gardening book" filled with all the tasks necessary to maintain a healthy, beautiful garden. She related each task to what she needed to continue to do to take care of herself in order to maintain her progress. She also potted seeds from the office garden to take with her.

A cooperative creation of a collage representing her personal growth, and a miniature trophy of a female karate champion as a symbolic gift, were aspects of the celebration for a woman whose empowerment in daily life often paralleled her lessons in karate.

A 7-year-old boy who became "prickly" (his parents' term) when he was upset and frustrated in his relationships received a small porcupine and a story about a porcupine's journey and discoveries about relating to others, including when to use what defenses.

A family learning to cope with the changes in relationships with the onset of adolescence read the book *Frederick* by Leo Lionni, in which the value of saving up positive memories is realized by a family of mice.

References

Barker, P. (1985). *Using Metaphors in Psychotherapy*. New York: Brunner/Mazel.

Gil, E. (1991). *The Healing Power of Play*. New York: Guilford.

Kramer, S. (1990). *Positive Endings in Psychotherapy*. San Francisco: Jossey-Bass.

Lionni, L. (1967). *Frederick*. New York: Dragonfly.

Mills, J. C., and Crowley, R. J. (1986). *Therapeutic Metaphors for Children*. New York: Brunner/Mazel.

Seuss, D. (1990). *Oh, the Places You'll Go!* New York: Random House.

97

The Feelings Center

Helen E. Benedict

INTRODUCTION

The Feelings Center is a useful adjunct to play therapy for the preschool child showing disruptive behavior in the classroom. By facilitating successful management of the child's distressing feelings, the center enhances self-control and a positive self-concept. These changes in the classroom in turn appear to facilitate therapy. In addition, the Feelings Center appears to be an effective way to help preschool teachers deal with the typically volatile feelings of preschoolers more effectively. Accepting children's feelings, coupled with teaching them appropriate ways to express those feelings, benefits all the children in the room.

RATIONALE

Preschool children with emotional and behavioral problems often have difficulty in preschool, day care, and Head Start classroom settings. It is not uncommon for children who present at clinical settings needing play therapy to have been expelled from one or more classroom settings for unmanageable behaviors, including aggressive activities, temper tantrums, oppositionality, and poor self-control (Trad 1990). Given the general immaturity of emotional expression in this age group, it is not surprising that these children are relatively undifferentiated and express emotional distress with both internalizing and externalizing symptoms. However, the experience of failure in the classroom typically compounds the child's problems, therefore a technique that increases the ability of the distressed preschool child to remain in the classroom setting has many potential benefits.

Many of the behavior problems seen at this age reflect underlying confusion, depression, anxiety, and negative internal representations of the self. For example, attachment disorders often present with symptoms of oppositionality and behavioral undercontrol (Speltz 1990, Zeanah, et al 1993). Similarly, children whose parents are separating or divorced show aggression and tantrums in a preschool classroom (Wallerstein and Kelly 1980). Trad (1990) points out the close relationship between aggression and depression at this age. Finally, James (1994) describes acting-out behavior in children exposed to trauma such as abuse. These children, faced with"failure" in the classroom, will often label themselves as "bad" or "unlovable." This negative self-evaluation begins a vicious circle where the child is angry and afraid of rejection, then behaves poorly, is placed in "time-out" or otherwise punished, and then labels him- or herself again as "bad," leading to increased anger and fear and subsequent out of control behavior. The Feelings Center supplements individual play therapy by offering a way to break this negative cycle in the classroom. Play therapy, by clarifying the child's feelings and helping the child express and resolve these feelings, helps the child use the Feelings Center in the classroom, which in turn facilitates therapy by providing experiences of beginning acceptance and control of negative feelings.

DESCRIPTION

The Feelings Center operates in the classroom like other activity-specific centers such as housekeeping, blocks, manipulatives, and library typically found in the preschool classroom. The Feelings Center, which works most effectively when well demarcated from other centers by dividers of low walls, should be equipped with a variety of materials conducive to expression of feelings. First, there should be pictures or posters on the walls of children expressing easily recognized feelings. In addition, there should be a collection of coloring-book-like line drawings of the common feelings such as mad, sad, scared, happy, and surprised for children to color. For sad feelings there should be several large pillows or a bean-bag chair to snuggle in and one or two cuddly stuffed animals. For angry feelings there should be a "mad" pad, where the child is encouraged to scribble vigorously and then crumple up the paper and throw it away. Rubber stamps (ideally showing feelings but also useful with pictures of familiar objects) and a stamp pad are excellent because the child can pound and draw at the same time, offering considerable control in expressing angry feelings. Some sort of pounding toy is also needed. While some children do best pounding on the pillows, other children respond well to a pounding board and hammer or a bop bag. However, these latter two can be disruptive of the larger classroom and should only be included when there is sufficient sound dampening available or sufficient privacy so that the bop bag is well contained in the Feelings Center.

The Feelings Center should be introduced carefully into the classroom, usually by the therapist working with the classroom teacher. Typically it is introduced during group time by reading one of the many books on feelings available for preschool children. A group discussion about feelings usually follows in which "hard" feelings and what you can do with them are emphasized. Then the area is shown to the children and each of the feelings activities is demonstrated for the children. Each child will want a turn in the area when it is first introduced.

The basic rule of the Feelings Center is that only one child may be there at any one time. Children may choose to go there when they feel a need and the teacher also can encourage children to go when they show strong feelings or signs of being about to lose control. It is important that the Feelings Center be a positive part of the classroom so any time-out chair should be in another part of the room. The goal is to help children go to the Feelings Center to deal with feelings before they lose control and act out their feelings in the room. If a child is overtly aggressive or otherwise violates classroom rules, the typical classroom behavior management procedures, such as time-out, should be used, not the Feelings Center. The teacher should notice and praise each child who successfully manages feelings with the center. Our experience with such centers in about eight preschool classrooms has shown that the Center, often originally opened to help one or two distressed children, ends up being used by many of the children with a generally positive impact on the classroom overall.

APPLICATIONS

The Feelings Center is effective with any preschool child whose acting-out behavior is closely tied to inner distress. We have found that children who are stressed at home (e. g., a recent move, a new sibling, a new parent figure, a divorce, parental fighting) use the Feelings Center for self-comforting and calming, especially on bad days when the classroom activity seems overwhelming to them. Many of the aggressive children in the classroom will use it as well, often going to the Center to pound awhile instead of hitting other children. For children in individual play therapy who have more serious problems, the Feelings Center provides a way for children to remain in the classroom and avoid frequent negative feedback about their behavior. Each time the child uses the Center to deal with feelings, he or she gets support for the idea that feelings are okay. This enables him or her to use the special safety of the playroom more effectively. By seeing other children use the Center and by being praised themselves for self-control, these children learn they are not "bad" and that they are like the other children.

Dustin, age 3, was referred for play therapy because of impulsive behavior, both aggressive, such as stealing other children's food, and affectionate, such as hugging and clinging to other children, poor attention span, and difficulty following directions. He also showed poor speech and was receiving speech therapy. Evaluation revealed a recent highly acrimonious divorce and frequent visits with the father from which Dustin returned agitated and bruised. In the play therapy setting, Dustin played out themes of monsters in the house, aggression toward an adult male figure, hurt baby play, and children hiding from the parent. His play initially was quite disorganized and his classroom behavior remained highly disruptive, despite the implementation of a behavior management plan in the classroom.

The Feelings Center was introduced by his teacher and play therapist after his third play therapy session. Dustin was initially intrigued and insisted on being first in the Center. However, he was angry when the other children took their turns, and did not return to the Center for several days, continuing his disruptive behavior. Several times, just as Dustin was about to intrusively hug another child, his teacher suggested he hug the bear in the Feelings Center. Dustin did so and received praise from the teacher. Over a period of several weeks, Dustin made increasing use of the Feelings Center, especially for angry feelings. He also began to talk more about feelings in the classroom and use words more to communicate with other children. As he did so, his classroom behavior improved considerably although he continued throughout the year to have difficult days, especially after visits to the father. On these days, he would often spend several periods in the Center during the day. Within therapy, his play became more organized and shifted to frequent demonstrations of his control of the situation in the play. He began to talk about his ability to "be good" in the classroom with considerable pride. It appeared that his improved self-representation enabled his work in therapy to proceed more quickly.

The presence of the Center also impacted the classroom as a whole. Teachers felt more comfortable helping children with feelings when they had actual tools for doing so. Observation of the room indicated that teachers were more sensitive to the children's feelings. Instead of assuming an oppositional child was simply willful, the teachers would often ask about feelings and suggest the Center. Children responded well to this shift, with the result that discipline techniques such as the time-out chair were employed less frequently. More books about feelings were read to the group than had been true of the classroom earlier as well. While the Center served as a playroom annex for Dustin, it served as a mini-playroom for several of the children in the class who were stressed but not to the extent that they needed individual therapy.

References

James, B. (1994). *Handbook for Treatment of Attachment-Trauma Problems in Children.* New York: Lexington Books.

Speltz, M. L. (1990). The treatment of preschool conduct problems: an integration of behavioral and attachment concepts. In *Attachment in the Preschool Years: Theory, Research, and Intervention ed.* M. T. Greenberg, D. Cicchetti, and E. M. Cummings, Chicago: University of Chicago Press.

Trad, P. V. (1990). *Conversations with Preschool Children: Uncovering Development Patterns.* New York: Norton.

Wallerstein, J., and Kelly, J. (1980). *Surviving the Break-up: How Children and Parents Cope with Divorce.* New York: Basic Books.

Zeanah, C. H., Jr., Mammen, O. K., and Lieberman, A. F. (1993). Disorders of attachment. In *Handbook of Infant Mental Health,* ed. C. H. Zeanah, Jr. New York: pp. 399–426.

98

The Disposable Camera Technique

Jo Ann L. Cook

INTRODUCTION

The need to provide children with a method for bringing in pictorial information about their world became more accessible with the availability of disposable cameras. Previous attempts to request the use of pictures had been limited to the child's use of pictures that frequently belonged to other people, with the limitations incurred by need to request and limit the types of use that could be allowed. There are many possibilities for use of the technique, with the initial introduction providing children with control, involvement, and ownership in the project and having pictures of their own when they are completed. In addition, the act of carrying the camera home and returning it symbolically extends the therapy into their world outside the office and assists them in making connections from their lives to the therapeutic process and back with them as they leave.

RATIONALE

The use of pictures in child therapy has often been applied in life story albums for children in foster care and adoption and in other situations where assisting the child to develop a pictorial history, depiction of present reality, and symbolic future signifies that their history is a meaningful part of who they are but does not define who they can become. It has been helpful in assisting children to recognize the sequence of events in their lives, as well as providing a vehicle to discuss their history with others. As in many techniques that are used with respect for children, it becomes the children who determine how it will serve them best. Having the control and ownership of the camera has resulted in evidence that children will bring in what they view as valuable and meaningful in their lives and which they would like to record, discuss, and save. This technique has proven to yield valuable information and experience for them, as well as to lend rich material to the ongoing process as they describe, assemble, and label the pictures they have taken.

DESCRIPTION

The technique is introduced to the children by discussing the idea of making an album or book about themselves with their choices about the pictures and narrative which they would choose. Children frequently offer ideas about what they might like to include and can be encouraged in the process of making a list of persons, activities, or events that they value. The materials needed are a disposable camera, scrapbook album with paper pages that allows fixing of photographs and also lends itself to artwork and writing. If the therapist has a polaroid camera the process can begin immediately by taking the child's picture, allowing the child to choose a setting that he feels signifies him, or other options that are available in the office setting or outdoors. The child can then affix his picture to the first page of the album and decorate and label it as he would like. If a polaroid camera is not available, the disposable camera can be used to make the first picture of the child. The other pictures will remain to be taken at home, school, or other settings of the child's choice. Their parent(s) or caregivers are advised of the project so they can assist in taking pictures in groups when the child would like to be included in the picture. The child's parent(s) or caregivers are requested to return the camera to the therapist prior to their next appointment so that pictures can be developed and the process can continue when the child is seen again.

APPLICATIONS

Many benefits are derived from this technique during the process, as well as from the finished product. Some books have included assisting the child to make a memory book of his foster or adoptive families, old and new homes, schools, neighborhoods, pets and friends, of himself learning new skills or sports, being successful in his goals, and in pictorial autobiographies as well as fictional and metaphorical stories with himself as a central character.

99

Use of Animals in a Play Therapy Setting

S. Eileen Theiss

INTRODUCTION

So often in the literature, the play therapist is encouraged to let the child lead the therapist in the play. Those of us trained in a client-centered approach learned from our instructors and from our supervisors that the child will let us know where she wants to go. In my work in a rural elementary school, I am continually (pleasantly) surprised that this is so.

However, in that elementary school setting, with time limitations and frequent interruptions to the schedule, practicing traditional play therapy is not always easy. After five years of working with children in an elementary school, I have come to realize that it is very difficult for traditional play therapy to be effective in a school setting.

But that is where I work, and the children who are referred to the school counselor are so often the children who most need intervention and for whom play therapy in a traditional therapy setting is simply unavailable. So the 50-minute session may only be a 35-minute session, sometimes interrupted by a fire drill, a holiday, or an assembly.

It is in this setting that I have come to find that having a few live animals in the room can stimulate conversation with a child, and often provide insight early on about the child's concerns.

RATIONALE

Children are naturally drawn to animals. An animal is nonthreatening, makes no demands of the child, and the child can choose whether to interact or simply observe. I find that when a child is observing or interacting with one of the animals in the play therapy room, she is at ease, relaxed, and often able to communicate just what it is about the animal that she recognizes in herself and/or others in her life.

DESCRIPTION

The animals that I have available in my play therapy room include an aquarium full of tropical fish, a few hermit crabs in an open tank and a small albino corn snake in a closed tank. The animals are in different parts of the room. I generally do not introduce the child to them, but allow the child to discover the animals.

Often I have children simply drop in, having heard about the animals, asking to see a particular one. Once there was a child, retained in second grade and generally regarded as somewhat immature, who took on the responsibility of dropping a weekend feeder cube in the aquarium every Friday. The child *asked* for this job and only forgot twice from September to December. I *never* reminded that "immature" child!

Another child, who was viewed by some teachers and students as a "tough" little kid, used the early play therapy sessions slowly working up the courage to hold Avalon, the albino corn snake. In the room, this child had permission to be afraid, and the child's fear could safely be expressed. We had the opportunity to talk about other fears while observing the snake—fears that were more seriously affecting this child's life: alcoholism and abuse in the home.

APPLICATIONS

I believe that there is no limitation to how an animal can be used with children in a play therapy session. The child will lead the therapist to the animal, will in some way indicate an interest in that particular animal, even simply by asking, "What is that?" Observing how the child responds when the therapist introduces the animal will determine how that animal might serve the therapeutic relationship.

I have seen children diagnosed with ADHD who will sit quietly for four to five minutes just to see the hermit crab tentatively emerge from its shell. Shy children will respond to a fish who prefers to "hide" behind a plant. A child who has experienced the intimidation of a bully will talk to a smaller fish, telling it to stand up to the larger one chasing it.

If a child is not interested, she will simply not show an interest. Often, the use of the animal is limited to simply putting the child at ease, giving the child something to occupy herself as she becomes comfortable. An aquarium is a great place to direct your gaze if you don't want to look at the adult sitting by you!

100

The Popcorn Walk

Allan Gonsher

DESCRIPTION

The Popcorn Walk is an excellent opportunity for the therapist to observe, evaluate, and interact with a child. On a Popcorn Walk, the child and I leave the office for a nearby store where I buy the child a bag of popcorn. (Depending upon the location of the therapist's office, another food, such as yogurt, ice cream, candy, or a doughnut, can be substituted.) During the first walk I evaluate the child's behavior in relation to the world around him. Subsequent walks are mobile therapy sessions where I focus on the presenting problem. Observing children in real-life situations helps the therapist determine the course of therapy. I seldom initiate a Popcorn Walk before establishing rapport with the child. This technique works best after two or three sessions, when I have defined the presenting problem and the therapeutic relationship was begun.

RATIONALE

The Popcorn Walk gives me the opportunity to build a relationship with the child outside the formal atmosphere of the office, observe the child's behavior, manage the child's behavior, and evaluate the progress of therapeutic interventions. Most times in this informal atmosphere the child is more willing to open up and talk about problems that are bothering him.

Before setting out on the walk, I meet privately with the parents to explain the technique and answer any of their concerns. Since the child and I are always in public, I've never had a parent refuse my request for a Popcorn Walk. I explain the ground rules to the child and the parent. Consequences are established for the child's failure to follow the clearly defined rules. The child must walk next to me and behave in a controlled, suitable manner. If the child is unruly or disobedient any time during the walk, we return immediately to the office.

It's my responsibility not to put myself or the child in a dangerous situation. If I have any doubts about a child's ability to behave, I don't use the Popcorn Walk. For instance, I don't use this technique with a child who has an attention deficit disorder unless he has a degree of self-control.

On the first Popcorn Walk I lead the way to the store and purchase popcorn. On subsequent walks, I encourage the child to take charge, including giving him the money to pay for his popcorn. During our time together, I ask the child questions in relation to the presenting problem, listen to his replies, and respond accordingly.

APPLICATIONS

The Popcorn Walk can be used as therapy for most children. The child is able to leave what he considers a threatening environment and spend time with a caring adult doing something fun. I have used this technique with children who are nonverbal in the confines of the office but will express themselves during an informal walk. For a child whose inability to share and cooperate prevents his building relationships with his peers, I include situations where the child must practice these skills.

Some children with learning disabilities have difficulty doing multiple tasks at the same time. In this case, I organize the walk so the child needs to concentrate on only one or two tasks at a time. For instance, we walk to the store without talking, then sit down to eat and talk. A child with an attention deficit hyperactive disorder will sometimes not be able to focus on what is going on around her. Having a goal for a particular activity, such as walking to buy a treat, helps the child concentrate for a short period of time. Being with an ADHD child in a real-life situation when she is taking Ritalin and when she isn't helps the therapist understand the dynamics of her relationship skills at home and at school.

On a Popcorn Walk an oppositional child is given the opportunity to protest by leading the walk, talking loudly, or disrespectfully or physically objecting to the interchange without having to suffer the consequences from a punitive parent. Accepting and not reacting to certain behaviors can be helpful to this child.

Karen, an 8-year-old girl from a divorced family, entered therapy because of oppositional defiant behavior at home and school. She was struggling with the aftermath of the divorce and the inconsistencies of her father's visitations. During our sessions in our office, Karen found it difficult to express her feelings. Even when she played with the toys in the playroom, she was guarded and not responsive to my prodding. After seven sessions Karen didn't make much progress in dealing with the problems that were disrupting her behavior.

I decided to take Karen on a Popcorn Walk. During the first walk, she was sullen and unresponsive. On each subsequent walk she responded more openly. She told me she wished her dad would spend time with her like I did. Karen finally expressed her anger that her parents were divorced and that her father didn't spend more time with her. During the remaining course of therapy, I was able to work with Karen in the office and playroom. I helped her understand how she could deal with her anger and build a life for herself without such reliance on her father.

Occasionally we took a Popcorn Walk together. These times were more of a socialization opportunity than a therapeutic session. At the end of the course of therapy Karen still felt anger toward her father, but she had learned how not to let her feelings control her behavior at home and at school.

In another case, 11-year-old Brad was suffering from depression as a result of his mother's treatment for cancer. Before his mother's illness he'd been outgoing and lively, and an important player on his soccer team. Now, he was quiet and withdrawn and preferred to stay in the house watching television rather than be with his friends.

During the initial sessions, I learned from Brad that he was extremely worried that his mother would die, but wasn't allowed to express his feelings at home. The mother wasn't able to work, so the family finances were severely strained and there was no money for extras like eating out or going to movies. His mother, physically weakened by her treatments, couldn't attend Brad's soccer games. Brad felt that all of the fun had been removed from his life.

I used play therapy techniques to help Brad work through his depression. While he was able to talk about his fears concerning his mother's illness and his anger about the changes in the family, he remained depressed. I decided to take Brad on a Popcorn Walk to show him that doing even a simple, inexpensive activity can be fun. On subsequent walks, I encouraged him to have a more positive outlook on the ordinary events in his life, like playing with his friends. Brad began to look forward to our walks together and had a new joke at every session.

His mother's health improved, and she was able to go back to work part-time. Although finances were still tight, the family was able to eat out or go to a movie occasionally. Once a week the parents organized a simple family activity, such as going for a walk in the park, making cookies, or renting a movie to watch at home. Brad's mother attended a few of his soccer games.

Brad gradually came out of his restrictive, hollow depression. He learned to appreciate his simple activities as well as major happenings in his life. He still worried about his mother's health but didn't let his feelings impact his daily life.

101

Co-Play Therapy

Ann C. Levinger

INTRODUCTION

Co-play therapy is a method designed to provide intense play therapy for a challenging client while simultaneously offering excellent supervision for peers or trainees. In co-play therapy, two therapists divide the therapeutic role. One therapist, following the child's lead, plays with the child as fully and intensely as seems appropriate; the second comments on their interaction and sets limits. The technique is appropriate for two situations: (1) dealing with a play therapy case at a stuck point, and (2) providing live supervision and modeling that allows a therapist-in-training to work with extremely difficult cases. Although co-play therapy is appropriate for meeting either of these challenges singly, it is ideal for meeting both simultaneously.

RATIONALE

Co-play therapy is a potent therapeutic tool, especially useful in difficult cases that are at an impasse, and for training and supervision. Its power for the child stems in part from the fact that the playing therapist is fully able to engage in the fantasy play, never having to step out of role to meet other therapeutic responsibilities. Thus the play can continue with undiluted intensity even while the commenting therapist is reflecting or setting limits. This structure provides the opportunity both for more intense play and a richer set of therapeutic interventions.

For therapists, the co-play format offers excellent training opportunities. It allows each co-therapist to concentrate on only part of the usual role, and provides immediate feedback on the impact of their actions and words. Both therapists directly interact with the child, though in different ways, and both are fully exposed to the emotion of the play. Their in-session collaboration and post-session discussion provide an intense form of live supervision that benefits not only apprentice therapists but experienced ones as well.

DESCRIPTION

Co-play therapy is most appropriate for cases in which the child asks for more direct play or for fewer comments from the therapist. It is then easy to introduce a second therapist by reflecting the child's wishes and saying, "For a while now ——— is going to meet with us. ——— will be the person who will play with you. I will sit over here and act like a TV commentator. "(Or alternatively, "——— is going to sit in this chair here and act like a TV commentator, while you and I play.")

This division of roles is adhered to firmly, thus creating a situation in which the child experiences clear boundaries. The person playing directly with the child responds freely, going along with the child's directions as fully as is comfortable. The second therapist reflects the actions, emotions, and verbalizations of the play and, when necessary, sets limits.

During the play time, the two therapists adhere basically to guidelines for client-centered play therapy suggested by such authors as Axline (1947) and Guerney (1983).

Because these sessions are intense, it is important to allow the child and the therapists a period of transition between the play time and the outside world. First, the room is put back in order. Both therapists take part in this. The child is expected to join in and usually does, but is not forced to do so.

After things are straightened up, the three participants sit down to write or draw about the play session. Both therapists have a chance to summarize the primary themes of the play, writing or drawing from their individual perspectives. All three participants then read or show and tell about what they have written or drawn.

In addition to this first debriefing session, the two therapists need a second session alone. After the child leaves, they review the play session, paying particular attention to their own emotional reactions. This discussion is crucial. For co-play therapy to work well, it is essential that the two therapists are comfortable with each other. Open discussion about what is happening externally and internally helps build this relationship. The therapists then look for emerging themes in the treatment and discuss their hopes for future sessions.

APPLICATIONS

Tim had lived most of his seven years in abusive situations, in homes of various relatives. He was currently in foster care. Play therapy was part of his treatment plan. His therapist (J. M.) brought up his case at a staff supervision session after his sixth session. Initially Tim had been suspicious and ill at ease in the playroom. Over the first three sessions he moved from sitting fiercely silent, as he did the first hour, through noticing things in the room and exchanging a few words with the therapist, into the very active play that began about halfway through the third session. He showed no interest in the doll house or small toys, but moved office furniture around, used the bop bag both to hit and argue with, and challenged the therapist to fights. He became intensely involved, but even the simplest comment from the therapist brought on an angry outburst or an abrupt shift in the play. After three sessions that basically followed this pattern, the therapist was feeling stymied and frustrated. Another staff member was intrigued by this case and volunteered to be a co-therapist for six sessions. Both therapists saw this collaboration as an opportunity to sharpen their own skills.

Tim was somewhat skeptical when a second adult was introduced, but he cautiously accepted the idea that for six weeks he would have a play partner who would let him be the director, while J. M. would act like a TV commentator. To emphasize the two roles, a very official-looking office chair was provided for J. M. while A. C. sat on one of the floor cushions.

Over the course of six weeks, Tim's play became both freer and more appropriately controlled. When he and A. C. were involved in a drama,

A. C. followed his wishes as fully as she could comfortably. If she felt uncomfortable in the play, she said so as a peer not an authority. J. M.'s commentary was usually tolerated and often seemed to help enhance and intensify the play, not interrupt it.

References

Axline, V. M. (1947). *Play Therapy*. Cambridge, MA: Houghton Mifflin.

Guerney, L. F. (1983). Client-centered (non-directive) play therapy. In *Handbook of Play Therapy*, eds. C. E. Schaefer and K. J. O'Connor, pp. 21–64. New York: Wiley.

Levinger, A. (1994). Co-play therapy. *International Journal of Play Therapy* 3(2) 53–62.

ABOUT THE EDITORS

Heidi Gerard Kaduson, Ph.D., specializes in evaluation and intervention services for children with a variety of behavioral, emotional, and learning problems. She is Past President of the International Association for Play Therapy and Co-Director of the Play Therapy Training Institute. She has lectured internationally on play therapy, attention deficit hyperactivity disorder, and learning disabilities. Dr. Kaduson co-edited *The Quotable Play Therapist* and *The Playing Cure*. Forthcoming books include *101 Favorite Play Therapy Techniques, Vol. 2,* and *Short-Term Play Therapy Interventions with Children*. She maintains a private practice in child psychotherapy in Hightstown, New Jersey.

Charles E. Schaefer, Ph.D., a nationally renowned child psychologist, is Professor of Psychology at Fairleigh Dickinson University and Director of its Center for Psychological Services in Hackensack, New Jersey. He is Director Emeritus of the International Association for Play Therapy. He has authored or edited more than forty books on parenting, child psychology, and play therapy, including *The Therapeutic Use of Child's Play, The Therapeutic Powers of Play,* and *Family Play Therapy*. Dr. Schaefer maintains a private practice in child psychotherapy in Hackensack.